ROMANTIC

DAYS AND NIGHTS™ IN

NEW ORLEANS

Romantic Cities Series

ROMANTIC

DAYS AND NIGHTS™ IN

New Orleans

INTIMATE ESCAPES IN THE BIG EASY

by Constance and Kenneth Snow

The Globe Pequot Press

OLD SAYBROOK, CONNECTICUT

Cover and text design by Mullen & Katz.
Chapter-opener illustrations by Maryann Dubé. Illustration on page 157 by Kenneth Snow. Other illustrations by Maryann Dubé and Mullen & Katz.

Romantic Days and Nights is a trademark of The Globe Pequot Press.

Library of Congress Cataloging-in-Publication Data

Snow, Constance.
     Romantic days and nights in New Orleans : intimate escapes in the Big Easy / Constance and Kenneth Snow. — 1st ed.
          p.   cm. — (Romantic cities series)
     Includes indexes.
     ISBN 0-7627-0121-8
     1. New Orleans (La.)—Guidebooks.   I. Snow, Kenneth.   II. Title.   III. Series.
     F379.N53S58   1997
     917.63'350453—DC21

                                                                    97-24501
                                                                    CIP

Manufactured in the United States of America
First Edition/First Printing

For our friend Ed Sherrill,
who introduced us to the
publishing business and each other.

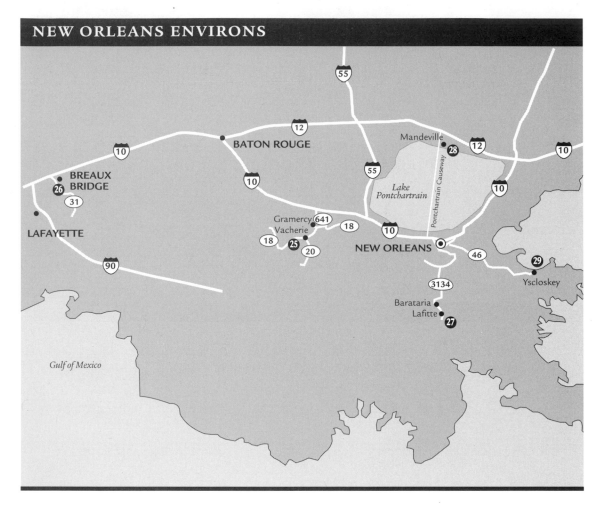

NEW ORLEANS ENVIRONS

55

12

BATON ROUGE

Mandeville

28

12

10

10

BREAUX
BRIDGE

26

31

55

10

Lake
Pontchartrain

Pontchartrain Causeway

10

LAFAYETTE

Gramercy 641

Vacherie

18

18

25

20

NEW ORLEANS

10

46

29

90

Yscloskey

3134

Barataria

Lafitte

27

Gulf of Mexico

Numbers on map correspond to itinerary numbers (see Table of Contents).

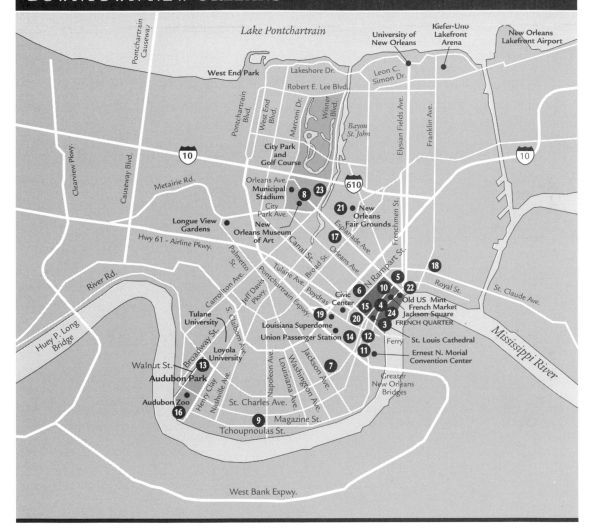

DOWNTOWN NEW ORLEANS

Lake Pontchartrain

University of New Orleans

Kiefer-Uno Lakefront Arena

New Orleans Lakefront Airport

West End Park

Lakeshore Dr.

Leon C. Simon Dr.

Robert E. Lee Blvd.

Pontchartrain Causeway

Pontchartrain Blvd.

West End Blvd.

Marconi Dr.

Wisner Blvd.

Bayou St. John

Elysian Fields Ave.

Franklin Ave.

Clearview Pkwy.

Causeway Blvd.

10

City Park and Golf Course

10

Metairie Rd.

Orleans Ave.
Municipal Stadium

610

8 **23**

City Park Ave.

21 New Orleans Fair Grounds

Frenchmen St.

Longue View Gardens

New Orleans Museum of Art

Esplanade Ave.

Hwy 61 - Airline Pkwy.

Palmetto St.

Canal St.

Broad St.

Orleans Ave.

17

River Rd.

Carrollton Ave.

Jeff Davis Pkwy.

Pontchartrain Expwy.

Tulane Ave.

Poydras

N Rampart St.

18

Royal St.

St. Claude Ave.

Huey P. Long Bridge

S. Claiborne Ave.

Civic Center

6 **10** **5**

22

Old US Mint
French Market
Jackson Square

Mississippi River

Tulane University

Broadway St.

Louisiana Superdome

19

15 **4** **24**
20 **3** FRENCH QUARTER

Loyola University

Union Passenger Station

14 **12**

St. Louis Cathedral

Ferry

Walnut St.

13

Henry Clay

Nashville Ave.

Napoleon Ave.

Louisiana Ave.

Washington Ave.

Jackson Ave.

11

Ernest N. Morial Convention Center

Audubon Park

Audubon Zoo

16

7

Greater New Orleans Bridges

9 Magazine St.

St. Charles Ave.

Tchoupitoulas St.

West Bank Expwy.

HELP US KEEP THIS GUIDE UP TO DATE

Every effort has been made by the author and editors to make this guide as accurate and useful as possible. However, many things can change after a guide is published—establishments close, phone numbers change, facilities come under new management, etc.

We would love to hear from you concerning your experiences with this guide and how you feel it could be made better and be kept up to date. While we may not be able to respond to all comments and suggestions, we'll take them to heart and we'll make certain to share them with the author. Please send your comments and suggestions to the following address:

The Globe Pequot Press
Reader Response/Editorial Department
P.O. Box 833
Old Saybrook, CT 06475

Or you may e-mail us at:

editorial@globe-pequot.com

Thanks for your input, and happy travels!

ACKNOWLEDGMENTS

We would like to thank Globe Pequot editors Laura Strom, Doe Boyle, and Paula Brisco for their guidance and patience; New Orleans writers Rick Atkinson, Rhoda Faust, Leigh Harris, Carolyn Kolb, and Priscilla Vayda for contributing sidebars; and our many friends and colleagues who helped out with advice and research, including Cary Alden, Sarah Burnette, Bill Curl, Sandra Dartus, Amy Hymel, Melissa Lee, Lee Sinclair, and Bonnie Warren.

CONTENTS

[*Contents*]

*L*ike any great beauty whose face is all the more alluring because of its flaws, New Orleans inspires both passion and respect, tender regard and exasperated affection. She's a grand old seductress—built for comfort, not speed—a virtuoso of temptation that beguiles willing subjects with heavenly food and wicked music. Under her spell, a lazy afternoon seems to stretch on for days, tropical nights brush eternity, and love can last forever.

Here, newcomers are greeted by centuries of hospitality and a joyful determination to "live and let live." Like a good house party, the line between guest and host is pleasantly blurred, and nobody bothers with make-up after the first day. The local diet may be reckless, but the pagan work ethic is definitely heart-healthy, as everyone's calendar is marked with Mardi Gras and 364 other excuses to give responsibility the slip.

L'amour is always on the front burner in this steamy environment, where you'll be the authors of your own potboiler, surrounded by moody moss-draped plantations, gaslit courtyards, and mysterious strangers. Even the cemeteries are sexy, lavished with crumbly tombs, voluptuous angels, and romantic atmosphere to die for—just ask Anne Rice.

Sound good? Then pack your bags with loose cottons and slouchy knits to suit the climate and cuisine. Bring sensible shoes for dodging mimes and dancing in the streets. Think unbridled excess. Truth is, after champagne for breakfast, muffulettas for lunch, and a few hours of subtropical sightseeing, your inner beauty will have ample opportunity to shine. Styling gel can't beat the humidity, so go with the frizz. Be who you is.

THE ITINERARIES

Spend a few hours people-watching in the French Quarter and you'll never again make the extravagant claim of "something for everyone." Even so, we have put together a diverse collection of itineraries that will help most couples explore one or more of their special interests. This old city has been in the business of pleasure for centuries, and your desires are bound to lead you to kindred spirits—whether your tastes run more to historical drama or romantic comedy, hiking boots or spike heels, hearts and flowers or booze and blues.

The Romantic Days and Nights™ format makes the most of offbeat paths, but these roads less traveled should also intersect with the main tourist track. Though we could hardly include them in every itinerary, a handful of all-time classics should be on any couple's to-do list: Stroll around the French Quarter by day and night; take a round trip on the St. Charles Avenue streetcar; cruise across the Mississippi aboard the Canal Street ferry; hit some live music clubs; eat po-boys, fried seafood, and gumbo; linger over chicory coffee and beignets at Cafe du Monde. And yes, everyone should walk down Bourbon Street at least once—if only to see how low we can go. If your budget (and arteries) can stand a strong dose of luxury, dine in the grand Creole tradition with breakfast at Brennan's, lunch at Galatoire's, dinner at Antoine's, or Sunday jazz brunch at Commander's Palace.

USING THIS BOOK

Rates and dates of operation are always subject to change, so it's best to call ahead and check. Hotels and restaurants are often booked months in advance for special events (Mardi Gras, Jazz Fest, Super Bowl), plus the city does a brisk convention business, so make your reservations as soon as possible. Listed prices do not include the 9 percent sales tax, plus an additional 2 percent hotel tax, which bumps room rates an extra 11 percent. You should also be aware that an amusement tax (which includes sales tax) tacks on a hefty 14 percent to concert and theater tickets and to cover charges in clubs that feature live entertainment.

Obviously, two or more itineraries may be linked together for longer trips. All of the recommended in-town accommodations are centrally located and (with minor adjustments) would be convenient for any of the New Orleans-based itineraries. The out-of-town drives are easily incorporated, as well, and most offer instructions for both day trips and overnight stays. Wherever possible, we've included detailed directions; but you should still pick up a good road map and seek additional advice from your hotel concierge or a visitor information office.

Restaurant prices are a tough call. Most menus offer entrées or sandwiches that fall above or below the designated range; but we've tried to give you an idea of the amount you can generally expect to spend. Because everyone's notion of a full meal differs, we've based our scale on the cost of a typical entrée during dinner hours. "Inexpensive" means you'll find a good selection of entrées under $10, "moderate" means $10 to $18, and "expensive" is $18 or more. Lunch entrées may cost less. In certain special cases (New Year's Eve parties or Christmas buffets, for instance), we designate the price range for that event, which may be higher than an everyday dinner. Many of the city's greatest restaurants offer bargain table d'hote menus at lunchtime and in the early evening (before 6:00 or 7:00 P.M.), a fine opportunity to soak up some romantic atmosphere and famous cuisine on a limited budget.

GETTING HERE AND GETTING AROUND

New Orleans International Airport is located in suburban Kenner, about a $21 cab ride from downtown. **Airport shuttles** (504–522–3500), which stop at several hotels, depart every ten minutes from the lower level near the baggage claim area and cost $10 per person one way. The **Airport/Downtown Express bus** (504–737–7433 or 504–737–9611) charges $1.50 per person and operates daily from 5:30 A.M. to 11:30 P.M., departing from the west side of the terminal's upper level every ten minutes during peak hours (6:00 A.M. to 9:00 A.M. and 3:00 P.M. to 6:00 P.M.) and every twenty-three minutes otherwise. By car, follow the airport access road to Interstate 10 East, which goes right through New Orleans.

Amtrak trains stop at **Union Terminal** (1001 Loyola Avenue at South Rampart in the Central Business District, 800–872–7245), connecting New Orleans with New York City, Chicago, Los Angeles, and Miami. Cruise companies that dock at the downtown Julia Street Wharf include **Commodore** (800–832–1122), **Carnival** (800–327–9501), and **Holland America Line** (800–426–0327). The **Delta Queen Steamboat Company** (800–543–1949 or 504–586–0631) schedules three- to fourteen-day river trips aboard authentic steam paddlewheelers.

Most city buses run around the clock, and the Regional Transit Authority will provide advice on routing and schedules for any destination if you phone the **RTA RideLine** (504–248–3900). VisiTour passes are available for one day ($4) or three consecutive days ($8) of unlimited travel on all public buses and streetcars.

If you're driving, be sure to heed posted parking regulations, especially downtown and in the French Quarter, where violators are certain to be towed—and pay a hefty fine. If you're walking, stick to populated areas and pay close attention to your surroundings, as neighborhoods can change dramatically within a couple of blocks. When in doubt, turn back.

FOR MORE INFORMATION

New Orleans Metropolitan Convention
  and Visitors Bureau
1520 Sugar Bowl Drive
New Orleans, LA 70112–1259
(800) 672–6124 or (504) 566–5011
http://www.neworleanscvb.com

Louisiana State Office of Tourism
P.O. Box 94291
Baton Rouge, LA 70804–9291
(800) 633–6970 or (504) 342–1969
http://www.louisianatravel.com

For a virtual visit to New Orleans, explore a fun and innovative website that offers live music (RealAudio) in a radio jukebox format, on-line hotel reservations, and regular contests with prizes ranging from Louisiana spices to recorded music to full-scale free trips (http://neworleansonline.com).

Bed and Breakfast, Inc., Reservation Service
1021 Moss Street, Box 52257
New Orleans, LA 70152–2257
(800) 729–4640 or (504) 488–4640

New Orleans Bed and Breakfast
  and Accommodations
671 Rosa Avenue, Suite 208
Metairie, LA 70005
(504) 838–0071

The prices and rates listed in this guidebook were confirmed at press time. We recommend, however, that you call establishments before traveling to obtain current information.

OVERINDULGENCES

ITINERARY 1
Three days and three nights

GRAND ILLUSIONS
LIVING LARGE IN LOUISIANA

*L*ong before you came to New Orleans in search of gilded romance and bygone opulence, "the Paris of the Americas" was the most exotic stop for the great riverboats, a pleasure island filled with fancy women, fashionable shops, and grand French restaurants. From fictional honeymooners Rhett and Scarlett Butler to real-life Texas oil-boom million-aires, wealthy travelers have prowled the Vieux Carré for centuries seeking European-style goods and services they couldn't find at home.

Even today, when most major cities offer at least as many amusements, and decades of hard times have dulled the ill-gotten glamour, pockets of old-world elegance still exist. If you've got the money, they've got what you desire. Read on and lose yourselves in luxury.

Practical notes: If it's in this itinerary, you need advance reservations and proper attire. Jackets separate the men from the tourists at dinner.

DAY ONE: EVENING

Of course, one simply cannot travel by taxi or (Ivana forbid!) public bus. Check the New Orleans *Yellow Pages* and you'll find about fifty limousine services. A couple of reliable companies are **A Touch of Class Transportation Service Inc.** (800–821–6352 outside Louisiana, 800–878–6352 inside Louisiana, or 504–522–7565) and **Limousine Livery Ltd** (504–561–8777 or 504–561–1000).

Like others of your ilk—Princess Anne, the Lord Mayor of London, Viscount Linley, Kathleen Turner, Julia Child—check into the **Windsor Court** (300 Gravier Street between South Peters and Tchoupitoulas Streets; 800–262–2662 or 504–523–6000; doubles $250 to $360, suites $325 to $1,100, ten-room penthouses $3,000). Consistently named among the world's top hotels by such tastemakers as *Condé Nast's Traveler,* the chic riverfront high rise is graced by marble floors, oriental rugs, gilded antiques, and an art collection worth millions. Spacious rooms and suites are decorated in sedate, traditional style with large marble baths and the ultimate in service. The indoor/outdoor health club facilities include an Olympic-sized pool.

Romance at a Glance

♥ *Discover a king's ransom of antiques and art along majestic Royal Street.*

♥ *Reserve the best seats in the house at the ballet, symphony, or theater.*

♥ *Dine in grand style at the Sazerac, Brennan's, Louis XVI, and the Grill Room.*

♥ *Fly right over the boring stretches on the road to Cajun country.*

♥ *Charter a captained sailboat for a sunset cruise on Lake Pontchartrain.*

Dinner

If you long for the days when a big dinner tab bought more than artsy squiggles on a plate and an overdose of attitude from your waiter, have we got an endangered species for you. Here a pianist performs nightly for dancing cheek to cheek, intricate tableside preparations are carried out with dash, and the intermezzo sorbet arrives in an illuminated ice swan. Welcome

With This Ring . . .

On one recent evening at the Sazerac, a young gentleman asked restaurant manager Ian Turkmen to help him surprise his date with an engagement ring. Turkmen centered the open box in a nest of rose petals, surrounded by other flowers, and covered the plate with a silver dome. When they ordered dessert, he placed it before the lady, announcing, "This is something special we do for couples." Then he lifted the dome. As she looked on in great surprise, the gentleman got down on one knee, professed his love, asked for her hand, and kissed her. By now dissolved in tears, she accepted. Turkmen broke out the champagne, and the happy pair requested that the flower petals be wrapped up for posterity.

Another young gentleman reserved a table for ten to make his grand proposal at the Sazerac. In addition to his intended, he brought along eight of his relatives, who looked on as he popped the question. Did she have a choice but to say yes? One old warning carries extra weight in this close-knit town: You don't just marry the man you love, you marry his family!

to the sumptuous **Sazerac** in the **Fairmont Hotel** (123 Baronne Street between Canal and Common Streets; 504–529–7111; expensive), where chandeliers glimmer above red velvet banquettes and tables are layered in ruby linens and white lace. Walls are lined with oil portraits of historic Louisiana luminaries who look down on a lively scene studded with today's political, financial, and social elite. Signature dishes include lobster bisque, turtle soup, hay-baked lamb, Dover sole, steak Diane, and Chateaubriand. Beluga Malossol caviar is served in a cradle of sculpted ice with Stolichnaya.

As for evening entertainment, schedules vary, but your trip may coincide with performances by the **New Orleans Opera** (504–529–2278), **Louisiana Philharmonic Orchestra** (504–523–6530), or **New Orleans Ballet** (504–522–0996). The Italian Renaissance **Saenger Theatre** (143 North Rampart Street at Canal; 504–524–2490) presents Broadway road shows in a majestic old movie palace. Golden doors open into the

150-seat **Southern Repertory Theatre** (in Canal Place Shopping Centre, 200 Canal Street at the river; 504–861–8163 or 861–5874), which produces works by established and emerging regional playwrights. To use your credit card for streamlined reservations at several major attractions, contact **Ticketmaster** (504–522–5555).

DAY TWO: MORNING

It may not be *Breakfast at Tiffany's,* but the local counterpart serves up a huge selection of dazzling treats that are great eye-openers at any time of day. **Coleman E. Adler and Sons Jewelers** (722 Canal Street between St. Charles Avenue and Carondelet Street; 504–523–5292) was founded in 1898 and now sprawls throughout a row of four classic buildings filled with romantic baubles and extravagant tableware. Don't linger too long, though, because you've got a date at one of Truman Capote's favorite restaurants.

Brunch

Another famous catchphrase, Breakfast at **Brennan's French Restaurant** (417 Royal Street between Conti and St. Louis Streets; 504–525–9711; expensive) is still a highlight of any trip to New Orleans. Today, the third generation operates this gorgeous French Quarter landmark, one of the few local restaurants still dedicated to classic dining in the Creole manner. Lunch and dinner are great, too, but the feasts presented each morning are a rare indulgence. Plenty of other kitchens prepare eggs Benedict, but here you'll also be offered a choice among eggs Hussarde (layered with Canadian bacon, marchand de vin sauce, and hollandaise); eggs Sardou (cradled on artichoke bottoms in a bed of creamed spinach with hollandaise); eggs Nouvelle Orleans (on a bed of lump crabmeat with brandy cream sauce); and eggs Ellen (on grilled salmon with hollandaise). Those who prefer to bypass the ubiquitous poached eggs can order fried oysters Benedict or crawfish Sardou. Sauteed baby veal is smothered in a spicy tomato sauce for grillades and grits. Indecisive types can even request a split platter with a half portion of two different breakfast entrées, a fun option for a whole table of tasters. Traditional eye-openers include brandy milk punch, absinthe suisse, Ramos gin fizz, and other historic concoctions too frothy for the cocktail hour. Ask to be seated on the balcony or terrace, which overlook one of the most beautiful patios in the city.

Even richer than your breakfast splurge, surrounding shops are packed with temptations. Although Royal Street was named long before anyone dreamed up the concept of an antiques store, it's the perfect label for the world-class eighteenth- and nineteenth-century trophies to be found in and around the first few blocks. If you want to furnish a love nest fit for a happy ending—you're in the right place.

Superb American and Continental pieces are beautifully displayed, along with eighteenth- and nineteenth-century paintings, at **Harper's Antiques** (610 Toulouse Street between Chartres and Royal Streets; 504–529–1996), which also provides an interior design service with an international following. Music boxes, jewelry, Victorian cut glass, porcelains, silver, and a host of other *objets* fills **M.S. Rau Antiques** (630 Royal Street between Toulouse and St. Peter Streets; 504–523–5660, 800–544–9440).

Somewhere back home is the perfect spot for a $58,000 burled-walnut grandfather clock, and you can pick one up at **The Manheim Galleries** (403–409 Royal Street at Conti Street; 504–568–1901). Ask to see the circa 1790 Louis XVI board of director's table in this former bank building. It was inlaid with every color of marble known at the time, and now dominates a room surrounded by one of the world's largest collections of archaic and antique hand-carved jade pieces.

Walnut and mahogany from Queen Anne through Georgian are the specialties at the 15,000-square-foot **Waldhorn Company, Inc.** (343 Royal Street between Bienville and Conti Streets; 504–581–6379), where tables are set with complete antique dinner services of porcelain and silver. To find the perfect chandelier or carved marble mantelpiece, head straight to **Keil's Antiques** (325 Royal Street between Bienville and Conti Streets; 504–522–

4552), where glittering window displays are especially beautiful at night. For nineteenth-century Chinese and Japanese objects, including exquisite cloisonné, visit **Diane Genre Oriental Art & Antiques** (233 Royal Street between Iberville and Bienville Streets; 504–525–7270). A huge inventory of museum-quality antiques spills over into two nearby annexes, but start at the main location of **Dixon and Dixon of Royal** (237 Royal Street between Iberville and Bienville Streets; 800–848–5148 or 504–524–0282) for heirloom jewelry and dozens of European grandfather clocks.

DAY TWO: EVENING

Drop your purchases back at the hotel, freshen up for a night on the town, and head out into the twilight in search of civilized pleasures. Begin with cocktails for two at **The Bombay Club** (830 Conti Street between Dauphine and Bourbon Streets; 504–586–0972), a pukka pub enriched by dark woods, polished brass, and tufted leather. In fact, the British atmosphere is so thick that New Orleans will seem like a distant dream. Sample too many of the house specialties (a staggering variety of ten-ounce martinis), and it will be.

Dinner

Rich hues of gold and burgundy, strolling guitarists, and award-winning European service reign at elegant **Louis XVI** (730 Bienville Street between Royal and Bourbon Streets; 504–581–7000; expensive). French-trained Agnes Bellet, who replaced the late Philippe Dufau as executive chef in 1993, has modernized the Continental menu, adding several new creations and updating a few established classics. Old favorites like rack of spring lamb and filet of beef Wellington remain, but some of Bellet's recent seasonal entrées have included fresh fish *Louisiane* (topped with sauteed banana, red bell pepper, tomato, parsley, and meunière sauce); cold seafood salad (shrimp, mussels, squid, scallops, and clams in a caper and basil vinaigrette);

and grilled chicken smothered in roasted garlic and rosemary. Fans of the flashier stuff can still finish up with one of the celebrated flaming desserts.

DAY THREE: MORNING/AFTERNOON

After light breakfast at the hotel, take off on a real Louisiana adventure with **Air Tours on the Bayou by Southern Seaplanes, Inc.** (504–394–5633). A half-day charter, which departs about thirty minutes from downtown New Orleans, sets down on water four times, starting with a stop at Lafitte, a small fishing village on Bayou Barataria that began as head-quarters for pirate Jean Lafitte. A one-hour layover in the Cajun village of Kraemer includes a close-up look at some indigenous wildlife and a walk through the trading post. Next it's on to the sugar cane fields of Napoleonville for a tour of the famous Greek Revival manor of Madewood Plantation. Finally, lunch at a casual seafood restaurant in the town of Golden Meadow is a casual feast of fresh seafood. The four- to five-hour trip costs $700. Bring along sunglasses and a camera.

Back in New Orleans, shop one of the country's largest selections of fine wines and liquors at **Martin Wine Cellar** (3827 Baronne Street between General Taylor and Peniston Streets; 504–899–7411). The warehouse-sized store also stocks a huge variety of regional products and imported gourmet goodies. Because Louisiana has one of the lowest alcoholic beverage taxes of any state, prices on some hard-to-find labels might astound you. (But, for once, sticker shock is a pleasant surprise.) After picking out several cases to ship home, choose a chilled bottle of champagne to take along for your sunset cruise on Lake Pontchartrain.

DAY THREE: EVENING

To set up your own private cruise, charter a captained 26-foot Pearson sloop from **Murray Yacht Sales and Boat Rentals** (402 South Roadway Drive at West End Park;

800–375–2507 or 504–283–2507). Sunset is best, especially during summer months, when you can drift beneath a huge flock of purple martins (up to 200,000) as they dive and wheel overhead before swooping under a bridge to roost for the night. Schedule your trip on a Wednesday to watch weekly sailboat races that draw from thirty to eighty participants.

Dinner

By now, you should be ready to head back to the hotel for one final splurge. Modeled after the famed Grill in London's Savoy Hotel, the **Grill Room** (504–523–6000; expensive) on the second floor at Windsor Court is filled with Important Art. A Lalique table stands at the entrance, and a marquetry screen of Windsor Castle was created expressly for the restaurant by Viscount Linley, son of Princess Margaret. The wine cellar is outstanding, and the seasonal menu changes every two weeks, featuring such exotica as chilled Kumomoto oysters with Absolut ginger ice; duck consommé with foie gras flan and duck confit; seared Maine scallops with Portobello mushroom and white truffle oil; and cinnamon-smoked quail with wild rice, Smithfield ham, maple pecan hash, and dried cranberry sauce. If you can't quite make up your minds, the chef also offers a seven-course tasting menu of each day's specials.

On the other hand, if you'd just as soon relax and dress down after your day's adventures, the same lavish food and service is available privately in your room. And what could be more luxurious than such a deliciously lazy night?

FOR MORE ROMANCE

A painstaking two-year restoration project brought a splendid 1884 mansion back to its original elegance at **The Melrose** (937 Esplanade Avenue at Burgundy Street; 504–944–2255; doubles, $225 to $250; suites, $325 to $425). Although the house is strictly formal in decor, the atmosphere is friendly and casual. Four double rooms have luxurious private baths, and four suites are fitted with whirlpool tubs. Plan to spend some time hanging around the tropically landscaped swimming pool. Rates include limousine pickup at the airport, a full breakfast, plus evening cocktails and hors d'oeuvres.

You'll feel like you've walked onto a lavish 1930s movie set if you check into the suite with double parlors, two hand-carved white marble fireplaces, towering ceilings, linen-draped four-poster bed, ebony grand piano, and oversized marble bathroom at **The Claiborne Mansion** (2111 Dauphine Street between Elysian Fields Avenue and Frenchmen Street; 800–449–7327 or 504–949–7327; doubles, $125 to $210; suites, $250 to $300). In fact, all seven rooms and suites in the historic Greek Revival mansion are unique and quietly elegant. A cottage is available for long-term stays. The lush garden is cooled by a swimming pool and waterfall. For extra privacy, you can pull your car into a brick courtyard and close the gates, just one reason why so many celebrities choose to stay here. Also, pets are welcome. Rates include full breakfast, evening cocktails and hors d'oeuvres, and other extras.

Both of the above properties are right on the edge of the French Quarter in Faubourg Marigny. For gorgeous accommodations in the French Quarter, see **Soniat House** (page 88) and **Hotel Maison de Ville** (page 15). To stay the night in an authentic plantation manor, see "Sugar Palaces and Sweet Dreams."

For physical pampering and top-drawer clothing shops, consult "Narcissus Does New Orleans." More great restaurants are detailed in "Magnificent Obsession." To feed your souls —or track down some great investments—see "Artful Seduction."

MAGNIFICENT OBSESSION
A COOK'S TOUR FOR LUSTY APPETITES

Casanova called oysters "a spur to the spirit and to love." Ancient Romans chewed whole bulbs of garlic for strength and endurance. The Marquis de Sade, Napoleon Bonaparte, and Madame Pompadour were enthusiastic consumers of truffles, as was French foodie Anthelme Brillat-Savarin, who claimed the elusive fungus "may in certain circumstances make women more affectionate and men more amiable."

In recent years, pragmatic souls have declared the ultimate aphrodisiac to be power (Henry Kissinger), diamonds (Lorelei Lee), or liquor (Dorothy Parker). But in New Orleans it will always be—even in these lean times—food, glorious food.

Outdoor markets and ethnic groceries are a feast for the eyes, and the air is rich with roasting coffee and molasses from creaky old plants along the river. Dining room chatter drifts from "what we ate yesterday" to "what we will eat tomorrow," always interwoven with serious analysis of the meal at hand. A few of the city's most celebrated restaurants will even make special arrangements for guests who want to venture beyond the swinging doors to a table in the kitchen for an insider's splurge of food sampling, wine tasting, and personal attention from the staff. If that stirs your appetite, read on for a behind-the-scenes guide to breakfast, lunch, dinner, and all points in between.

Practical notes: The restaurants in this itinerary are often booked weeks in advance, especially the chef's tables, so phone well ahead to reserve a place. If you strike out, try to join one of the occasional kitchen parties in the posh **Grill Room at Windsor Court** (300 Gravier Street between South Peters and Tchoupitoulas Streets; 504–523–6000; expensive) or ask to be seated at the chef's bar in Emeril Lagasse's spinoff restaurant **NOLA** (534 St. Louis Street between Decatur and Chartres Streets; 504–522–6652; moderate).

Romance at a Glance

♥ *Dine face to face with world-famous chefs.*

♥ *Hide away in a landmark Vieux Carré cottage with a private courtyard.*

♥ *Shop for antique cookware and the latest gourmet gadgets.*

♥ *Linger over the world's first cocktail in a grand and historic bar.*

♥ *Prowl the ancient French Market for succulent souvenirs.*

DAY ONE: LATE MORNING
Lunch

Arrive hungry before noon for an early lunch, so you'll have a few hours to walk it off in time for dinner. (See, you're thinking like natives already.) Head straight for a window table at **Sapphire** (228 Camp Street at Gravier Street; 504–571–7500; expensive) for street-level views of the business district action. The sophisticated Venetian-style interior is graced by Mario Villa's sculptural chandeliers and cushy metal chairs, plus specimens from the chef's own gem and mineral collection.

Before he racked up walls of awards at nearby Windsor Court, Kevin Graham did time at London's Savoy Hotel and the Hotel Negresco in Nice, among others—and even rustled up a private meal in the home of H. R. H. Princess Margaret. In 1994 the British-born superchef (and author of four cookbooks) opened his first New Orleans restaurant, Graham's, and followed up with Sapphire in 1996. His menu changes biweekly, offering anything from braised pheasant with creamed foie gras to Chinese lacquered duck with coffee mandarin glaze. Graham is also well known for his elaborate grain dishes and "Body-Conscious" specials, a fine choice to pace yourselves for the full schedule ahead.

DAY ONE: AFTERNOON

Check into **Hotel Maison de Ville** (727 Toulouse Street between Royal and Bourbon Streets; 504–561–5858 or 800–634–1600; doubles, $195 to $315; cottages, $245 to $555), a sophisticated French Quarter beauty with a lush brick patio and twenty-three high-ceilinged guest rooms furnished in antiques, four-poster beds, and period paintings. Though it's not among the most luxurious, number 9 comes with the best story: Tennessee Williams once lived and worked there. A few blocks away, the hotel's seven Audubon cottages are gracefully renovated with polished wood floors, exposed beams, and private or semi-private courtyards. More history here: John James Audubon lived in number 1 while painting *Birds of America* in 1821. Just in case you need a little pick-me-up between meals, **The Bistro** (504–528–9206; expensive) is the jewel box house restaurant, a proving ground for the city's up-and-coming young chefs. For details, see "Narcissus Does New Orleans."

Back on the streets, tease your senses with a cook's safari through the Quarter. Begin at lavish **Lucullus** (610 Chartres Street between Toulouse and St. Peter Streets; 504–528–9620) to marvel at museum-quality kitchen and dining gear from the seventeenth to early twentieth centuries and meet owner Patrick Dunne's bulldog, Alphonse. **Arius Art Tiles** (504 St. Peter Street on Jackson Square; 504–529–1665) are handcrafted with Louisiana and Southwestern motifs to brighten your kitchen back home. Step into tiny **Rendezvous, Inc.** (522 St. Peter Street on Jackson Square; 504–522–0225) for fine table linens and antique lace. **La Cuisine Classique** (439 Decatur Street between Conti and St. Louis Streets; 504–524–0068) is one of the largest culinary stores in the United States, a gleaming jumble of copper pots, rustic crockery, and European imports.

Among other temptations at the towering **Canal Place Shopping Centre** (333 Canal Street at Tchoupitoulas Street; 504–522–9200) you'll find the local outpost of **Williams-Sonoma** (504–523–3993), regional foods and cookbooks at **Louisiana Potpourri** (504–524–9023), imported European napery at **Linens** (504–586–8148), plus a stellar collection of pottery and hand-blown glassware crafted "Right Here In New Orleans" at **RHINO** (504–523–7945).

DAY ONE: EVENING

Before you head back to Maison de Ville to dress for dinner, cross Canal Street to drink in a little history at the **Sazerac Bar** in the grand old **Fairmont Hotel** (123 Baronne Street between Canal and Common Streets; 504–529–7111). Just off the lobby, the sedate den is lined with dark walnut paneling and Paul Ninas' 10-foot murals of New Orleans scenes, reclaimed from the 1939 New York World's Fair. It's a plush backdrop for intimate talk, a provocative spot to speculate on the pleasures to come as you toast one another with the specialty of the house.

According to local legend, the Sazerac was the world's first cocktail, mixed in 1859 in a French Quarter apothecary shop by Antoine Amadée Peychaud. The pharmacist served his wildly popular "stomach tonic" in a *coquetier* (French for "egg cup"), a term that was mangled by his American customers to "cock-tay," and after downing a few, to "cocktail." Monsieur Peychaud's original recipe contained Sazerac-de-Forge cognac and a dash of absinthe. The modified version still presented at bars all over town dates from 1870, an intensely flavored blend of rye whiskey, Herbsaint (an anise-flavored liquor), and Peychaud bitters.

Dinner

Shortly after its debut in 1991, **Emeril's** (800 Tchoupitoulas Street at Julia Street; 504-528-9393; expensive) was anointed "Restaurant of the Year" by *Esquire* critic John Mariani.

Kitchen Sink Romance

Before the days of star chefs and cooking as theater, the region of the dining room nearest the kitchen was known as Siberia, a remote place to banish noisy yahoos and an insult to everyone else. Now it's not uncommon for connoisseurs to compete for the best seats in the house, where they can watch the master of the moment at work and observe all the backstage bustle. The chef's table at Emeril's has been the scene of more than one engagement, as well as a favored dining spot for movers, shakers, and celebrities. (Politically correct lovebirds Tim Robbins and Susan Sarandon, predictably enough, insisted on meeting the dishwashers.)

"In Europe it's considered an honor to be invited back into the heart of a kitchen," says Emeril's general manager Mauricio Andrade. "To hear the sounds, to smell the smells, to watch the whole machine being managed and directed—it's a tremendous physical and emotional experience. Not everyone can appreciate it, but 90 percent of the time they're blown away. They have the opportunity to get up and watch items being prepared, to ask questions. Even if they're a little apprehensive, the chef and his staff wait on them hand and foot. Generally we serve a tasting menu. We usually do seven or eight courses, sometimes just five—but the record is eighteen, held by brothers in the restaurant industry from Chicago."

However, New Orleans' love affair with Emeril Lagasse had already begun a decade earlier, when he took the helm as executive chef at Commander's Palace in 1980, succeeding Louisiana cooking guru Paul Prudhomme. Today the Massachusetts-born Lagasse is almost as famous as his Cajun predecessor, thanks to his exuberant *Essence of Emeril* program on the Food Channel.

Sky-high ceilings and plate glass windows create a lofty atmosphere that's just right for a prime location on Gallery Row in the Warehouse/Arts District. The effect is softened by warm wood furnishings and service that's efficient without being chilly. The chef's table is privately situated inside the kitchen. It's a comfortable fit for two or four; six is a little tight, but worth the squeeze. Emeril's also seats up to ten aficionados at the galvanized steel "chef's food bar" in the dining room, which overlooks the entrée line and has become one of the hottest tickets in town.

The food is as spectacular as the presentation, with seasonal offerings that feature stacked salads, seafood parfaits, smoked salmon cheesecakes, and fire-roasted vegetables. You could encounter jumbo scallops in a truffle herb crust or a homey veal chop simmered in a cast-iron skillet with sweet potato/pecan gravy. The desserts are legendary, especially the signature banana cream pie with banana crust, caramel sauce, and chocolate shavings. Ask for two forks and dive in together.

Take a cab back to the hotel for a little stargazing in your courtyard before drifting off to bed.

DAY TWO: MORNING

All guests at Hotel Maison de Ville are treated to continental breakfast in bed, delivered on a silver tray with a newspaper and a rose, a light and elegant appetizer for a full day devoted to the pleasures of the palate. Begin with a short walk to Jackson Brewery to pick up a few basics.

Brunch

Touristy, but substantial, the **Louisiana General Store** (Jackson Brewery, 620 Decatur Street at Jackson Square; 504–525–2665) peddles iron skillets, spices, books, Cajun/Creole foodstuffs, and regional cooking classes. The three-hour seminars (daily from 10:00 A.M. to 1:00 P.M.) are relaxed and chatty, a fun introduction to such homestyle standards as gumbo, jambalaya, rich bread pudding, and pecan pralines. All cooking is done by staff chefs, cheered on by the comfortably seated audience. Generous tastings make a meal, plus you'll go home with a couple of fattening new skills, all for about $20 per person. It's best to reserve in advance. Ask for a mail-order catalog.

DAY TWO: AFTERNOON

The historic **French Market,** oldest in the U.S., follows the riverfront from Jackson Square to Barracks Street. It began more than 200 years ago as an Indian trading post. The elegant colonnaded structure was erected in 1813 for a Gascogne butcher's market. In those days it was a combination grocery store and shopping mall, an exotic and noisy flurry of parrots, monkeys, livestock, caged fowl, fishmongers, patent medicines, and household contraptions. Native Americans still roamed the grounds, along with bargemen, fur traders, and buccaneers. Dentists would operate alfresco, minus anesthetic, accompanied by brass bands to drown out the screams of their patients—a favorite with spectators.

Health codes and Wal-Marts put an end to such extravaganzas, but today you'll still find anything from Omar's fresh-baked pies to alligator skulls in the crowded stalls that are open around the clock in the section known as the **Old Farmer's Market** (between Ursulines and Barracks Streets). A popular tourist attraction, it also remains a major produce source for area restaurants and a fun place to rummage for tasty souvenirs. Here's the spot to pick out potent fruits and vegetables for an intensive course of aphro-loading as a prelude to love. (Ancient sources recommend asparagus, tomatoes, strawberries, figs, and peaches.)

Cross the street to stock up on rare imported cheeses, olive oils, salamis, coffees, spices, and other Mediterranean goodies at a couple of beloved local institutions. The two jam-packed Sicilian *alimentaris* have been competitors on the same block for nearly seventy-five years. **Central Grocery Company** (923 Decatur Street between Dumaine and St. Philip Streets; 504–523–1620) was established by the Tusa family in 1906. **Progress Grocery** (915 Decatur Street between Dumaine and St. Philip Streets; 504–525–6627) has been operated by the Perrone family since 1924. Both have mail-order catalogs.

Return to the hotel in time for a doze under the banana trees or a quick plunge in the pool before you dress for dinner. Maybe snack on a few of those aphrodisiacs . . .

DAY TWO: EVENING
Dinner

Ask a New Orleanian to recommend the city's greatest restaurant, and chances are he'll answer **Commander's Palace** (1403 Washington Avenue at Coliseum Street; 504–899–8221; expensive). In fact, the grand old Creole institution was named number one in the U.S. by *Food & Wine* in 1996, along with countless other awards over the years.

The Garden District mansion, painted a startling bright turquoise, has been in business since 1880, when it was established by Emile Commander. During the 1920s sporting gentlemen were entertained in the bordello upstairs, while families were routed into the first-floor dining room through a separate entrance. The Brennan family took over in 1974, showcasing the famous tropical courtyard with glass walls and garden decor, and launching the much-imitated weekend jazz brunch.

Though newer dishes can compete with the most creative in town, Creole classics are at their best here. Order a traditional feast of turtle soup with sherry, shrimp rémoulade, Gulf fish with roasted pecans, and bread pudding soufflé. Afterward, linger on that famous courtyard and bid farewell to New Orleans with brandy and hot chicory coffee under the stars.

FOR MORE ROMANCE

Since 1992 the **New Orleans Wine and Food Experience** has presented vintner dinners at famous local restaurants, receptions in French Quarter antiques shops and art galleries, educational seminars, and grand tastings. To request an information packet or registration forms for the annual June event, contact the organizers at P. O. Box 70514, New

Orleans, LA 70172; (504) 529–WINE. Packages available from Travel New Orleans (800–535–8747) include accommodations at selected downtown and French Quarter hotels.

Dozens of freewheeling food-related festivals are scheduled all over Louisiana throughout the year. Contact the **Louisiana State Office of Tourism** (504–568–5661) for a calendar.

For a fascinating glimpse into the past, **The Historic New Orleans Collection** (533 Royal Street between St. Louis and Toulouse Streets; 504–523–4662) maintains extensive files of early menus and photos (interior and exterior) from local restaurants. Though not on display, the documents are accessible to the public at the facility's new **Williams Research Center** (410 Chartres Street between Conti and St. Louis Streets; 504–523–4662).

NARCISSUS DOES NEW ORLEANS
LOVE IN VAIN

*S*elf-love is the sincerest love of all, especially when you can share it with someone else, so here's a quest for partners in vogue who dream the impossible dream: to actually look better after a trip to New Orleans.

Right away you're ahead of the game, certain to appear thinner against a backdrop of locals and tourists who have abandoned their figures to fried seafood and pecan pie. No need to feel deprived, though, when you can feed your desires with delta aphrodisiacs like chilled oysters on the half shell, spicy boiled shrimp, hot and crusty baguettes, ripe Creole tomatoes, homegrown strawberries, and Sicilian fruit ices.

Even exercise is a luxury when your power walk is shaded by the ancient oaks of Audubon Park or serenaded by freelance musicians along the Mississippi River levee. Mild winter days are fine for golf or tennis. And summer transforms the entire town into an enormous steam bath, wonderfully hydrating for the skin and a liberating experience for the hair. (Whatever the condition of your head on the inside, on the outside you'll look like a regular Einstein.)

It's a great excuse to buy a hat in one of the few cities where romantic millinery and haberdashery still flourish, along with perfumeries, portraitists, mask makers, and other masters of illusion.

Practical notes: Phone ahead to make appointments for spa treatments at the Canal Place branch of **Lulu Buras** (504–523–5858) and at **Belladonna** (504–891–4393). You'll also need to set up a date with **New Orleans School of GlassWorks & Printmaking Studio** (504–529–7277) to have your hands casted in sand for the sculpture. Reservations are recommended for **The Bistro at Maison de Ville** (504–528–9206).

DAY ONE: AFTERNOON

Romance at a Glance

♥ *Luxuriate in the pleasures of the flesh at two fashionable day spas.*

♥ *Hold hands forever in a glass sculpture.*

♥ *Commission a custom fragrance from a 150-year-old perfumery.*

♥ *Feast on Louisiana seafood with an exotic twist at sexy Shalimar.*

Check into the **Westin Canal Place Hotel** (100 Iberville Street at the River; 504–566–7006 or 800–228–3000; doubles, $259 to $289; suites $379 to $3,000), where you can bed down in a riverfront room with dazzling views and a big marble bath, secure in the knowledge that more than thirty shops are located just under your pillows. Below the 11th-floor lobby lie Saks Fifth Avenue, Gucci, Polo/Ralph Lauren, Bally Switzerland, Brooks Brothers, Ann Taylor . . . aaaah, better than counting sheep.

The high-rise hostelry is perched atop **Canal Place Shopping Centre** (333 Canal Street at Tchoupitoulas Street; 504–522–9200), a sleek vertical mall where you'll also find one of the city's toniest day spas, **Lulu Buras** (504–523–5858). Stop here first to pamper yourselves with European facials and paraffin nail treatments, then ask one of the consultants to customize a take-home regimen from the exclusive line of skin care products.

Now's the time to preserve your perfect manicures for posterity, so hail a cab for a quick trip to **New Orleans School of GlassWorks & Printmaking Studio** (727 Magazine Street between Girod and Julia Streets; 504–529–7277). By prior arrangement, artisans will have a box of casting sand ready and waiting to make an impression of your hands for a glass sculpture. The casting takes about thirty minutes, plus three days to complete the piece. It can be shipped to you at home, inscribed with your names and the date, if you wish. Staffers will photograph you making the imprint, even scan the image into a computer to create an E-mail postcard for your friends.

The South's largest glassmaking and printmaking facility also creates hand-blown hearts and elegant glass gift boxes (complete with inscribed glass tags), as well as hand-embossed wedding invitations on handmade paper. Mischievous fiancés have been known to commission a champagne flute or goblet with an engagement ring encircling the stem. (Unfortunately, it must be broken to retrieve the prize.)

DAY ONE: EVENING

On your way out tonight, loiter in the lobby over a cup of herbal tea (or splurge on a glass of champagne in the Green Bar) while you drink in one of the best views in town. The illuminated twin bridges and skyline are spectacular after dark, fading into soft gaslight from the French Quarter and ghostly reflections of the ships gliding along the Mississippi. Angle your vantage point just so, and you'll also be able to admire your own reflections in the massive plate glass windows.

Dinner

The Bistro at Maison de Ville (727 Toulouse Street between Royal and Bourbon Streets; 504–528–9206; expensive) is a see-and-be-seen spot for chic cuisine, praised by

Food & Wine, Esquire, Gourmet, and *Time,* among others. The youthful kitchen staff has earned that international reputation with a creative but substantial menu that changes with the seasons. You could be offered anything from roasted Portobello mushrooms stuffed with crabmeat and goat cheese to grilled shrimp on Asian-style orzo pasta in a lemongrass curry vinaigrette.

The noisy Parisian-style Bistro is lined with mirrors, dark wood paneling, red leather banquettes, and fashionable upstarts. Tiny tables are squeezed close together, which can present a challenge for the plus-sized.

DAY TWO: MORNING

Breakfast in bed on fresh berries and melon from room service, before you head uptown to buff your bodies from scalp to toe. You'll need to phone weeks in advance to set up a couple's appointment at exclusive day spa **Belladonna** (2900 Magazine Street at Sixth Street; 504–891–4393) for a double whammy that includes a private Jacuzzi for two and a light lunch, usually pasta and salad, in the Japanese garden. Choose your antitoxins from a full menu of herbal wraps, salt rubs, seaweed body envelopment, marine hydro-massage, shiatsu, aromatherapy, cool gel leg treatments, reflexology pedicures . . .

DAY TWO: AFTERNOON

All polished up and someplace to go: Take a cab to Jackson Square for a late afternoon promenade and treat yourselves to some baubles and bows.

A picturesque shop now operating on the square was first established on Bourbon Street in 1843, hence the name **Bourbon French Parfums** (525 St. Ann Street on Jackson Square; 504–522–4480). The original proprietors built their business on the secret formula for Eau

de Cologne, a European fragrance favored by Napoleon Bonaparte. Along with another all-time bestseller, Kus Kus (based on the green undertones of a local root known as vetivert), it is still part of a fascinating inventory graced by dozens of other vintage scents.

Custom blends are a specialty. A one-hour sitting entails a body chemistry analysis, personality profile, and assessment of your likes and dislikes before the mixing of the fine oils begins. When the perfect combination is isolated, "secret" formulas for the two of you will be recorded and available for special order in an entire wardrobe of toiletries, including perfume, cologne, eau de toilette, body powder, lotion, shampoo, foaming shower gel, and bath salts.

At any rate, be sure to sample a few of the eighty historic house blends before you go. Try a whiff of Alessandra, Honeysuckle, Olive Blossom, Magnolia, Voodoo Love, Wildest Dreams . . . and, of course, Narcisse.

A few blocks away, you can select a basic felt or straw hat, plus assorted plumage, for ladies' custom millinery at elegant **Fleur de Paris** (712 Royal Street at Pirate's Alley; 504–525–1899). **Gallery I/O** (829 Royal Street between St. Ann and Dumaine Streets; 504–523–5041) is home base for nationally known artist Thomas Mann and his "techno-romantic" jewelry that incorporates hearts, eyeballs, and other startling images.

Finally, before the sun goes down, stroll back around **Jackson Square** (bordered by Decatur, St. Ann, St. Peter, and Chartres Streets) and choose a lucky sidewalk artist to capture your magnificent mugs on canvas.

DAY TWO: EVENING

If you can turn a blind eye to the tourists, slip into the bar at **Fashion Cafe** (619 Decatur Street between Toulouse Street and Wilkinson Row; 504–522–3181; moderate) for a quick Evian and pay homage to the Gaultier mesh dress worn by Madonna in her video "Fever," Vivienne Westwood shoes once modeled by Naomi Campbell, Diana Ross' Aghayan gown, and other ab-fab duds on display.

Dinner

Just around the corner, even the healthiest vegetarian cuisine seems decadent at **Shalimar** (535 Wilkinson Row between Decatur and Chartres Streets; 504–523–0099; moderate). The multilevel restaurant, formerly a stable for Jax Brewery's draft horses, was renovated by owners Har and Anila Keswani, who traveled throughout their native India to collect the furnishings and fittings. The ultra-romantic result even captivates pedestrians, who stop to peer into the front window as though it were a shop display. Diners sit in intimate nooks, secluded by hand-carved wooden screens painted with scenes from Hindu mythology. Golden threads woven into antique tapestries still gleam. Soft lighting glows through rough-hewn slabs of glass (etched with Indian goddesses) and handmade copper fixtures.

Begin with a nonalcoholic mango cocktail, then tank up on Omega-3 with fresh Louisiana seafood seared at more than 800 degrees in the *tandoor* clay oven. Better yet, kick-start your senses with a tongue-torching *vindaloo.* Remember, hot and spicy foods stimulate your body's own endorphins for a natural high, a sexy prelude to a night exploring the mysteries of the *Kama Sutra.*

FOR MORE ROMANCE

Ride the streetcar uptown to **Riverbend** (at the intersection of St. Charles and Carrollton Avenues), a cozy neighborhood of historic cottages, shops, and restaurants cradled in a curve of the Mississippi. Scout out consignment couture for resale at **On the Other Hand** (8126 Hampson Street between South Carrollton Avenue and Dublin Street; 504–861–0159), custom baubles at **Symmetry Jewelers** (8136 Hampson Street between South Carrollton Avenue and Dublin Street; 504–861–9925), and designer fashions at **Ballin's Ltd.** (721 Dante Street at Hampson Street; 504–866–4367).

Frame your fresh new complexion in world-class millinery, frilled with antique feathers from Germany and turn-of-the-century flowers from France. Hats by local designer **Yvonne LaFleur** have starred in *The Great Gatsby, Pretty Baby, Chanel Solitaire,* and other films. You'll also find frou-frou lingerie and her exclusive line of YLF fashions at the Riverbend boutique that bears her name (8131 Hampson Street at Dublin Street; 504–866–9666).

Don't miss the main store and atelier of nationally known jeweler **Mignon Faget Ltd.** (710 Dublin Street between Hampson and Maple Streets; 504–865–1107), which also has a branch right under your hotel room (Canal Place Shopping Centre; 504–524–2973).

Dozens of other shops are right across the street from your hotel at the panoramic

Riverwalk Marketplace (follows the Mississippi from Canal Street to Girod Street; 504–522–1555). Other downtown malls worthy of your attention include the festive complexes known collectively as **Jax Brewery and The Millhouse** (620–24 Decatur Street at Jackson Square; 504–587–0749). Adjoining the Superdome is the more serious **New Orleans Centre** (1400 Poydras Street between Loyola Avenue and LaSalle Street; 504–568–0000), a postmodern marble-and-glass temple where you can worship at Macy's, Lord & Taylor, Victoria's Secret, and more than fifty other shops and eateries.

ITINERARY 4
One day and two nights

THE BIG LAZY:

TWO DAYS OF SUBTROPICAL SLOTH

*N*atives claim New Orleans has two seasons, summer and February, but you don't need a fireplace on a snowy night for romance. Just crank up the air conditioner, turn on the ceiling fan, and close the shutters for a cool and sexy siesta illuminated by dim slats of sunlight shafting across the bed.

Better yet, check into a big hotel with luxurious services and great views, a little corner of heaven where you don't have to do anything but eat, drink, sleep, and pay 11-percent tax (gotta give the devil his due). On this lazy dream vacation, you'll never walk more than a block at a time and you definitely won't dress for dinner, because it's too darn hot. Along the way, if there's anything you want to skip, go right ahead. It'll still be there *mañana*.

Practical notes: Reservations are recommended for dinner at K-Paul's Louisiana Kitchen (504–524–7394) and brunch at The Court of Two Sisters (504–522–7291).

DAY ONE: AFTERNOON

To kick back in the heart of the French Quarter, check into the **Omni Royal Orleans** (621 St. Louis Street at Royal Street; 800–THE–OMNI or 504–529–3333; I.T.'s, $109 to $129; doubles, $139 to $364; suites, $239 to $389). Accommodations range from bargain priced "I.T.'s" (smaller "individual traveler" rooms) to luxury suites with whirlpool baths and private balconies. The lobby is a luxe oasis of marble, gilded furnishings, and crystal chandeliers; in-house services range from a barber shop to a florist; and rooms are cozily fitted out with Irish linen sheets and thick terry bathrobes. More importantly, the world is at your feet. Just walk a block or less for Bourbon Street clubs, Royal Street galleries, and several of the city's greatest restaurants and bars. If you really get ambitious, hike 1½ blocks to reach the festive attractions surrounding Jackson Square.

On second thought, have the concierge contact **Good Old Days Carriages** (504–523–0804). A driver will pick you up at the front door for a guided tour of the French Quarter in a horse-drawn buggy, then return you to the hotel for a nap before dinner.

Romance at a Glance

♥ *Lounge around the rooftop pool and get high on the view at the Omni Royal Orleans.*

♥ *Let your horse do the walking and your driver do the talking on a languid buggy tour.*

♥ *Kick back with celebrated cuisine in country comfort at K-Paul's Louisiana Kitchen.*

♥ *Drift off over nightcaps and a lullaby in ragtime at Maxwell's Toulouse Cabaret.*

♥ *Doze through the afternoon to recover from brunch at The Court of Two Sisters.*

DAY ONE: EVENING

You don't know it yet, but one of the reasons you chose this hotel is the incredible view from the rooftop pool and observation deck. Bestir yourselves in time for a little eye-opener at the cabana bar before dinner.

"Start slow and taper off."
—Walt Stack

"Never put off until tomorrow what you can do the day after tomorrow."
—Mark Twain

Dinner

You've seen the world's most famous Cajun chef on television and magazine covers, now you can amble over and sample Paul Prudhomme's spicy creations at **K-Paul's Louisiana Kitchen** (416 Chartres Street between Conti and St. Louis Streets; 504–524–7394; expensive). The menu changes daily to take advantage of the freshest regional ingredients for a sophisticated country feast of dark and smoky gumbos, complex *etouffées,* peppery roasted duck with pecan gravy, rabbit tenderloin with Creole mustard, fried eggplant *pirogues* (Cajun canoes) loaded with fresh shellfish, and rustic pies. Presented in a comfy country-style cafe lined with old brick walls and no-nonsense wood furnishings, here's one lazy pleasure that dances on the palate and goes easy on the nerves.

On your way back to bed, get yourselves in the mood with a jazz session at **Maxwell's Toulouse Cafe** (615 Toulouse Street between Chartres and Royal Streets; 504–523–4207), where you might be serenaded by the Jimmy Maxwell Orchestra, the Dukes of Dixieland, or Harry Connick, Sr. (who daylights as the New Orleans District Attorney). Shows are scheduled on the hour nightly and the $15 cover charge includes the first round of drinks.

On the other hand, if you're too damn lazy to leave the hotel room—or even to travel to

Carolyn Kolb's Top 10 New Orleans Romantic Movies

What could be better than watching a classic movie unroll between your toes, with a bit of New Orleans charm thrown in for spice? All are available on videotape.

10. **The Pelican Brief,** *1993. Julia Roberts at the peak of fragile vulnerability, racing through French Quarter crowds to escape an assassin. Leaves you panting.*

9. **Tightrope,** *1984. Clint Eastwood and Genevieve Bujold prowl the seamy edges of New Orleans nightlife in this tale of a cop and the sexual predator he pursues.*

8. **Interview with the Vampire,** *1994. Passion can be a draining experience as Tom Cruise, in lace cuffs and tight satin pants, nibbles his way through the centuries.*

7. **The Big Easy,** *1987. Dennis Quaid, the cop, and Ellen Barkin, the prosecutor, explore new law enforcement positions in this steamy yarn. The accents aren't authentic, but the scenery is.*

6. **Angel Heart,** *1987. Robert DeNiro, Mickey Rourke, Charlotte Rampling, Lisa Bonet. Do do that hoodoo that you do, etc. The X-rated scenes were put back into the videotape.*

5. **King Creole,** *1958. Elvis himself, crooning and hip-twitching his way through the Vieux Carré with sultry Carolyn Jones.*

4. **Cat People,** *1982. Malcolm McDowell and Nastassia Kinski. The feline sensuality of this eerie thriller colors every frame.*

3. **Easy Rider,** *1969. Dennis Hopper, Peter Fonda, Jack Nicholson. '60s nostalgia with a New Orleans destination.*

2. **Pretty Baby,** *1978. Susan Sarandon, Brooke Shields, Keith Carradine. Tale of a child prostitute, lush and authentic settings, and a musical score with a sensuous beat.*

1. **Double Feature**

Panic in the Streets, *1951. Richard Widmark, Barbara Bel Geddes, Jack Palance. The all-time greatest New Orleans movie—Elia Kazan's superbly photographed film noir. Health officer Widmark tracks the plague through the back alleys of the Vieux Carré and the riverfront. Hold hands and be spellbound.*

A Streetcar Named Desire, *1951. Tennessee Williams's play is Kazan's other great New Orleans movie, the quintessential romantic film set in the city. Marlon Brando is incandescent as the virile Stanley Kowalski, with Vivien Leigh playing Blanche Dubois, the moth to his flame; great performances by Kim Hunter and Karl Malden.*

"It was such a lovely day I thought it was a pity to get up."
—W. Somerset Maugham

New Orleans at all—you could just watch the parade pass you by on video. The sidebar lists a stack of great flicks to get you started, recommended by local historian and film lover Carolyn Kolb. (For details on her Movie Sites Tour, see "Between the Covers.")

DAY TWO: Morning
Brunch

What could possibly be more enticing than breakfast in bed? How about a sinfully decadent buffet laid out amongst tropical blooms and strolling jazz musicians on one of the most lavish courtyards in town? More than fifty regional dishes, from jambalaya to shrimp Creole, are offered every day from to 9:00 A.M. to 3:00 P.M. at **The Court of Two Sisters** (613 Royal Street between Toulouse and St. Peter Streets; 504–522–7261; expensive). This romantic setting was once occupied by the *rabais* (notions shop) of sisters Emma and Bertha Camors, who dealt in imported lace, perfumes, and other fripperies from 1886 to 1906. Touristy, yes, but truly beautiful, and casual dress is (unfortunately) the norm.

Before you head back to your room for a nap, step into the neighboring **Martin LaBorde Gallery** (631 Royal Street between Toulouse and St. Peter Streets; 504–587–7111) to take inspiration from Bodo, the little magician who floats through LaBorde's moonlit landscapes, a master of dreams.

DAY TWO: AFTERNOON

When you're ready to face the world again, walk across the street to poke around the nearby shops and galleries. Of special interest are the French Impressionist paintings at **Kurt E. Schon, Ltd.** (523 Royal Street between St. Louis and Toulouse Streets; 504–524–5462), elaborate Carnival masks at **Rumors** (513 Royal Street between St. Louis and Toulouse Streets; 504–525–0292), miniature warriors at **Le Petit Soldier Shop** (528 Royal Street between St. Louis and Toulouse Streets; 504–523–7741), antique weaponry at **James H. Cohen & Sons** (437 Royal Street between Conti and St. Louis Streets; 504–522–3305), and valuable oddities at **Raymond H. Weill Co., Rare Stamps** (407 Royal Street between Conti and St. Louis Streets; 504–581–7373). Even if you can't afford to buy, the time travel is a romantic freebie.

DAY TWO: EVENING
Dinner

Whatever you've been doing assiduously, it's time to think about food again. One of the better places to chow down on fresh Louisiana shellfish is **Ralph and Kacoo's** (519 Toulouse Street between Decatur and Chartres Streets; 504–522–5226; moderate). Order the crawfish or crab platter for generous tastings of several traditional dishes or sample exotica like fried alligator and stuffed softshell crawfish. The decor is cheery and pleasantly cluttered, sort

of like an old boathouse, and an enormous saltwater aquarium is filled with luminous beauties. Think beach music and summer love.

You won't need to exert yourselves too strenuously to join the conversation at **O'Flaherty's Irish Channel Pub** (514 Toulouse Street between Decatur and Chartres Streets; 504–529–1317), where good listeners are always welcome. The Celtic Folk are on the program nightly, along with occasional performances by visiting bands, even lessons in Irish dancing and Scottish bagpipe.

FOR MORE ROMANCE

If you are willing to abandon one of the basic tenets of this itinerary (dressing down for dinner) four of the city's greatest restaurants are also within a block of the Omni Royal Orleans. Haute Creole cuisine is on the menu at historic **Antoine's** (see "Past Imperfect") and **Brennan's French Restaurant** (see "Grand Illusions"). Both food and clientele are fashionably turned out in the **Bistro at Maison de Ville** (see "Narcissus Does New Orleans"). Dressy casual is the code at chef Emeril Lagasse's stylish **NOLA** (see "On the Prowl").

Three local hotels are directly connected to downtown malls, creating maximum comfort zones with air-conditioned access to dozens of shops and casual restaurants. The **New Orleans Hilton Riverside** (2 Poydras Street at the river; 800–445–8667 or 504–561–0500) hooks up with festival shopping along the Mississippi at **Riverwalk Marketplace** (on the river between Canal and Girod Streets; 504–522–1555). The **Hyatt Regency** (500 Poydras Plaza between Loyola Avenue and LaSalle Street; 800–233–1234 or 504–561–1234) joins the **Louisiana Superdome** (1500 Poydras Street at LaSalle Street; 504–587–3810) by way of the spectacular glass palace known as **New Orleans Centre** (1400 Poydras Street between Loyola Avenue and LaSalle Street; 504–568–0000). The **Westin Canal Place Hotel** (100 Iberville Street at the river; 800–228–3000 or 504–566–7006) is panoramically situated atop high-rise **Canal Place Shopping Centre** (200 Canal Street at the river; 504–522–9200), which is also home to a cinema multiplex and **Southern Repertory Theatre** (504–861–8163).

For more details on French Quarter galleries and antiques shops, see "Artful Seduction" and "Grand Illusions."

ITINERARY 5
Two nights and no days

ON THE PROWL

DARK CORNERS FOR MIDNIGHT RAMBLERS

*B*ourbon Street is for amateurs. Whooping fraternity boys, conventioneers on an annual toot, traveling salesmen, tour groups—it's a heckish vision, Six Flags over Sodom and Gomorrah. Wholesale sin looks so much cooler in the brochures.

Maybe you don't care to work so hard at having fun. What you crave is a little relaxed debauchery (minus the barkers and oil wrestling), a night crawl through some offbeat joints that are loaded with dark romance, fresh sounds, and intriguing strangers. Along the way, you'd like a couple of good meals, because you slept through breakfast, lunch, and dinner. And you look forward to jumping back in bed just before dawn.

Welcome to the city that rocks around the clock, where life begins after midnight and the bars never close. Whether your idea of a good time is club hopping through the wee hours or a marathon coffee jag, here are a couple of road maps to lead you to some kindred spirits.

Practical notes: Music clubs and coffeehouses draw the biggest crowds and keep the latest hours on Friday and Saturday nights; otherwise call ahead to check on closing times. As always, pay attention to your surroundings and stick to well-populated areas when walking after midnight.

Night owls will appreciate a cozy five-room inn that's ideally located for exploring Faubourg Marigny and the French Quarter in the wee hours, but well away from daytime tourist traffic. The mid-1800s Creole townhouse, made ready for the twenty-first century by an artist who renovated it as his studio/gallery, was recently converted by new owners to **Parkview Marigny Bed and Breakfast** (726 Frenchmen Street between Royal and Dauphine Streets; $87 to $107, doubles; 800–729–4640 or 504–488–4640). Ask for the main-floor room with an extra-large bathtub and dual-head shower for two, or the second-floor charmer with a dormer window overlooking Washington Square. Sleek updates blend beautifully with original architectural details and quality traditional furnishings. Complimentary continental breakfast is served in the dining area. Be sure to ask for touring and entertainment tips from hosts Christopher Liddy and Larry Molaison, an expert on Louisiana history.

Romance at a Glance

♥ *Dine fashionably late at superchef Emeril Lagasse's stylish NOLA.*

♥ *Meet the press and other hard-boiled company in Molly's at the Market.*

♥ *Cool your heels with off-duty musicians at R Bar and Fritzel's European Jazz Pub.*

♥ *Rub shoulders with the young and the restless at Café Brasil and the Dragon's Den.*

♥ *Greet the dawn over coffee and beignets at Cafe du Monde.*

NIGHT ONE: LATE

You may be the sort of lascivious layabouts who eat breakfast at dusk, but you don't have to punish yourselves with a midnight lunch at I–HOP. **NOLA** (534 St. Louis Street between Decatur and Chartres Streets; 504–522–NOLA; moderate) is open until midnight on Friday and Saturday nights. Star chef Emeril Lagasse's second local restaurant is set in an art-filled renovated warehouse, casual in manner but serious in purpose. A raving perfectionist, Lagasse employs a full-time butcher (who prepares sausages, bacon, pastrami, tasso, terrines, and pâtés) and pastry chef (for fresh breads, desserts, ice creams, and sorbets). Even the Worcestershire sauce and ketchups are made on the premises. All contribute to a style Lagasse characterizes as "new New Orleans cooking," a lightened version of Creole cuisine with various ethnic twists. The best seats in the house are at the concrete-topped "chef's counter," where diners perch on bar stools for front-row views of the busy scene around the wood-burning ovens, complete with occasional samples and running commentary from the cooks.

NIGHT ONE: LATER

Molly's at the Market (1107 Decatur Street between Ursulines and Governor Nicholls Streets; 504–525–5169) is the traditional watering hole for local and visiting journalists, a great place to solve the world's problems and make some new friends. Television newscasters, politicians, and other New Orleans personalities are occasionally pressed into service as celebrity bartenders. Walls are crammed with mementos and photographs; there's even a portrait autographed by Pope Pius XI in 1923. The beloved old pub is also headquarters for one of the city's three St. Patrick's Day parades.

NIGHT ONE: LATEST

After winding up their final sets at other clubs around town, off-duty musicians flock to the **R Bar** (1431 Royal Street at Kerlerec Street; 504–948–7499), a no-nonsense haunt that's also popular with artists, writers, and freelance philosophers. If you're more comfortable on the beaten path, **Fritzel's European Jazz Pub** (733 Bourbon Street between Orleans and St. Ann Streets; 504–561–0432) is an after-work stop for many traditional jazz musicians, who sometimes join the house band for impromptu jam sessions. The old-fashioned beer garden is a favorite with international Dixieland fans and traveling performers.

By now you should be ready for a predawn snack to fortify your walk back to bed. **Poppy's Grill** (717 St. Peter Street between Royal and Bourbon Streets; 504–524–3287; inexpensive) is open around the clock, promising "simple food for a complex neighborhood." Besides the campy diner atmosphere, the big attraction is a bit of showbiz that employs an everyday power drill to transform a whole spud into a single spiraling potato chip several feet long. This operation, which takes thirty seconds at most, has been photographed by visitors from around the world. Omelets and waffles are billed as "a Platonic dish, just like your Mama." Hand-formed burgers are grilled under a hubcap.

"An American hubcap," emphasizes manager Chuck Miller. "We use one from a GMC truck for two or three burgers. For more than that, we use a full wheel cover from a Cadillac. It steams in the natural flavors."

NIGHT TWO: LATE

When you woke up earlier this evening, you probably promised yourselves you'd never drink again, so tonight's itinerary makes the rounds of some outré coffeehouses that are sure to keep you wide awake until the wee hours. (Café Brasil and the Dragon's Den also serve liquor, in case you tumble off the wagon.)

Just about anyone will feel comfortable at **Kaldi's Coffeehouse** (941 Decatur Street at St. Philip Street; 504–586–8989). A lofty old-world oasis, located in a nineteenth-century bank building, it's a great place to kick-start your night over a late breakfast of cappuccino and croissants. Named for the mythological goatherd who got the first coffee jolt (from nibbling beans), this funky meeting spot attracts a genial and diverse crowd that ranges from disaffected youth to after-theater swells. You just know a future James Joyce is lurking in one of the corners. Occasional live entertainment features jazz, gospel, poetry readings, even opera.

Stalking the Midnight Snack

Great food and romantic ambiance: It's a lot to expect after 11:00 P.M., but New Orleans has plenty of tempting hideaways for an apres-prowl feast. Here's a short list of scenic feeding spots for late birds.

For atmosphere at any time of day, you can't beat **Napoleon House** (500 Chartres Street at St. Louis Street; 504–524–9752; inexpensive), a moody retreat for classical music and emperor-sized sandwiches until midnight Monday through Thursday, and until 1:00 A.M. on Friday and Saturday.

Walls of French doors and an antique bar also turn on the charm at **Cafe Maspero** (601 Decatur Street at Toulouse; 504–523–6250; inexpensive), but two-fisted sandwiches on chargrilled French buns are the main attraction for long lines of tourists and locals. Food is served until midnight Friday and Saturday.

Authentic Creole breakfasts are a late-night luxury at **The Old Coffee Pot** (714 St. Peter Street between Royal and Bourbon Streets; 504–524–3500; inexpensive). Pull up a chair in the shelter of the carriageway for omelet Rockefeller or traditional callas (rice cakes with pecans and syrup) until midnight Sunday through Thursday and until 1:00 A.M. on Friday and Saturday.

Fat chargrilled burgers, Polynesian drinks, and shadowy nautical atmosphere draw longtime regulars to **Port of Call** (838 Esplanade Avenue; 504–523–0120; inexpensive). Food is served until 1:00 A.M. from Sunday through Thursday, and until 3:00 A.M. on Friday and Saturday.

Open around the clock in a former corner grocery, **La Péniche** (1940 Dauphine Street at Touro Street; 504–943–1460; inexpensive) is a homey mix of greenery and old wood with a dependable menu of breakfasts, burgers, and seafood. The restaurant is closed from 7:00 A.M. on Wednesday until 9:00 A.M. on Thursday.

Still a sentimental favorite for outstanding burgers, breakfasts, house-baked pies, and crisp service, the stately white-columned **Camellia Grill** (626 South Carrollton Avenue between St. Charles and Hampson Streets; 504–866–9573; inexpensive) celebrated its fiftieth anniversary in 1996. Food is served until 1:00 A.M. from Sunday through Thursday, and until 3:00 A.M. on Friday and Saturday.

NIGHT TWO: LATER

When his father died in 1800, Bernard Xavier Philipe de Marigny de Mandeville became the wealthiest fifteen-year-old in America. Unfortunately, he also had a bit of a dice problem and rolled away the family fortune by the time he was twenty-three. To cover his losses, he subdivided his plantation and sold lots to create the early *faubourg* (suburb) that still bears his name. Today Faubourg Marigny is populated by struggling artists and literati—a fate that would have amused the young Creole aristocrat whose own poetry was so bad it once provoked a duel.

Your love is sure to find expression in this raffish old neighborhood, which adjoins the French Quarter at Esplanade Avenue. The sidewalks are alive with the sort of bohemian nightspots and ethnic restaurants that have been forced out of the Quarter by high rents and rampant tourism. Follow your ears along Frenchmen Street to sample the avant-garde offerings at an ever-changing collection of clubs and coffeehouses.

Attune your courting rituals to a world beat at one of the city's best alternative music venues, **Café Brasil** (2100 Chartres Street at Frenchmen Street; no phone), which hosts bands from South America, Africa, the Caribbean, and the U.S. The stark storefront coffeehouse also presents plays, poetry, art shows, and political events. Weekend crowds usually spill outside along the curb, which the management has lined with classic junkers ('58 DeSoto, '62 Lincoln, '65 Chrysler) to discourage customers from sitting on other parked cars.

NIGHT TWO: LATEST

Just around the corner, **Siam Cafe** (435 Esplanade Avenue between Frenchmen and North Peters Streets; 504–949–1750; inexpensive) is authentically third world, a murky and mysterious haunt splashed with red paint, wooden idols, and gold-embroidered black tablecloths. The first-floor dining room locks up around 2:00 A.M. on weekends, but live bands still rattle the ceiling from the second-floor **Dragon's Den,** where late-late diners dig into artfully arranged noodles studded with jumbo shrimp, roasted chiles, crushed peanuts, and orange slices. After 10:00 P.M. in the upstairs music bar, "Chef Tee" Thaingtham offers an abbreviated version of his regular menu, a spicy lineup of spring rolls, satay, soups, curries, and noodle dishes. Nightly entertainment is a mixed bag, anything from modern jazz to belly dancers. The clientele is mostly under thirty and strenuously hip.

Finally, **Cafe du Monde** (800 Decatur Street at Jackson Square; 504–525–4544; inexpensive) is a lovely place to end a night on the town, the traditional last stop for generations of New Orleanians. Fragrant chicory coffee is blended with steamed milk and pillow-shaped French doughnuts are served hot, dusted with powdered sugar. Busy around the clock, the twenty-four-hour sidewalk cafe is calmed by river sounds and soft views of the moon-splashed spires of St. Louis Cathedral. (You could even stagger over and repent your sins at 6:00 A.M. Mass.)

FOR MORE ROMANCE

More late-night attractions are detailed in "Howling at the Moon," "A Day of Low Culture and High Camp," and "A Feast for the Ears."

SOUL MATES

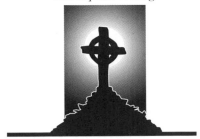

SAINTS AND SINNERS
A DAY OF MIRACLES AND MAGIC

*V*oodoo practitioners call on Christian saints for assistance. Devout church ladies burn "Lucky Bingo" candles and carry fetishes to the game in their handbags. Young girls gaze into mirrors at midnight on Good Friday to see their future husbands. Pharmacies sell "Money House Blessing" spray and "Law Stay Away" incense.

You want logic, vacation in Silicon Valley. The New Orleans web is a crazy tangle of Catholic dogma, ancient tribal custom, blind faith, and superstition that weaves throughout the local landscape. Cemeteries are guarded by stone angels and ragtag hex signs. Altars great and small are crowded with candles and icons. Decent citizens abandon all that's holy for the pagan rites of Mardi Gras, then troop into St. Louis Cathedral the next morning to get their throbbing foreheads dabbed with ashes. Overall, the effect is simply luminous. Disorganized religion has such a gorgeous influence on society.

Do you want to beguile a new paramour? Is marriage in the stars? Has the magic begun to fade? Then you've come to the right place. Just follow local tradition and cover all bets on this daylong pilgrimage that ranges from the sublime to the idolatrous.

Practical notes: The historic cemeteries of New Orleans are fascinating, but long rows of aboveground tombs provide plenty of hiding places for evildoers (and we don't mean vampires). Never wander around the grounds alone day or night, only with a guided group.

MORNING

Take a cab to **St. Roch Cemetery** (1725 St. Roch Avenue at Derbigny Street; 504–945–5961) and tell the driver to wait for five minutes while you view the famous chapel just inside the front gate. Modeled on Campo Santo dei Tedeschi (Holy Field of the Germans) near St. Peter's in Rome, it was built following the yellow fever epidemic of 1868 by a local Catholic priest. Father Thevis prayed to St. Roch (who was canonized for his work with plague victims during the Middle Ages), promising to erect this memorial with his own hands in exchange for the health of his parishioners. Over the years, hundreds have claimed miraculous cures after visiting the shrine, donating their crutches, braces, plaster casts of vital organs, glass eyes, and other tokens to the ever-changing collection that crowds the walls and altar. It's a spectacular scene in the grand and mystical tradition of Catholicism, New Orleans style, at once gruesome and inspiring.

Of special interest to lovers and lonely hearts, single men and women still make pilgrimages to the chapel on Good Friday to petition St. Roch for mates. Though the lighthearted custom was initially discouraged by the Catholic Church, Father

Romance at a Glance

♥ *Avow your love before five spectacular altars, three Catholic and two voodoo.*

♥ *Leave your mark—if you dare—on the tomb of black magic priestess Marie Laveau.*

♥ *Bewitch your mate with an authentic ju-ju bag, custom blended to do your bidding.*

♥ *Chart the course of your union with the fortune-tellers at a charming old tearoom.*

♥ *Grace a table at Christian's Restaurant, a renovated church with heavenly chow.*

Thevis insisted, "Why shouldn't they pray to God to direct them in the most important step of their lives?"

Breakfast

Afterward, tell the cab driver to drop you in the French Quarter at **Cafe Beignet** (334–B Royal Street between Bienville and Conti Streets; 504–524–5530; inexpensive). You must show up ten minutes early to join the walking tour that departs from the premises daily at 10:00 A.M. Allow a bit longer to relax over coffee and the namesake French doughnuts, served hot with a generous dusting of powdered sugar. The menu also features an assortment of pastries, egg dishes, and cereals.

❧

The two-hour **Cemetery and Voodoo History Tour** (504–947–2120) is a fun and credible ramble led by Robert Florence, a former ranger for Jean Lafitte National Park, or one of the accredited guides from his staff. First stop is lovely **Our Lady of Guadalupe Chapel** (411 North Rampart Street at Conti Street; 504–525–1551). Originally known as the Church of the Dead, it was built in 1826 to hold funerals for yellow fever victims outside the gates of the old city (now the French Quarter). Today it's the official chapel of the New Orleans Police and Fire Departments, as well as the national shrine of St. Jude, patron of hopeless causes.

Next, among the wonders of sun-baked **St. Louis Cemetery** (Basin Street at St. Louis Street), you'll see the alleged tomb of 19th-century voodoo priestess Marie Laveau, still cluttered with hex marks and fresh offerings from her latter-day disciples. The tour also visits a private voodoo shrine and **Congo Square** (North Rampart Street at Orleans Street), an ancient gathering spot that is still the scene of occasional moonlit rituals. The walk ends in front of **Marie Laveau's house** (1020 St. Ann, between Burgundy and Rampart Streets).

AFTERNOON

Continue on your own to explore the small, but authentic, collection of spiritual exotica on display at **New Orleans Historic Voodoo Museum** (724 Dumaine Street, between Royal and Bourbon Streets; 504–523–7685). Adventurous souls can pay a small fee to creep through a couple of back rooms crammed with handmade icons and fetishes, plus the odd human skull or petrified cat. Otherwise, just commission one of the in-house practitioners to mix a magical "ju-ju bag" to strengthen your union while you peruse the wild inventory of love potions and herbal cures on display in the front shop. Either way, be sure to leave an offering on the altar for Exu, an earthy spirit who likes candy bars and cigars.

Lunch

This being New Orleans, food plays a big role in local voodoo tradition. Some practitioners still employ garlic or bay leaves to guard against witchcraft. Others cook okra for Shango, African deity of thunder and lightning, to invoke his protection from evil and unseen enemies. And modern priestesses stir up spicy shrimp dishes to woo blessings from love goddess Oshun, a surefire prescription for divine sex.

Clearly, all signs point to a steaming bowl of shrimp gumbo, a dark and complex brew zapped with an extra whammy of garlic, bay leaves, and okra. **The Gumbo Shop** (630 St. Peter Street between Chartres and Royal Streets; 504–525–1486; moderate) is a quaint and cozy cafe with a brick-walled courtyard and a dependable menu that also features jambalayas, etouffées, and other Louisiana mainstays.

⌘

The **New Orleans Pharmacy Museum** (514 Chartres Street, between St. Louis and Toulouse Streets; 504–565–8027) maintains a small collection of voodoo artifacts and handwritten formulas, including ancient herbal cures that have since been proven effective by modern research. Old newspaper ads for local drugstores promote love potions, lucky

Spellbound: Prayers and Potions to Bewitch Your Mate

How's your love life? Before you call in a plastic surgeon or spin doctor, try one of these natural remedies, just a few of hundreds collected for the WPA Louisiana Writers Program by Lyle Saxon, Robert Tallent, and Edward Dreyer. Their 1945 Gumbo Ya-Ya: Folk Tales of Louisiana *was reprinted in 1987 by Pelican Publishing.*

To win the woman of your dreams, sleep with a few strands of her hair under your pillow or carry a piece of St. John the Conqueror root in your pocket. (One of the most common talismans, it's still sold at local voodoo shops and spiritual supply houses.)

To catch the man you desire, hide his picture behind a mirror. You might also tuck a silk-wrapped thimble into your pocket for three days and make a wish on it every time you enter or leave a house. (Calling Dr. Freud . . .)

To insure a good match, join the hands of two dolls with a ribbon and place them in a mound of sand surrounded by nine candles. Sprinkle champagne over all, chanting, "St. Joseph, make this marriage and I'll pay." After your wedding, leave a plate of food under a tree in Congo Square to settle the debt.

To get rid of a man, "pick a rooster naked" and feed it a spoonful of whiskey; then place in its beak a piece of paper inscribed nine times with the name of the offending male. Thus prepared, the poor bird must be set loose in a cemetery. Within three days, Mr. Wrong will be out of your life—and his.

If all else fails, at least you can charm your cat into staying home. Just sprinkle sugar in its mouth on a Friday morning, rub grease on its paws, or make it look in a mirror.

powders, St. John the Conqueror root, and other bizarre sundries that were stocked under the counter and requested by number to insure privacy. You'll also find more conventional remedies—and some outlandish relics of quackery—in the restored 1823 shop that was originally operated by Louis Dufilho, Jr., one of the first licensed pharmacists in America. Be sure to notice the antique marble soda fountain (unfortunately defunct) and the courtyard garden of medicinal plants.

Oldest in the U.S., **St. Louis Cathedral** (Jackson Square between Père Antoine's Alley and Pirate's Alley; 504–525–9585) is the city's most famous landmark, named for Louis IX, saint-king of France. (You'll see him announcing the Seventh Crusade in the huge mural behind the altar.) Tours last about fifteen minutes, but you can linger quietly in one of the pews to meditate on the sublime architecture, statuary, and stained glass. While you're there, any single ladies who'd like to petition yet another holy matchmaker can light a candle for St. Ann, patroness of unmarried women and inspiration for the old jump-rope chant: "St. Ann, St. Ann, send me a man!"

Afterward, pop into the enchanting **Bottom of the Cup Tearoom** (732 Royal Street between Père Antoine's Alley and St. Ann Street; 504–523–1204) for a little tea and prophecy. Since 1929 this quirky old curiosity has welcomed lovers and others for private readings in curtained booths. Staff psychics consult your choice of leaves, palms, crystal balls, tarot cards, handwriting, and other cosmic pipelines. The shop also sells assorted fortune-telling paraphernalia for do-it-yourselfers.

EVENING

On the way to dinner in Mid-City, ask your cab driver to detour along beautiful Bayou St. John, past **Pitot House** (1440 Moss Street, between Esplanade Avenue and Grand Route St. John; 504–482–0312). Formerly home to the great-grandmother of French Impressionist painter Edgar Degas, then to James Pitot (first mayor of incorporated New Orleans), it was purchased in 1904 for a convent by Mother Frances Xavier Cabrini, the first U.S. citizen to be canonized as a saint by the Catholic Church. In 1962 the convent donated the 1799 building to the Louisiana Landmarks Society. Today it's restored as a country home furnished in period antiques, a favorite setting for weddings.

Dinner

Speaking of formal ceremonies, wear your Sunday best to dine in one of the city's temples of contemporary Creole cuisine. **Christian's Restaurant** (3835 Iberville Street at North Scott Street; 504–482–4924; expensive) is set in a renovated church, graced by dark wood paneling, stained glass windows, classic art, and crisp service. Start with Crawfish Caroline in a brandy cream sauce or try the bacon-wrapped oysters *en brochette*. Shrimp Marigny is sauteed (with pearl onions, mushrooms, sundried tomatoes, and garlic), then flamed in brandy, and finished with a Dijon butter sauce. Veal Madeira is pan-sauteed with mushrooms and garlic. Fresh fruit sorbets are a righteous dessert, but sinners will succumb to baked Alaska or *profiteroles au chocolat* filled with house-made ice creams. If the rest of the night goes as well, you'll have plenty more to repent by morning.

FOR MORE ROMANCE

Devotees can put together quite an amorous arsenal at **F&F Botanica** (801 North Broad Street at St. Ann Street; 504–482–9142), just a short cab ride away from the tourist traps of the French Quarter. Serious practitioners do their shopping at this spiritual supermarket in a working-class neighborhood, where a few dollars buys anything from love potions to "Domination Triple Fast Action Bubble Bath and Floor Wash." While you're there, be sure to stock up on that household essential for every successful couple, his and hers "Keep Your Mouth Shut" candles.

Phone **Save Our Cemeteries** (504–525–3377) for a schedule of their guided tours to various sites. Proceeds fund preservation of the historic "cities of the dead."

You'll find other spooky amusements in the "Haunting Honeymoon" itinerary. For more on local churches and convents, see "Rich in Love," and "Haute Creole." The construction of elaborate food-laden altars, and other St. Joseph's Day rituals observed by the local Sicilian community, is detailed in "Moonstruck on the Mississippi."

ITINERARY 7
Two days and two nights

BETWEEN THE COVERS
AN INTRIGUING PLOT FOR LITERARY LOVERS

*N*ew Orleans has provided a very attractive setting for both writers and their works for centuries. William Faulkner, F. Scott Fitzgerald, Tennessee Williams, Truman Capote, and Walker Percy are but a few of the luminaries who have lived and worked here. In the past few decades, the city has played a major role in the novels of native authors Anne Rice, Shirley Ann Grau, Nancy Lemann, Sheila Bosworth, Chris Wiltz, and other established stars. Meanwhile, there are rumblings that we may soon experience a literary renaissance to rival the boom days of the 1920s.

You'll need to route your affair via the St. Charles Avenue line, instead of the now-defunct *Streetcar Named Desire,* but you can still court one another over *Dinner at Antoine's* and take *A Walk on the Wild Side* during *The Witching Hour.* You may be *Almost Innocent* in a town where everyone else is skilled at *Handling Sin,* but true lovers can usually depend upon the kindness of strangers.

Practical notes: Reserve well in advance for Heritage Tours (504–949–9805 or 504–524–2940) and Carolyn Kolb's Film Site Tours (504–861–8158).

DAY ONE: AFTERNOON

New Orleans's answer to the Algonquin, the sedate and stately **Pontchartrain Hotel** (2031 St. Charles Avenue at Josephine Street; doubles $145–$175, suites $165–$270; 800–777 –6193 or 504–524–0581) is favored by visiting literati, old-line celebrities, and academics with business at nearby Tulane, Loyola, and Xavier universities. Featured in several novels by Anne Rice, who lives just a few blocks away, it's convenient for exploring the outstanding architecture of the Garden District, and the French Quarter is just a short ride away on the St. Charles Avenue streetcar. The European-style lobby is a study in grace, from the oriental rugs to the barrel-vaulted ceiling. Rooms are spacious and elegantly furnished; those above the fifth floor have great views of the river or skyline. A few smaller "pension rooms" (showers instead of bathtubs) are available at reduced rates.

Ask the concierge for a walking map and set off to view nearby historic houses. (The maps are also available from any tourist information office.) Be sure to search the shelves where Rice does, at her neighborhood **Garden District Book Shop** (2727 Prytania Street at Washington Avenue; 504–895–2266), which stocks many limited and autographed editions of her work. Owner Britton Trice, a knowledgeable guide to the local literary scene, also offers signed volumes by other regional and national authors, as well as used and rare books on New Orleans and Louisiana. It's too far to walk, but you'll also find an excellent selection of regional titles at nearby **Beaucoup Books** (5414 Magazine Street between Jefferson Avenue and Octavia Street; 800–543–4114 or 504–895–2663).

Romance at a Glance

♥ *Sleep in the Tennessee Williams suite or spot Anne Rice at the Pontchartrain Hotel.*

♥ *Explore old haunts of literary lions and famous film sites on two walking tours.*

♥ *Dig through the stacks for rare finds and regional titles at well-loved book shops.*

♥ *Soak up some real New Orleans atmosphere at restaurants favored by local writers.*

♥ *Drink in the dark Victorian mood and racy film history at the Columns Hotel.*

Louisiana Love Stories

"I've read all of these books set in New Orleans and Louisiana and love them," says literary leader Rhoda Faust, owner of Maple Street Book Shop. *"Although none would come close to being classified into the 'romance novel' category, they are all books of love. Some do tell a story of romantic love, or people searching for love, but others are about people who love in a different sense of the word, or who love an ideal."*

Her recommendations:

The Emerald Lizard, *Chris Wiltz (Dutton)*

A Confederacy of Dunces, *John Kennedy Toole (LSU Press)*

The Thanatos Syndrome, *Walker Percy (Farrar, Straus, Giroux)*

The Last Gentleman, *Walker Percy (Farrar, Straus, Giroux)*

Big Time, *Marcel Monticino (Morrow)*

Handling Sin, *Michael Malone (Little, Brown)*

Sleeping Dog, *Dick Lochte (Arbor House)*

Lives of the Saints, *Nancy Lemann (Knopf)*

Midnight Lemonade, *Ann Goethe (Delacorte)*

Victory Over Japan, *Ellen Gilchrist (Little, Brown)*

Net of Jewels, *Ellen Gilchrist (Little, Brown)*

A Lesson Before Dying, *Ernest Gaines (Knopf)*

The Exact Image of Mother, *Patty Friedmann (Viking Penguin)*

Black Cherry Blues, *James Lee Burke (Little, Brown)*

Almost Innocent, *Sheila Bosworth (Simon & Schuster)*

Catch the streetcar uptown to **Maple Street Book Shop** (7523 Maple Street between Cherokee and Hillary Streets; 504–866–4916), a long-standing local favorite surrounded by charming cottage shops, coffeehouses, and restaurants. Two side-by-side Victorian houses are filled floor to ceiling with thousands of regional cookbooks, children's stories, and works from more than 120 Louisiana natives (some first editions), including an impressive collection by Walker Percy.

DAY ONE: EVENING
Dinner

While you're on Maple Street, choose your spot from an inviting collection of homey eateries. Among the best: **Chicory Farm Cafe** (723 Hillary Street between Hampson and Maple Streets; 504–866–2325; moderate) showcases handmade cheeses and imaginative vegetarian fare stocked with fresh produce from the state's most respected growers; **Jamila's** (7808 Maple Street between Burdette and Fern Streets; 504–866–4366; moderate) is a family-run charmer with beautifully presented Tunisian and Mediterranean fare; **Figaro's** (7900 Maple Street at Fern Street; 504–866–0100; moderate) serves up imaginative gourmet pizzas and Italian dishes in a sleekly renovated gas station.

✧◌◌◌◌✧

Afterward, continue on the streetcar to talk the night away at **Maple Leaf Bar** (8316 Oak Street between Dante and Cambronne Streets; 504–866–9359). A hangout for writers and bookworms, the scruffy storefront pub also presents readings and live music.

DAY TWO: MORNING
Breakfast

A couple of scenes in Anne Rice's *The Witching Hour* were set in your hotel's **Cafe Pontchartrain** (moderate). The tranquil coffee shop has been a meeting ground for Uptown ladies and the power breakfast crowd for generations, many of whom are pictured in the photographs that line the walls. The soft gray-blue interior is brightened by flowers on every table and large windows that overlook oak-shaded St. Charles Avenue. Splurge on a crabmeat au gratin omelet or poached eggs St. Croix on grilled crawfish cakes with hollandaise. The blueberry muffins are great.

⌘

Before you left home, you made advance reservations to join a couple of fascinating walking tours tailored to literature lovers. A research professor at University of New Orleans and nationally known expert on Tennessee Williams, Dr. Kenneth Holditch's **Heritage Tours** (504–949–9805 or 504–524–2940) explore French Quarter haunts of Williams, William Faulkner, Truman Capote, Sherwood Anderson, Katherine Anne Porter, Lillian Hellman, and others who lived and worked here. Holditch also offers a walk dedicated exclusively to Williams. The two-hour tours cost $20 per person and groups are limited to 20 participants. Custom tours for two are available, priced at $60 total. The walks are under two miles, with plenty of stops.

Carolyn Kolb's Film Site Tours (504–861–8158) visit French Quarter backdrops from *Interview with the Vampire, Angel Heart, Walk on the Wild Side, Panic in the Streets,* and more. (See her top-ten list of romantic New Orleans movies on page 34.) The 25-block stroll takes about ninety minutes and costs $12.50 per person, or $75 minimum for two to twenty-five participants. A fun and knowledgeable guide to local history, Kolb also offers custom-tailored walks that focus on literature, politics, or other subjects of interest.

DAY TWO: AFTERNOON
Lunch

You could spring for an old-line splurge at **Galatoire's** (see page 91), one of the aristocratic backdrops in *Almost Innocent* by Sheila Bosworth. **Bailey's** serves attractive lunches in the lobby of the majestic old **Fairmont** (123 Baronne between Canal and Common Streets;

504–529–7111; moderate), which was the real-life model for Alex Hailey's *Hotel*. **The Pearl** (119 St. Charles Avenue between Canal and Common Streets; 504–525–2901; moderate) is more than a little frowzy, but the hot pastrami sandwiches and oyster bar are good, and the walls are decorated with framed references from Nancy Lemann's *Lives of the Saints* and James Lee Burke's *A Stained White Radiance* and *A Morning for Flamingos*. Easiest of all, fans of John Kennedy Toole's *Confederacy of Dunces* can just stop on a corner in the French Quarter to buy **Lucky Dogs** (inexpensive) from one of the roving wiener-shaped carts that were piloted by Ignatius J. Reilly in the Pulitzer Prize–winning novel.

After lunch, visit **Faulkner House Books** (624 Pirate's Alley between Chartres and Royal Streets; 504–524–2940). Namesake William lived in this lovely townhouse, which overlooks St. Louis Cathedral, while he wrote his first novel, *Soldiers' Pay*. Today the shop specializes in his works, including first editions and other rare volumes. You'll also find a good stock of New Orleans and Louisiana histories.

A few blocks away, Frances Parkinson Keyes penned several of her romance novels while in residence at **Beauregard-Keyes House** (see "Haunting Honeymoon"). The 1826 showplace, once home to Confederate General P. G. T. Beauregard, is open for tours daily, on the hour, from 10:00 A.M. to 4:00 P.M. Admission is $4. A gift shop sells works by Keyes.

Two of the city's greatest sources for used and rare books are **Librarie** (823 Chartres Street between St. Ann and Dumaine Streets; 504–525–4837) and **Beckham's Bookshop** (228 Decatur Street between Iberville and Bienville Streets; 504–522–9875), which stocks more than 50,000 volumes and 10,000 classical phonograph records. Chain giant **Bookstar** (414 North Peters Street between St. Louis and Conti Streets; 504–523–6411) offers an enormous variety, including a special section of regional titles.

Dinner

For a *Times-Picayune* survey during a recent writers' conference, we asked local literary stars which restaurants they would advise the attendees to visit for great New Orleans atmosphere. The most recommendations by far went to **Commander's Palace** (1403 Washington Avenue at Coliseum Street; 504–899–8221; expensive). The grand old landmark got the nod from novelists Anne Rice, Sheila Bosworth, and Peter Feibleman; historian Stephen Ambrose; and cookbook author/chef Paul Prudhomme. For details on this worthwhile splurge, see "Magnificent Obsession."

On the other hand, if you're making this trip on a scribbler's salary, the survey also turned up a couple of cozy old neighborhood eateries that are located off the tourist track in Mid-City. No-nonsense Creole fare is reasonably priced at bustling **Mandina Restaurant and Bar** (3800 Canal Street at South Cortez Street; 504–482–9179; moderate), another favorite of Ambrose and novelist Patty Friedmann, who pronounced it "the place for voyeurs and gourmands, and most writers are both." A former police detective turned crime novelist, John Dillman fingered nearby **Liuzza's Restaurant and Bar** (3636 Bienville Street at North Telemachus Street; 504–482–9120; inexpensive), a downscale Creole/Italian joint he labeled "unique, about as New Orleans as you can get."

※

If you saw the scandalous Louis Malle film *Pretty Baby,* which starred Brooke Shields as a child prostitute, you'll recognize the setting of the cavernous old bordello, which is actually the very respectable **Columns Hotel** (3811 St. Charles Avenue between General Taylor and Peniston Streets; 504–899–9308). The dark and moody 1883 interior, with its mahogany staircase and stained glass skylight, should fire your imaginations, and **The Victorian Lounge** is a clubby and pleasantly worn watering hole that was named best bar in New Orleans by *Esquire.* (Incidentally, if the Pontchartrain is too rich for your blood, guest rooms here are inexpensive, though the heavy Victorian furnishings and ancient clawfoot tubs may have a bit too much character for some.)

FOR MORE ROMANCE

Each year, around the third weekend in March, the **Tennessee Williams Literary Festival** features three days of plays, lectures, and readings, plus such lighthearted events as a "Stella!" hollering contest. For details, contact 504–581–1144.

These days Chef Frank Brigtsen, star pupil of best-selling cookbook author Paul Prudhomme, brings home his own national awards to **Brigtsen's** (723 Dante Street at the river; 504–861–7610; expensive). His renovated nineteenth-century cottage is just steps from the Mississippi River levee, a storybook setting for modern Creole/Cajun cuisine. Handwritten menus change nightly and eager diners fill every table. You could be offered anything from pan-roasted snapper in crab broth to roast duck with cornbread dressing and pecan gravy. Complementary wines are sold by the glass. If you're on a budget, a special three-course meal is available for $14.95 Tuesday through Thursday from 5:30 to 6:30 P.M.

ARTFUL SEDUCTION
FROM DEGAS TO YA/YA

*F*rom the sidewalks around Jackson Square to the hushed galleries of New Orleans Museum of Art, the "Paris of the Americas" is awash in visual poetry. Royal Street storefronts frame centuries of treasures and trash. Bars and coffeehouses all over town showcase emerging masters and urban primitives. Even the humblest lunch is laid out with unconscious style, a moody still life of frosted beer bottle and fried oysters on French.

The throbbing heart of the contemporary scene is the Warehouse/Arts District, a riverfront commercial zone previously occupied by ship chandlers, cotton and sugar presses, iron foundries, and light manufacturers. Restoration of historic townhouses and industrial lofts has reawakened these sleepy back streets to their former life as a busy residential neighborhood where locals live, work, and play. The "SoHo of the South" remains more than a little rough around the edges, but its galleries and restaurants are among the best in the country. They provide sleek and sophisticated backdrops for a fashionable fling, a lustrous setting for your study in romance.

Practical notes: Reservations are recommended for tea at Windsor Court (800–262–2662 or 504–523–6000) and lunch at Bizou (504–524–4114), as well as dinner at Upperline (504–891–9822) and Mike's on the Avenue (504–523–1709). An advance appointment is required to view works in progress and completed pieces for sale at Estudio/Gallery (504–524–7982).

Romance at a Glance

♥ *View works by masters of the past and future along Julia and Royal Streets.*

♥ *Raise a glass with the famous couple who live and paint at Estudio/Gallery.*

♥ *Take afternoon tea surrounded by the Windsor Court's $8 million collection.*

♥ *Indulge your appetite for art, romance, and whimsy at Upperline Restaurant.*

♥ *Immerse yourselves in love through the ages at New Orleans Museum of Art.*

DAY ONE: Afternoon/Evening

Check into the **Lafayette Hotel** (600 St. Charles Avenue at Girod Street; 800–733–4754 or 504–524–4441; doubles, $155 to $350; suites, $285 to $650) in the Warehouse/Arts District, directly on the St. Charles Avenue streetcar line. Rooms are decorated in English country style with polished dark woods, upholstered club chairs, king-sized beds, lavish drapery, botanical prints, and marble baths with brass fittings and Swiss-milled soaps. Some suites have four-posters and whirlpool baths. A small marble-lined lobby is surrounded by the three stylish dining rooms of **Mike's on the Avenue** (628 St. Charles Avenue at Girod Street; 504–523–1709; expensive).

Tea

Walk six blocks to **Le Salon in the Windsor Court Hotel** (300 Gravier Street between South Peters and Tchoupitoulas Streets; 800–262–2662 or 504–523–6000; moderate) for an elegant afternoon tea, served daily from 2:00 to 6:00 P.M.

Linger over finger sandwiches, scones with clotted cream, and tiny pastries. Rich woods, oriental rugs, green marble floors, and live chamber music create the perfect setting for viewing the hotel's $8 million dollar art collection.

On display throughout the hotel's public areas, many of the artworks are connected with the British royal family. Curator Sarah Jumel, also on staff at the New Orleans Museum of Art, leads free guided tours every Saturday at 3:00 P.M. for guests of the Windsor Court or its restaurants.

Continue five blocks to yet another hotel lobby that offers some unexpected treasures. The **Fine Arts Gallery** (504–522–0691) in the grand arcade of **Le Meridien** (614 Canal Street between Camp Street and St. Charles Avenue; 800–543–4300 or 504–525–6500) sells museum-quality works by such big names as Renoir, Rodin, and Corot.

Dinner

And now for something completely different: Cross Canal Street and walk two blocks to **House of Blues** (225 Decatur Street between Iberville and Bienville Streets; 504–529–BLUE; inexpensive), where one of the largest collections of its kind crams the walls with Southern primitive art. Down-home eats are a class act, especially authentic Tennessee-style barbecue from the smokehouse out back. First stop by the box office, located at the front entrance of the complex, to check the roster of nightly performances and buy your tickets for the after-dinner show in the music room. Then grab a table in the dining area to elevate your souls (and cholesterol counts) in the midst of wild images created by Leroy Alom, Archie Byron, Jimmy Lee Sudduth, and other mean-street masters. Some pieces are for sale in the adjoining gift shop.

DAY TWO: MORNING

Breakfast

Whenever you awaken, dress casually for a day of gallery hopping. For breakfast, head straight to the lobby for an eye-opening treat at Mike's on the Avenue. Try the crawfish rémoulade Napoleon (with smoked salmon, crisp bagel chips, cream cheese, capers, and red onion); frittata (layered with potatoes, grilled Creole sausage, and salsa fresca); or quiche flavored with exotic mushrooms and spicy Cajun ham.

⌒◌⌒

The vast and energetic **Contemporary Arts Center** (900 Camp Street at St. Joseph Street; 504–523–1216) transformed a 40,000-square-foot warehouse into showplace and unofficial university for the local arts community, a collaborative masterpiece all the way from the undulating glass-plate reception desk created by sculptor Gene Koss to the highest web of catwalks and exposed wooden beams. In addition to 10,000 square feet of gallery space, two theaters present plays, dance, music concerts, and other special events throughout the year. Admission to visual arts exhibits is free on Thursdays.

DAY TWO: AFTERNOON

To see art in the making, watch master glassblowers at work in the **New Orleans School of GlassWorks & Printmaking Studio** (727 Magazine Street between Girod and Julia Streets; 504–529–7277). The hot shop is closed from June to September, but the front gallery continues to sell pieces made on site, along with others by internationally known masters. The cavernous facility also houses a printmaking, papermaking, and bookbinding studio and offers workshops for beginning and experienced crafters. You can even clasp hands eternally in a custom-made glass sculpture. For details, see "Narcissus Does New Orleans."

Lunch

A short walk away, **Bizou Restaurant** (701 St. Charles Avenue at Girod Street; 504–524–4114) is open for lunch Monday through Friday only. Chic bistro fare features a creative lineup of salads and sandwiches, plus seasonal entrées like pan-seared salmon (with flash-fried spinach and tomatoes in a reduced balsamic vinaigrette). Better yet, take a seat near local artist Zella Funck's wall mural *The Kiss,* and enjoy the sexy view over a plate of Zella's Crabcakes, named in her honor by Chef Daniel Bonnot.

⤖⤖⤖

If—and only if—you have called ahead for an appointment, you can stop for wine or coffee with the artist herself at **Estudio/Gallery** (630–B Baronne Street between Girod and Lafayette Streets; 504–524–7982), the working studio and home of Funck and partner Martin LaBorde. The celebrated couple's second-floor loft also serves as a gallery for Funck, who has exhibited her paintings and ceramics at the National Museum of Women in the Arts and the World Trade Center in Hong Kong. LaBorde continues to paint on the premises but is now represented exclusively by a new French Quarter gallery that bears his name (see pages 35 and 72).

Jana Napoli's **628 Gallery** (628 Baronne Street between Girod and Lafayette Streets; 504–529–3306) is home to the internationally acclaimed Young Artists/Young Aspirations. YA/YA's furnishings and decorative items, splashed with bright colors and bold designs, are also exhibited in New York, Paris, Tokyo, Amsterdam, and other major cities. The private, nonprofit arts organization provides an outlet for talented inner-city youths ranging in age from fourteen to twenty-six, while setting aside funds for their college educations. It's a great way to feather your nest while you help young talent spread its wings.

Most of the action in the Warehouse/Arts District is concentrated along "Gallery Row," a few blocks of Julia Street between (appropriately enough) Church and Commerce Streets. Regional and international works on display at **Wyndy Morehead Fine Arts** (603 Julia Street between Church and Camp streets; 504–568–9754) include Sandi Grow's elongated horses, ceramics by Louise Hopson, Nofa Dixon's oversized ceramic fruits and vegetables, and surreal miniatures of pre-Columbian architectural details by Bernard Mattox. **Marguerite Oestreicher Fine Arts** (626 Julia Street between Camp Street and St. Charles Avenue; 504–581–9253) represents American master Milton Avery, as well as Gregory Amenoff, Stephen Mueller, Balthus, and Joseph Cornell. A Warehouse/Arts District pioneer, **Galerie Simonne Stern** (518 Julia Street between Camp and Magazine Streets; 504–529–1118) features established mid-career artists and regional stars, such as George Dunbar, Margaret Evangeline, Jacqueline Humphries, Lynda Benglis, and John Scott (recipient of the MacArthur Foundation genius grant). Nationally known curators occasionally oversee exhibitions at prestigious **Arthur Roger Gallery** (432 Julia Street at Constance Street; 504–522–6999), which showcases masters like Ida Kohlmeyer (as well as emerging talents at an annual June exhibit). New collectors will find a stellar inventory of outsider art, pottery, jewelry, crafts, and fine arts by fresh regional talents at **LeMieux Galleries** (332 Julia Street between Tchoupitoulas and Commerce Streets; 504–522–5988), including Shirley Rabé Masinter's urban landscapes and Pat Benard's whimsical ceramics. **Still-Zinsel Contemporary Fine Art** (328 Julia Street between Tchoupitoulas and Commerce Streets; 504–588–9999) is a brilliant white backdrop for powder graphite drawings by Gregory Saunders and nudes by Ronna S. Harris. Heralded by *Metropolitan Home* and *Vogue,* **Christopher Maier Furniture Design** (329 Julia Street at Commerce Street; 504–586–9079) produces functional exotica such as the funerary *Vault of Drawers,* sculpted *Torso Cabinet,* and dazzling Egyptian-style armoire with bronzed wings for doors.

DAY TWO: EVENING
Dinner

Step right outside your hotel and board the streetcar to dine with the locals and feast your eyes on a premiere collection of Southern folk art. Imagine visiting the home of a sophisticated yet easygoing friend who loves Creole food, great wines, and lively conversation. At **Upperline Restaurant** (1413 Upperline Street between Prytania and Pitt Streets; 504–891–9822; expensive) you'll walk past a cottage garden into three lightsome dining rooms filled with fresh flowers, exuberant artworks, and owner JoAnn Clevenger's BIG laugh. Service is smart but genial, and regulars range from French Quarter bohemians to Uptown Brahmins. Order the "tasting dinner" for generous samplings of seven house specialties, including fried green tomatoes with shrimp rémoulade, seafood gumbo, duck and andouille gumbo, spicy shrimp with jalapeño cornbread, duck etouffée with corncakes, roasted duck, and pecan pie. Be sure to notice Martin LaBorde's whimsical *Magic of the Moment* paintings splashed across the facade.

DAY THREE: MORNING

Create you own masterpiece over breakfast (*Reclining Nudes with Room-Service Fruit and Croissants*) before heading out to view more romantic tableaux. Oak-shaded **City Park** (City Park Avenue at Esplanade Avenue) is home to 30,000 trees, plus some 35,000 manmade beauties at **New Orleans Museum of Art** (1 Collins Diboll Circle in City Park; 504–488–2631). Stop by the front desk for floor plans of the forty-six galleries displaying treasures worth more than $200 million. In addition to traditional European masterpieces and contemporary works, NOMA is strong on Japanese paintings of the Edo period, as well as Chinese, Indian, African, pre-Columbian, Native American, and Oceanic art. Don't miss the outstanding collections of photography, glass, Newcomb pottery, and Southern self-taught artists.

And be sure to see the *Portrait of Estelle Musson Degas* painted by her cousin, French Impressionist Edgar Degas, when he lived with her family about a mile from the museum. While in residence, Degas also painted *The Cotton Market in New Orleans,* his first work—and the first by any Impressionist—to be purchased by a museum. (It's still on display at the Musee des Beaux Arts in Pau, France.)

DAY THREE: AFTERNOON/EVENING
Lunch

When all that lust and yearning works up your appetites, cool off in the museum's **Courtyard Cafe** (lunch only; inexpensive). Outdoor sculptures are framed by towering plate-glass windows, original paintings line the walls, and imaginative sandwiches and salads are served at a walk-up counter.

⌒⌒⌒

Afterward, head for the French Quarter to lose yourselves in the remarkable range of art for sale along Royal Street. **906 Gallery** (906 Royal Street between Dumaine and St. Phillip Streets; 504–525–4527) offers a good selection of local etchings, prints, and works on paper. For collectible Jazz Fest and Carnival posters, plus paintings by regional self-taught artists, stop at **Bergen Galleries** (730 Royal Street at Orleans Street; 504–523–7882).

Just across the street, you'll recognize a familiar blue dog staring from dozens of bayou landscapes in the **Rodrigue Gallery of New Orleans** (721 Royal Street at Orleans Street; 504–581–4244). Riding the wave of success he helped to create for Cajun artist George Rodrigue and that ubiquitous icon, impresario Richard Steiner opened the neighboring **Martin LaBorde Gallery** (631 Royal Street between St. Peter and Toulouse Streets; 504–587–7111) in the spring of 1997. Here you'll be among the first to meet yet another superstar in the making: the little magician named Bodo who floats through dark and ethereal landscapes, a gentle champion for romance. LaBorde's work has been exhibited in Tokyo, Chicago, Munich, and Mexico City. He was awarded the Pushkin Medal of Honor from the Hermitage Museum in Leningrad.

If you liked the outsider art at House of Blues, there's plenty more where that came from at **Barrister's Gallery** (526 Royal Street between Toulouse and St. Louis Streets; 504–525–2767). At the other end of the spectrum, **Kurt E. Schon, Ltd.** (523 Royal Street between St. Louis and Toulouse Streets; 504–524–5462) is an elegant showcase for 150 nineteenth-century European paintings, supplemented by a neighboring annex with six floors of

Visions of Love: A Dozen Sexy Showpieces at NOMA

The Toilette of Psyche, *Charles Joseph Natoire. Would that we all had seven or eight naked handmaidens to help us get ready for a date and sixty extra pounds to reach the ideal of female beauty— not to mention Cupid himself for a boyfriend.*

Whisperings of Love, *William-Adolphe Bouguereau. A luminous backdrop for hundreds of wedding photos over the years, it's Cupid again, murmuring sweet nothings into the pink-tinged ear of another woman.*

Portrait of a Young Lute Player, *Francesco d'Ubertino (Bacchiacca). His song celebrates The Triumph of Love, as famous couples (Daphne and Apollo, Sampson and Delilah) cavort in the background; but that big hourglass out front is a reminder to get it while you can.*

Romeo and Juliet, *Benjamin West. "Farewell, farewell! One kiss, and I'll descend."*

The Surprise (Woman with a Cat), *Francois Boucher. A voyeur peeks around the drapery to observe a fleshy young lady at play with her pet.*

Female Figure of the Eleventh Century, *North Central India. With voluptuous breasts and erotic posture that promise fertility, she may be a likeness of Amibika, worshiped on behalf of mothers and infants.*

Bijin (Courtesan), *Yamaguchi Soken. Eyes modestly downcast, clad in a brilliant red and blue kimono with leaves of gold, she sways above the ground on lacquered clogs.*

Storyville Photos, *Ernest James Bellocq. Ladies of the evening posed for these black-and-white stunners, haunting images of love for sale in New Orleans bordellos, circa 1913.*

Faberge Eggs, *Peter Carl Faberge. Just some little Easter baubles from a czar to his wife . . .*

Louisiana Federal Bedchamber, *various craftsmen. The most inviting display in the furniture gallery could have graced a French Quarter townhouse or River Road plantation in the early nineteenth century.*

Exhibit of Portrait Miniatures, *various artists. Portable paintings of loved ones, encircled by gold and pearls, were small enough to be slipped in a pocket or clasped over the heart.*

Renaissance Boy Chastising a Monkey, *Alfred Thompson. Oh, those English!*

Neoclassics, Preimpressionists, Impressionists, and Postimpressionists. One of the country's largest collections of sleek graphics and sculpture by Erté is on display at **Dyansen Gallery** (433 Royal Street between Conti and St. Louis Streets; 504–523–2902). **Galerie Royale, Ltd.** (312 Royal Street between Bienville and Conti Streets; 504–523–1588) launched self-taught star William Tolliver and continues to represent an eclectic group of emerging artists. The **Vincent Mann Gallery** (713 Bienville Street between Bourbon and Royal; 504–523–2342) offers works by lesser-known nineteenth- and twentieth-century Impressionists and Postimpressionists, such as Françoise Gilot (mother of Paloma Picasso). Contemporary painting, sculpture, and photography at **Hanson Gallery** (220 Royal Street between Iberville and Bienville Streets; 504–524–8211) includes works by pop idol Peter Max.

Dinner

If the right regional ingredients are in season, you may be able to order some of the celebrated food art that chefs Greg and Mary Sonnier prepared during their guest stint at the James Beard House. Convenient to NOMA, but only open for dinner, the menu at **Gabrielle** (3201 Espianade Avenue at Mystery Street; 504–948–6233; expensive) changes weekly according to local markets. The cooking couple earned their toques in the kitchens of Chef Paul Prudhomme, and they carry on his dedication to the freshest Louisiana fare. Other than bread, everything (including the andouille sausage) is made in house. You'll always be offered Gulf fish, and usually rabbit, both dressed to thrill. This thoroughly modern restaurant, named for the Sonniers' young daughter, is softened by romantic lighting and French Country style, an oak-shaded charmer frilled with flowers, white linen, and lace.

Another good place for a farewell champagne toast is right under your room. Mike's on the Avenue is a stylish backdrop for East-meets-Southwest cuisine. Try crawfish spring rolls with a chile-lime dipping sauce or Jamaican jerked breast of chicken stuffed with shrimp, edged with coconut fried rice and mango salsa.

FOR MORE ROMANCE

If you prefer a homier setting with an artsy history, **The Degas House** (2306 Esplanade Avenue between Rocheblave and Tonti Streets; 504–821–5009; doubles $75 to $150, including Creole breakfast), where Edgar Degas lived with the family of his maternal uncle during 1872–73, is now a sunny bed-and-breakfast inn decorated with prints of his work.

If you'd like to create a masterpiece of your own, **Dixie Art and Drafting Supplies** (319 Magazine Street between Gravier and Natchez Streets; 504–833–2612) has everything you need. You'll find great subjects all over town, especially in the French Quarter, City Park, and on the Mississippi River levee. Audubon Park (bordered by St. Charles Avenue, Exposition Boulevard, Walnut Street, and the river) was formerly the estate of wildlife artist John James Audubon.

For a self-guided walking tour of outdoor sculpture gardens, see "Rich in Love."

ITINERARY 9
Two days and two nights

HOWLING AT THE MOON
A DUET FOR JAZZ CATS AND BLUES HOUNDS

*O*n the prowl for hard listening, it's great to be with your soul mate. A raunchy old blues song about a lover's special prowess could inspire both of you. Or if it's a boozy lament of paradise lost, dance a little closer and be glad you're still together.

You won't run out of sound with dozens of clubs to choose from, plus even more musicians spilling out onto the streets. The birthplace of jazz continues to nurture its ever-growing brood, along with hundreds of foster children. And they all find plenty of inspiration in this indulgent old city, which has always smiled fondly on rambling rogues, hard-headed women, and cheatin' hearts.

Practical notes: For club schedules, check listings and reviews in the daily *Times-Picayune* and newsweekly *Gambit*. *Offbeat* covers the local music industry. Call ahead to join one of the Cradle of Jazz Tours (504–282–3583) or book a private jaunt for two.

DAY ONE: AFTERNOON

You'll find lots of backstreet romance in the favored nesting spot for a long list of international performers. **Le Richelieu Hotel** (1234 Chartres Street at Barracks Street; 800–535–9653 or 504–529–2492; doubles, $95 to $150; one-bedroom suites, $170 to $205 for the McCartney Suite) is located at the quieter downtown edge of the French Quarter, a less crowded residential area that's also convenient for late-night rambles among the bohemian music clubs, coffeehouses, and restaurants of Faubourg Marigny. Ask for the McCartney Suite, where Beatle Paul once stayed for several months while familiarizing himself with New Orleans bands and cutting an album at a local studio. Large rooms are graced by towering ceilings and huge windows that open onto a balcony. The hotel's intimate bar overlooks a small, tropically landscaped pool. There's even plenty of free self-parking, a rare amenity in the Quarter.

After checking in, walk up Chartres Street toward the skyscrapers of the Central Business District. Six blocks along, you'll come to **Jackson Square** (bounded by Chartres, Decatur, St. Ann, and St. Peter Streets), one of the most popular hangouts for street musicians. Expect anything: classical woodwinds, lone saxophonists, wineglass xylophones, a five-instrument one-man band, even a determined performer tugging a full-sized piano on wheels. And don't be surprised to see professional-quality brass bands of young children belting out jazz standards, a longtime local tradition. Vagabond entertainers also work the tourist crowds a block over on Royal Street and atop the Mississippi levee in Woldenberg Riverfront Park. Just be sure to wear comfortable shoes for dodging mimes and dancing in the streets.

Romance at a Glance

♥ *Twist and shout in a Beatle's bed at Le Richelieu Hotel.*

♥ *Flip through stacks of rare labels at Louisiana Music Factory.*

♥ *Drift away to a slower time with living legends at Palm Court Jazz Cafe.*

♥ *See where Bolden blew and Storyville stomped on a Cradle of Jazz Tour.*

♥ *Get real, dance the night away, and learn to say Tchoupitoulas at Tipitina's.*

Had Enough of Silly Love Songs?

If so, try one of these classic heart-stoppers recommended by local R&B royalty, vocalist Leigh "Little Queenie" Harris:

I Sold My Heart to the Junkman, *Patti Labelle and the Bluebelles. Few people realize that before the silver spacesuits and Frank Lloyd Wright coifs she sported in the '70s and '80s, Patti had already had a whole career in this part of the world.*

Just a Gigolo, *Louis Prima. Anything by this local dynamo knocks me out, and the duets with his wife Keely Smith are all sublime. Cinephiles should be on the lookout for an obscure, but unforgettable (and at least vaguely biographical) 1950s musical starring the Primas called* Hey Boy! Hey Girl!

Lipstick Traces, *Benny Spellman, accompanied by some of the most atonal but heartfelt backing vocals in history. Whenever this song is played on a jukebox in New Orleans, every bar patron over thirty sings along at the top of his lungs, often with tears in his eyes.*

Big Chief, Parts 1 and 2, *Professor Longhair. My most vivid and resonant musical memory of childhood in New Orleans is hearing this song on WTIX and WNOE during every Carnival season. It hypnotized me then, and that effect has only slightly diminished today.*

Walk on Gilded Splinters, *Dr. John. Still among the most mystical rock 'n' roll tunes ever written. The chant "Tee Alberta" is as hair-raising in the '90s as it was in 1970.*

I Get a Kick out of You, *Louis Armstrong with Oscar Peterson. I'm including this very left-field choice just because of the way Satchmo sings the line, "Then I suddenly turn and see your fabulous face." Heaven!*

There's Got to Be a Girl, *Mike and the Jokers. When this song was a local favorite, I was about five years too young to attend the dances where Mike Ancona sang it live, but every time I heard it on the radio, its dreamy quality filled the air with starry teenage promise: "If there's a boy for you, there's got to be a girl, too."*

Jackson Square is a great hopping-off point for an unguided tour of the French Quarter, where you can just follow your ears and eyes through ninety square blocks of music clubs, shops, and galleries. **Beckham's Bookshop** (228 Decatur Street between Iberville and Bienville Streets; 504–522–9875) is great for atmosphere and serious research, with worn display cases and a creaky old staircase, not to mention more than 10,000 old classical records and newer CDs, plus a great collection of hard-to-find books on regional musicians and music history.

Just a few doors up, **Louisiana Music Factory** (210 Decatur Street between Iberville and Bienville Streets; 504–586–1094) is the best place in town to search for local and regional music. The first floor is stocked mostly with CD's; the second is exclusively for vinyl, with one entire wall devoted to jazz. Staffers are knowledgeable, but not snooty, great sources for club recommendations and tracking down obscure recordings. Says one partner, "Our Japanese and European customers tell us we have the largest selection of traditional jazz in the world."

DAY ONE: EVENING

Head back to the hotel along Bourbon Street (everyone has to peek into the notorious bars, strip joints, and novelty shops at least once) and Barracks Street, one of the prettiest residential blocks in the French Quarter. Drop off your treasures, maybe take a nap, then fluff up your ears for a night of true sound and no-nonsense dining.

Dinner

One of the most popular evening venues for the New Orleans Jazz & Heritage Festival each spring, **Palm Court Jazz Cafe** (1204 Decatur Street between Barracks and Governor Nicholls Streets; 504–525–0200; moderate) is also a year-round showcase for top local and international performers. In addition to younger talent, the schedule often features the city's living jazz legends, many now in their late seventies and eighties. You might see the same performers who usually appear for twenty-minute sets at the renowned Preservation Hall (see page 150), but here you'll have your own table, drinks, and food service. Mosaic tile floors, mahogany bentwood chairs, a carved antique bar, and ceiling fans add plenty of period romance. The menu features a reasonable lineup of classic Creole/Cajun fare, like gumbo and jambalaya, but also steaks and vegetarian pasta dishes. The tropical salad is a cool mix of shrimp, artichokes, eggs, and olives with a colorful splash of exotic fruits. Before you leave, fill a doggy bag with take-out music from the adjoining shop, where you'll find a wide-ranging selection of CDs and vinyl recordings on rare labels that include Jazzology, Audiophile, and GHB.

DAY TWO: Morning/Afternoon
Breakfast

Order a full breakfast in bed, head down to the hotel restaurant, or walk about two blocks to neighborhood hangout **Croissant d'Or** (615–17 Ursulines Street between Chartres and Royal Streets; 504–524–4663). If you choose the last, first check the newspaper boxes outside for the *New York Times* and *New Orleans Times-Picayune,* which features good music coverage in the Friday "Lagniappe" section; then choose European pastries to go with your coffee, head for the rear courtyard, and relax . . .

Just four blocks away, the **Old US Mint** (400 Esplanade Avenue at Decatur Street; 504–568–6968) houses an outstanding permanent exhibit on jazz history. A member of the Louisiana State Museum system, the stately facility dedicates several rooms to photographs and memorabilia, including Louis Armstrong's first cornet and a fascinating display on "Women in Jazz." Meanwhile, the vintage soundtrack helps transport you back in time. One of the two gift shops specializes in rare recordings.

You may have listened to Jelly Roll Morton's "Sidewalk Blues" for decades, but it will never sound quite the same once you've seen the sidewalk in front of his house. This ain't Hollywood, but a peek at early jazzmen's homes could be even more unforgettable. Native-born news photographer and jazz historian John McCusker has spent years tracking down stories and rumors to piece together his moving picture of the city's musical heritage. Schedule one of his intimate **Cradle of Jazz Tours** (504–282–3583), and you'll hear recordings keyed to the sites as he drives you around town in an air-conditioned van. McCusker's narration is sensitive and well informed, plus he welcomes questions from neophytes or experts. In fact, he says some queries have led him to valuable research. Most tours last between two and three hours, depending upon the enthusiasm of participants, and carry four to six passengers. The cost is $25 per person.

Lunch

An antiquated sign across the top of the Italianate/Baroque building still reads "Philip Werlein Ltd., Everything Musical, est. 1842." Generations of New Orleanians bought their pianos, band instruments, and sheet music here until an extravagant renovation transformed the downtown monument into a Parisian-style bistro. The Brennan family of restaurateurs created the ultra-stylish **Palace Cafe** (605 Canal Street between Chartres and Royal Streets; 504–523–1661; expensive), a lively retreat for Creole seafood, imaginative salads, and pasta dishes, not to mention the infamous white-chocolate bread pudding. The grand staircase leads to a second-floor dining area splashed with wall murals of local jazz legends. Many of those musicians carried their first instruments through these doors and some even took lessons in the glass cubicles upstairs.

❧

Walk back to the hotel on Royal Street, past world-class antiques stores and galleries, as well as kitschy gift shops. Along the way, you'll encounter plenty of music-inspired merchandise, from ashtrays and T-shirts to inlaid Louis XVI grand pianos. Be sure to stop at

Galerie Royale, Ltd. (312 Royal Street between Bienville and Conti Streets; 504–523–1588), which introduced self-taught artist William Tolliver to the world. His brilliantly colored oils, especially those populated by classic jazz figures, have an international following.

DAY TWO: Evening

Get off to a rocky start with a couple of tall drinks in the shade of Fats Domino's piano, which is perched over the guitar-shaped bar at **Hard Rock Cafe** (418 North Peters Street at St. Louis Street; 504–529–5617; inexpensive). In addition to the usual paraphernalia from international pop icons, the collection also includes such local treasures as Professor Longhair's jackets; outrageous costumes from the Mardi Gras Indians; and Dr. John's cape, top hat, and cane.

Dinner

A tough crowd of locals (who initially resented these Hollywood outsiders jumping into their music scene) has been won over by the outstanding schedule and easy atmosphere at **House of Blues New Orleans** (225 Decatur Street between Iberville and Bienville Streets; 504–529–BLUE; inexpensive). The 1,000–capacity music hall offers standing room only and lines are long for big-name acts, but you can walk past to dine in the cavernous restaurant and bar area. Nearly every flat surface is plastered with authentic outsider art, service is warm, and the food is good and plentiful. Don't miss the barbecue from the backyard smokehouse or the righteous mashed potatoes. Sunday gospel brunch is the perfect marriage of a big down-home buffet with bigger sounds from top homegrown performers.

If you prefer to support a true original, an absolute must on every music lover's visit to the city is a night at **Tipitina's** (501 Napoleon Avenue at Tchoupitoulas Street; 504–895–

8477). Named for the song by Professor Longhair, immortalized in bronze near the front door, there's not a bad spot to stand or dance on the entire first floor of this intimate, 700-capacity club. For a bit more elbow room, watch the fray from the balcony. Recent news of renovations at Tip's put a scare into some purists, but we haven't heard anyone complaining about the air-conditioning or new sound system. And slick, it still ain't.

FOR MORE ROMANCE

For accommodations with a quieter location and lower rates than Le Richelieu, **The Lefevre Home Bed and Breakfast** (6022 Pitt Street between State and Webster Streets; 800–729–4640 or 504–488–4640; doubles, $51 to $76) is a good choice for classical music lovers. The owner is a harpist who offers four guest rooms that share two and one-half baths and a communal living area filled with antique harps and a grand piano. Your fellow occupants could be students or symphony conductors, and it's a lovely walk to Audubon Park or the campuses of Tulane and Loyola universities, which always feature full schedules of concerts, recitals, and other entertainments. A short ride on the St. Charles Avenue streetcar will take you to a neighboring trio of major uptown clubs, **Jimmy's** (8200 Willow Street at Dublin Street; 504–861–8200), **Carrollton Station** (8140 Willow Street at Dublin Street; 504–865–9190), and the **Maple Leaf Bar** (8316 Oak Street between Dante and Cambronne Streets; 504–866–9359).

More of the city's greatest music clubs are featured in "On the Prowl," "From Gumbo to Gospel," "Cheap Thrills," "A Day of Low Culture and High Camp," and "The Big Lazy."

"A Feast for the Ears" also details the New Orleans Jazz & Heritage Festival, which attracts multitudes of visitors each spring for a ten-day blowout that has become an even bigger draw than Mardi Gras. Less well known, but musically significant, the annual **French Quarter Festival** (800–673–5725 or 504–522–5711) is an enormous block party that also showcases famous local restaurants via dozens of food booths for "the world's largest jazz brunch."

NATIVE CHARMS

ITINERARY 10
Two days and one night

HAUTE CREOLE
THE FRENCH CONNECTION

*D*espite what you may have heard, mostly in Hollywood films and television shows, the typical New Orleans resident does *not* speak with a Cajun accent. Cajuns are country people from southwestern Louisiana, descendants of *Acadiens* who were forced out of Canada by British invaders. The city was settled much earlier by French and Spanish Creoles, not to mention the hordes of Germans, Irish, Italians, and Asians who followed.

Creole architecture and cuisine are sophisticated and complex, urbane in style and heavily influenced by African slaves, as well as those later immigrants from other European cultures. The Hollywood crowd hit town last, but at least they got one thing right, steamy sexy romance in an unmistakable atmosphere. You've seen it in the movies. Now's your chance to bid *au revoir* to American shores in the Gallic heart of New Orleans.

Practical notes: Advance reservations are essential for The Soniat House (800–544–8808 or 504–522–0570) and all of the restaurants listed in this itinerary, except Napoleon House. Call the box office to reserve tickets for a production at Le Petit Théatre du Vieux Carré (504–522–2081).

DAY ONE: AFTERNOON

First you walk through the sheltered flagstone carriageway, a short time tunnel that opens onto a courtyard draped with tropical blooms. A favorite hideaway for visiting stars, including a certain blond vampire, **The Soniat House** (1133 Chartres Street between Ursulines and Governor Nicholls Streets; 800–544–8808 or 504–522–0570; doubles $145 to $250, suites $250 to $475) is lush and moody, a luxurious nest from the wide pine floors to the 14-foot ceilings. The intimate French Quarter hotel is named for the wealthy sugar planter who built it as his town home in 1830. (The massive mahogany bed in Suite 64 was custom made in Europe to showcase antique embroidered panels, a lavish frame softened by fine linens and goosedown pillows.) Breakfast in bed brings fresh-baked buttermilk biscuits, homemade strawberry preserves, and steaming cafe au lait—not to mention an extra helping of Southern hospitality from a staff of thirty that caters to just thirty-one rooms.

Romance at a Glance

♥ *Hang your Panama hats in the posh city home of a sugar planter at Soniat House.*

♥ *Marvel at treasures from Napoleon's death mask to the teeth of Beauregard's horse.*

♥ *Lunch in an old-world bistro with the crème de la Creoles at Galatoire's.*

♥ *Tap your toes to a classic musical at historic Le Petit Théatre du Vieux Carré.*

Within the same block, the **Old Ursuline Convent** (1100 Chartres Street between Ursulines and Governor Nicholls Streets; 504–529–3040; guided tours $4) is the only pure French Colonial architecture remaining in what should be called the Spanish Quarter. This majestic beauty, with its square portico and formal gardens, is crowned by a steep roof with rows of dormer windows. Of national historic significance, it is the oldest building in the Mississippi valley. Aristocratic Creole children of the eighteenth and nineteenth centuries were educated here, but the sisters of Ursula also established the country's first school for black and Indian children.

After your 45-minute guided tour, relax over cafe au lait and French pastries in the pleasant little courtyard of **Croissant**

d'Or (615–17 Ursulines Street between Chartres and Royal Street; 504–524–4663; inexpensive). In rainy weather, choose one of the indoor tables nestled in a bay window.

DAY ONE: EVENING
Dinner

Oblivious to modern food fads, **Brennan's French Restaurant** (417 Royal Street between Conti and St. Louis Streets; 504–525–9711; expensive) remains true to the rich and elegant New Orleans cuisine that made the city's reputation, a splendid choice for Creole dining in classic style. The formal service complements romantic dazzlers such as oysters Rockefeller, piquant turtle soup, escargots, tournedos with three sauces, trout Nancy smothered in lump crabmeat, rack of lamb, and veal Kottwitz atop diced artichokes and mushrooms in a lemon butter sauce. Signature bananas Foster is just one of the flaming desserts. (For details on the famous breakfast at Brennan's, see "Grand Illusions.") The Vieux Carré landmark is still owned and managed by founder Owen Brennan's sons and grandchildren.

Just two blocks away, their cousins operate **Mr. B's Bistro** (201 Royal Street at Iberville Street; 504–523–2078; moderate), a fashionable and clubby retreat that makes good use of regional ingredients for a fresh take on Creole tradition. If you prefer a more informal atmosphere, stop here for enlightened creations like pasta jambalaya, oysters Diablo in herbed pepper crust, elaborate salads, or wood-fired goodies from the hickory grill. Whether you choose to cast your eyes over French Quarter sidewalks or the bustling open kitchen, it's a lively scene and a favorite with local couples.

❧❧❧

It's hopelessly corny, but those horse-drawn buggies are the best way to view the French Quarter as it was seen by grand ladies and gentlemen in slower times. Climb aboard at the carriage stand by the Decatur Street entrance to Jackson Square. A thirty-minute circuit of the Vieux Carré costs about $20 per person.

DAY TWO: MORNING

After ringing for hot biscuits and homemade jam in your room, head back to Jackson Square to amble through centuries of Creole history in three neighboring landmarks of the Louisiana State Museum complex. The **Cabildo** (701 Chartres Street at Jackson Square; 504–568–6968) is most famous as the site where the documents for the Louisiana Purchase were signed over from France to the U.S. in 1803. Inside the magnificent colonnaded structure, you'll also find Napoleon's death mask, artifacts from the Battle of New Orleans, and mementos of the city's history under various European governments. Be sure to notice the portrait of voodoo priestess Marie Laveau, whose magic was often sought in the service of dangerous liaisons.

Local color continues at the Cabildo's twin, known as the **Presbytere** (751 Chartres Street at Jackson Square; 504–568–6968). Among countless romantic visions, you'll see *Elegance After Dark: Evening Wear in Louisiana, 1896–1996* and a 1929 portrait of Longfellow's tragic lovers, Evangeline and Gabriel, which bears a suspicious resemblance to the stars who played the roles in that year's epic film (Dolores del Rio and Roland Drew). A number of treasures on exhibit reflect the city's ongoing love affair with Creole general P. G. T. Beauregard, including his horse's teeth.

The Cabildo and Presbytere flank lovely **St. Louis Cathedral** (615 Père Antoine Alley at Jackson Square; 504–525–9585). Be sure to walk around back to gaze through the iron fence into St. Anthony's Garden, site of countless nineteenth-century duels.

DAY TWO: AFTERNOON

A few steps along the square is another Louisiana State Museum property that's worth a visit. The **1850 House** (523 St. Ann Street at Jackson Square; 504–568–6972) is fully restored in the style of a nineteenth-century Creole family of the middle class, down to the table settings and dolls in the nursery.

In Louisiana's feudal society of the eighteenth and nineteenth centuries, young Creole gentlemen lived like princes, with egos to match. Tempers flared over the tiniest slight, and friends were pressed into service as "seconds" to observe sword or pistol fights provoked by anything from an impudent glance to competition for a lady's affections. Though many died in these affaires d'honneur, *the French Creoles traditionally obtained satisfaction at first blood. Americans who came along later began the custom of fighting to the death. In fact, the governor himself, W. C. C. Claiborne, won the first duel under the American regime in 1803.*

Grave markers in older cemeteries identify occupants who were killed in duels with such glorious euphemisms as victime de son honneur *(victim of his honor),* mort sur le champ d'honneur *(died on the field of honor), or* pour garder intact le nom de famille *(for defending the family name). St. Vincent de Paul Cemetery (poetically situated between Piety and Desire Streets) was even owned for a time by a colorful local character known as Señor Pépé Lulla, a fencing master and expert marksman. According to legend, the celebrated duelist needed the extra space to dispose of his many unsuccessful challengers.*

Lunch

One of your best chances to get a look at a contemporary Creole aristocrat is a late afternoon lunch at **Galatoire's** (209 Bourbon Street between Iberville and Bienville Streets; 504–525–2021; moderate), when this grand old Parisian-style bistro is filled with members of upper-crust families who have been regular customers for generations. One of the last native strongholds in the tourist-happy French Quarter, the classic French Creole menu and Continental service have changed little since the doors first opened in 1905. The walls are lined with dark wood and mirrors, the antique chairs are hard, and a floor covered with tiny white tiles only amplifies the noise level. In a world gone mad over mango salsa and blue corn polenta, here is a sane oasis where you can still find great turtle soup, escargots bordelaise, lamb chops béarnaise, and crepes Suzette.

Now you're faced with a choice. Do you return to the hotel for a nap or to freshen up and visit the neighbors? If it's the latter, you'll get an eyeful of haute Creole style touring the 1857 **Gallier House Museum** (1118–32 Royal Street between Ursulines and Governor Nicholls Streets; 504–525–5661, guided tours $5), which was built for his own family by celebrated local architect James Gallier. The 1826 **Beauregard-Keyes House** (1113 Chartres Street between Ursulines and Governor Nicholls Streets, 504–523–7257, guided tours $4), is named for two illustrious former tenants, that beloved Civil War general and romance novelist Frances Parkinson Keyes.

DAY TWO: EVENING

Tonight you could abandon yourselves to classic romantic comedy or lavish love songs. Either way, you won't need to *parler français* to enjoy the English-language presentations at the little playhouse with the Gallic name. The country's oldest continuously operating community theater, established in 1916, still stages presents first-class productions at **Le Petit Theatre du Vieux Carré** (616 St. Peter Street at Chartres Street; 504–522–2081). The gray stucco building is a 1922 replica of the eighteenth-century house that formerly stood on this site, residence of the last Spanish governor of Louisiana. Intermissions are lovely on an inner courtyard graced by a tiered fountain and tropical blooms. Broadway musicals are a favorite at this small theater, where the curtain usually goes up at 8:00 P.M. Tickets cost $18 for musicals, $14 for straight plays.

After the theater, soak up the old-world atmosphere at **Napoleon House** (see "Past Imperfect") with a midnight supper of wine, cheese, and crusty sandwiches on French bread. Soon you'll be ready to exile yourselves to that magnificent bed. *Bon nuit.*

FOR MORE ROMANCE

Steal a kiss—or settle a lovers' quarrel once and for all—under the infamous dueling oaks, where 19th-century gentlemen met at dawn over pistols for two and brandy for one. The ancient trees are located in **City Park** (City Park Avenue at Esplanade Avenue; 504-482-4888), also home to such romantic backdrops as Popp's Fountain, an antique carousel, the classic peristyle overlooking a lagoon, and the lavish display of native blooms in the **New Orleans Botanical Garden.** All are favorite sites for local weddings.

Two other stellar restaurants have established a national reputation with their contemporary Creole cuisine. **The Pelican Club** (312 Exchange Alley: 504-523-1504; expensive) offers chic and cosmopolitan fare in the French Quarter. **Gautreau's** (1728 Soniat Street; 504-899-7397; expensive) is a sedate and polished beauty, set in a renovated 19th-century pharmacy in an Uptown residential neighborhood.

Creole plantation life is detailed in "Sugar Palaces and Sweet Dreams." For more on regional Cajun culture, see "Cajun Rendezvous."

ITINERARY 11
Two days and two nights

FROM GUMBO TO GOSPEL
THE AFRICAN/CARIBBEAN CONNECTION

From the roots of jazz to the seeds of the civil rights movement, New Orleans has been largely defined by its African-American culture. To see its influence on the city, look anywhere: Food, music, art, dance, language, literature, fashion, and government. The mystique of the Big Easy remains inseparable from its racial history, whether you choose to immerse yourselves in the romance of the past or indulge in the abundances of today.

Lend your ears to living legends or stars of the future at local jazz and blues clubs. Revel in the exotic flavors of African-born gumbo and jambalaya, or Caribbean-inspired shrimp Creole and crab soup. Abandon yourselves to sinful goodies and joyful noise at a down-home gospel brunch. Court each other with carriage rides, gallery hopping, and moonlit rambles on the river levee. Everywhere you turn, you'll find another course in this feast for the senses. Like Louis Armstrong sang, "It's a wonderful world."

Practical notes: Phone in advance to reserve spots on the "Roots of New Orleans" Heritage City Tour (888–337–6687 or 504–596–6889).

DAY ONE: AFTERNOON

The **African-American Accommodation Reservation Service** (888–232–1785 or 504–522–1785) represents around a dozen black-owned properties, including bed and breakfast in private homes, some cottages, one penthouse, and a group of corporate apartments. The **Greater New Orleans Black Tourism Network** (504–523–5652) also maintains a list of accommodations and provides information on area attactions.

Romance at a Glance

♥ *Follow the famous musicians and movie stars who dine at Dooky Chase.*

♥ *Feed your hungry eyes on African-American art at galleries and museums.*

♥ *Dip into diaries of Harlem Renaissance poets at Amistad Research Center.*

♥ *Search for new favorites among the classic jazz exhibits at the Old US Mint.*

♥ *Get off the tourist track for BBQ and brass bands at Donna's Bar & Grill.*

Lunch

After checking in, make the pilgrimage to an internationally known landmark of Creole cuisine. Before Edgar "Dooky" Chase and wife Emily Tenette opened for business in 1941, there was no fine dining restaurant available to the local black community. **Dooky Chase** (2301 Orleans Avenue at North Miro Street; 504–821–2294 or 504–821–0600; moderate) soon became one of the city's institutions. Now operated by Dooky Chase, Jr., and his wife, celebrated chef Leah Chase, it's also home to a premier collection of regional folk art. The menu offers a feast of seafood, gumbos, etouffées, stuffed peppers, and other regional specialties. (Unfortunately, the surrounding neighborhood has deteriorated, so it's best to take a taxi right to the door.)

⊙⊙⊙

Everyone has to get a look at the French Quarter, so direct your cab driver to drop you on Decatur Street at Jackson Square. If you prefer to let someone else do the walking, snuggle up in a mule-drawn buggy for a narrated tour. Different companies operate from the same stand, but **Mid-City Carriages** (Decatur Street at Jackson Square; 504–581–4415) are black owned. The thirty-minute tour costs $40 for up to four passengers.

From the square, it's only about five blocks to **La Belle Gallerie & The Black Art Collection** (309 Chartres Street between Bienville and Conti Streets; 504–529–3080, 504–529–5538). Explore the 6,000-square-foot exhibit area for everything from French posters of Josephine Baker to intricately beaded Haitian voodoo flags and antique African artifacts. You'll find original works by both national and regional artists, along with limited edition posters, lithographs, and serigraphs.

Cross Canal Street and continue six blocks to the Warehouse/Arts District, where you can pick up colorful treasures to feather your nest from the **628 Gallery** (628 Baronne Street between Girod and Lafayette Streets; 504–529–3306). This is the workshop and home gallery for **YA/YA** (Young Aspirations/Young Artists), a private nonprofit organization that provides an outlet for gifted inner-city artists ages fourteen to twenty-six. Their bold designs transform ordinary wooden furniture and decorative items into striking, functional art that has been exhibited in Amsterdam, Paris, Tokyo, Milan, and major U.S. cities. In addition to their paychecks, a portion of each youth's sales is placed in trust to fund a college education.

DAY ONE: EVENING
Dinner

Hope you made arrangements for all of those wonderful finds to be shipped directly home (it saves on sales taxes), because you are in the right neighborhood to feast on some of the best Creole soul food around. Stroll eight blocks on Julia Street, window-shopping "Gallery Row," then take a right onto South Peters Street for dinner at **The Praline Connection** (901 South Peters Street at St. Joseph Street; 504–523–3973; inexpensive). An efficient staff dressed in black slacks, starched white shirts, and black fedoras delivers the freshest fried seafood, spicy gumbos and etouffées, stewed or fried chicken, and homestyle meatloaf with your choice from three different greens and five varieties of beans on the side. Cornbread and sweet potato pie round out the splurge.

⋘⊙⊙⋙

Savor the goods at your leisure, because you're right next door to some rousing entertainment, offered nightly except Monday and Wednesday, at **The Praline Connection Gospel and Blues Hall** (907 South Peters Street between St. Joseph and North Diamond Streets; 504–523–3973). Set in a 9,000-square-foot space that formerly housed a steamboat engine factory, the showpiece is a massive, 50-foot, carved bar that was hauled downriver by barge from one of Al Capone's Chicago speakeasies. The 20-by-30-foot stage, flanked by the actual facades of two New Orleans houses, is usually ruled by Raymond Myles & Friends. A local favorite, this natural-born performer will have you clapping, swaying, and shouting for joy in no time. Myles shows his spiritual side for the weekly Sunday Gospel Brunch, a feast for both body and soul. The brunch costs $19.95. There's no cover charge for evening shows, usually scheduled on Tuesday and Saturday nights.

DAY TWO: MORNING

Linger over breakfast with your B&B host, who is sure to recommend personal favorites for Big Easy romance, then retire to the privacy of your room for a little unguided sightseeing before you dress for the day.

If it's Thursday, Friday, or Saturday, check into Gwen Carter's **Roots of New Orleans Heritage City Tour** (888–337–6687 or 504–596–6889). The two-and-a-half-hour motor-coach circuit, $28 per person, stops at three historic landmarks. You'll visit St. Augustine Church, the first to be built by free people of color, and St. Louis Cemetery Number One, where brave petitioners can chalk an X on voodoo priestess Marie Laveau's tomb and turn

Sealed with a Kiss

Not all of the letters on file at the Amistad Research Center are signed by famous names, but even the unsung authors can capture your heart. Besides, it's a delicious opportunity to get your hands on someone else's mail.

"Dear Sophronia," begins a flowery billet-doux penned by one lovestruck guy in 1889, "The impression you have made upon me is so deep and powerful that I cannot forego writing to you in defiance of all rules of etiquette." The genteel pleading climaxes four pages later with, "I think you are the sweetest girl on the globe, and unless I greatly deceive myself, I believe you are a permanent girl . . ."

A 1943 message of support from writer Zora Neale Hurston to Harlem Renaissance poet Countee Cullen condemns "stale phrases and bodiless courage" and favors the hard road of reality to "the rattling wagon of wishful illusions."

In a 1940 letter to her pastor, a man recalls his family's nurse, a tiny woman who "bossed" both the children and their parents. When she was nearly 100 years old, she could still thread a needle by candlelight and breakfast on three quarts of iced tomatoes with sugar. He remembers her as "a court of authority for my conduct and of security for my physical wellbeing" and his five-page tribute reads like a lively short story. It is signed by William Faulkner.

around three times to make a wish. (It's said that Laveau only helps those who swear their wishes to secrecy, so don't tell even each other.) The last stop is the Amistad Research Center at Tulane University, which houses an outstanding African-American art collection and the world's largest archive on U.S. ethnic history and race relations. Meanwhile, the journey meanders through old neighborhoods, past such points of interest as the first black YMCA and a monument to Dr. Martin Luther King, Jr.

If no tours are offered during your visit, catch the St. Charles Avenue streetcar and get off at **Tulane University** (6823 St. Charles Avenue, facing Audubon Park; 504–865–5000) to explore the collection at the **Amistad Research Center** (Tilton Hall; 504–865–5535) on your own. More than 250 artworks showcase such African-American masters as William H. Johnson, Henry O. Tanner, and Ellis Wilson. However, the main attraction for scholars from around the world is a monumental collection that includes the personal papers of hundreds of civil rights leaders, writers, artists, educators, politicians, and musicians. None of the documents may leave the building, but all are open to study by the public. Ask one of the archivists to direct you to some love letters or diaries.

Lunch

For an authentic African meal, complete with national dress and music, continue to the end of the line on the streetcar and transfer to the Carrollton bus to reach **Bennachin Restaurant** (133 North Carrollton Avenue between Canal and Iberville Streets; 504–486–1313; inexpensive). In their simple storefront dining room, partners Fanta Tambajang of Gambia and Alyse Njenge of the Cameroon offer the crisp and delicate black-eyed pea fritters known as *akara*, a ginger-scented cousin of shrimp Creole called *shipa-shipa,* and beef chunks simmered in a rich peanut gravy for *domoda.* Several weekday lunch specials are priced under $5.

If you'd prefer to go Caribbean, step right next door to **Palmer's Jamaican Creole Restaurant** (135 North Carrollton Avenue between Canal and Iberville Streets; 504–482–3658; inexpensive). The lunchtime buffet on weekdays is a spicy and exotic bargain of jerked chicken, pepperpot soup, and other island goodies.

ॐ

Afterward, continue on the Carrollton bus to view the works in the African and Southern folk art galleries at **New Orleans Museum of Art** (1 Collins Diboll Circle in

City Park; 504–488–2631); then head back to the French Quarter on the Esplanade bus to explore the jazz exhibits at the **Old US Mint** (400 Esplanade Avenue at Decatur Street; 504–568–6968). While you're there, be sure to see the display of splashy costumes from the Mardi Gras Indians, various local marching groups who still honor the Native American tribes that gave runaway slaves sanctuary and a life of freedom. Their intricately beaded and plumed extravaganzas remain one of the highlights of Carnival.

Dinner

Take your pick from two good choices for dinner and dancing, depending upon the music schedules at local clubs. Check listings for neighboring **Jimmy's** (8200 Willow Street at Dublin Street; 504–861–8200), **Carrollton Station** (8140 Willow Street at Dublin Street; 504–865–9190), and **Maple Leaf Bar** (8316 Oak Street between Dante and Cambronne Streets, 504–866–9359). If the shows look good, begin your evening of club hopping with an uptown meal at **Zachary's Creole Cuisine** (8400 Oak Street at Cambronne Street; 504–865–1559; moderate). The second and third generations of a celebrated local family of restaurateurs continue the culinary tradition begun by patriarch Eddie Baquet. Wayne Baquet's large pink cottage is graced by starched linens, smooth service, and soft jazz CDs. Try piquant shrimp rémoulade and fresh speckled trout topped with lump crabmeat in lemon butter sauce. The gumbos are famous.

On the other hand, you could aim yourselves right at the downtown heart of the city for barbecue and brass bands across the street from Armstrong Park in **Donna's Bar & Grill** (800 Rampart Street at St. Ann Street; 504–596–6914; inexpensive). It's basic, but the red beans and rice are wonderful, and live music heats up around 10:00 P.M. Regulars include Kermit Ruffins & the Barbecue Swingers, Treme Brass Band, Tuba Fats & The Chosen Few, Leroy Jones, and the New Birth Brass Band. This is the real thing!

FOR MORE ROMANCE

As fascinating as a small museum, but more liberal with visitors who want to touch or hold the works on display, **Davis Gallery** (3964 Magazine Street at Constantinople Street; 504–897–0780) exhibits a wealth of ethnographic art imported from West and Central Africa. Here you can run your hands over exotic antiques, worn smooth and softly polished from centuries of use by members of the represented cultures. Of special interest for lovers are various fertility icons, jewelry, textiles, and household implements. However, collectors at every level will find treasures, from $50 baskets to museum-quality masterpieces. The gallery's international client list even includes the Smithsonian Institution.

Plenty of other music clubs are featured in "Howling at the Moon," "On the Prowl," "Cheap Thrills," and "A Feast for the Ears." For more visual stimulation, see "Artful Seduction."

MOONSTRUCK ON THE MISSISSIPPI
LOVE ITALIAN STYLE

*F*rench yes, but the most Mediterranean city in the U.S. is also home to a huge community of Italian-Americans, who have played a major role in creating our colorful local cuisine, music, architecture, politics, business climate, hand gestures, and strangely un-Southern accent. You'll sense their spirit everywhere you go on this quick dip into *la dolce vita.*

From the art treasures of Florence to the ice creams of Palermo, here's your chance to escape on a Roman mini-holiday without leaving town. Read on to find romantic music, *ristorantes, alimentari,* and other appetizers for *amore.*

Practical notes: Reservations are recommended for Bella Luna (504–529–1583). Seating is strictly first come, first served at Irene's Cuisine, so plan an early dinner (before 7:00 P.M.) for the shortest wait at this popular restaurant.

DAY ONE: EVENING
Shoemaker Antonio Monteleone worked so hard after he immigrated to New Orleans

from Contessa, Italy, that he eventually purchased the old Commercial Hotel in 1886 and gave it his name. Today the **Monteleone** (214 Royal Street between Iberville and Bienville Streets; 800–535–9595 or 504–523–3341; doubles, $145 to $250; suites, $290 to $840) is a plush French Quarter landmark with a baroque granite facade, uniformed doormen, rooftop pool, and 600 individually decorated rooms, some with four-poster beds and mirrored canopies.

Start your social whirl with cocktails in the hotel's revolving **Carousel Bar.** Clubby and sedate, the piano bar is a popular meeting spot for local businesspeople, politicos, and other power drinkers.

Romance at a Glance

♥ *Toast the enterprise of shoemaker Antonio Monteleone at his grand hotel.*

♥ *Discover Italian-American jazz masters in local music clubs and record stores.*

♥ *Explore love among the ruins at Piazza d'Italia.*

♥ *Mangia! Feast in style at two historic delis, a cozy trattoria, and a moonlit dazzler.*

♥ *Splurge on Sicilian gelati and fresh fruit ices from Angelo Brocato's grandchildren.*

Dinner

Promise one another the moon in a romantic setting that's out of this world at **Bella Luna** (914 North Peters Street at the river; 504–529–1583). Located in the French Market overlooking the Mississippi, big views of the river are balanced by luminous grey decor, elegant service, and tables that are well spaced for plenty of privacy. Horst Pfeiffer's seasonal menu is a sensuous marriage of housemade pastas, regional ingredients, and fresh herbs from the chef's own garden. You could be offered anything from house-cured pork chops in pecan crust to penne tossed with sun-dried tomatoes and white truffle oil. The wine list won the 1994 *Wine Spectator* Award of Excellence.

⌘

After dinner, don't just head for the nearest Bourbon Street joint. Jazz roots also run deep in the Italian community, so check club listings in the French Quarter for Al Belletto, Rene

Netto, James LaRocca, Frank Frederico, and other native performers with melodic last names. Order a nightcap of amaretto to sweeten your dreams.

DAY TWO: MORNING

After you awaken, walk to Decatur Street to pick out a picnic brunch and exotic souvenirs at three Mediterranean markets. For generations **Central Grocery Co.** (923 Decatur Street between Dumaine and St. Philip Streets; 504–523–1620) and **Progress Grocery** (915 Decatur Street between Dumaine and St. Philip Streets; 504–525–6627) have occupied the same block of Decatur Street, colorful and crowded *alimentari* jammed to the rafters (literally) with dried salamis and fish, garlic braids, fresh breads, coffees, bulk spices, and a dizzying range of imported foodstuffs and housewares. A chic newcomer, **Bella Luna Pasta Shop** (914 North Peters Street at the river; 504–529–1583) stocks European kitchenware, along with many of the temptations you saw on the restaurant's menu last night, including house-made pastas and baked goods.

Along they way, check the shops for the contemporary musicians listed above, plus classics by Louis Prima, Sam Butera, and Sharky Bonnano, among others. In fact, the world's first jazz recording, the original "Dixieland One-Step," was cut in 1917 by Nick LaRocca (father of James) with the Dixieland Jass [*sic*] Band. You'll find outstanding regional inventories at **Louisiana Music Factory** (210 Decatur Street between Iberville and Bienville Streets; 504–586–1094) and in shops adjoining **Palm Court Jazz Cafe** (1204 Decatur Street between Governor Nicholls and Barracks Streets; 504–522–0200) and the permanent jazz exhibit at **The Old U.S. Mint** (400 Esplanade Avenue at Decatur Street; 504–568–6968). You could also uncover rare finds among the used stacks at the two locations of **Record Ron's** (1129 Decatur Street between Ursulines and Governor Nicholls Streets; 504÷524–9444 and 239 Chartres Street between Iberville and Bienville Streets; 504–522–2239).

Drop your take-home goodies at the hotel; then carry your picnic brunch across Canal

Street into the Central Business District to play Apollo and Daphne in the sunlight and shadows of a landmark monument to the Italian heritage of New Orleans. Superstar architect Charles Moore created the postmodern **Piazza d'Italia** (Poydras Street between South Peters and Tchoupitoulas Streets) in 1979, a pastel fantasy "ruin" with archway, campanile, pavilion, and boot-shaped fountain.

DAY TWO: AFTERNOON

By now you're probably ready for a cool dessert. From Piazza d'Italia, walk back to catch the Canal Street bus, disembarking at Carrollton Avenue to scoop up on another authentic Sicilian treat at **Angelo Brocato Ice Cream and Confectionery** (214 North Carrollton Avenue between Iberville and Bienville Streets; 504–486–0078; inexpensive).

Ever since the founder and namesake brought his recipes from Palermo more than eighty years ago, New Orleanians have loved the authentic *gelati, canoli,* and Sicilian pastries. Now operated by the third generation, the family company still produces fresh ices from seasonal fruit (don't miss the mango or blueberry), *torrincino* flavored with almonds and cinnamon, and *stracciatella* spiked with fine shreds of chocolate. Signature *spumoni* is an eye-catching pastel wedge of pistachio, tutti-frutti, and lemon *gelati* with a whipped cream center. Despite a few moves over the decades, the current shop retains an authentic turn-of-the-century atmosphere, with marble-topped tables, ceiling fans, and huge old jars brimming with brilliant Italian candies. Share a cool treat with two spoons.

Continue on the Carrollton Avenue bus to **City Park** (City Park Avenue at Esplanade) to view centuries of Italian masterworks on display at **New Orleans Museum of Art** (1 Collins Diboll Circle in City Park; 504–488–2631). Be sure to celebrate the triumph of love with Bacchiacca's *Portrait of a Young Lute Player* and bask in the dreamy affection of Il Pesarese's *Madonna and Child with Goldfinch.* (For a romantic road map through the rest of the collection, see "Artful Seduction.") When you're ready to move on, the Esplanade Avenue bus will get you back to the French Quarter.

DAY TWO: EVENING
Dinner

First promise to return, then bid *ciao bella* to "America's most European city" at a wonderfully charming hideaway. Tucked away on a Vieux Carré side street is a sweet nook and local favorite, **Irene's Cuisine** (539 St. Philip Street at Chartres Streets; 504–529–8811; moderate). Two smallish dining rooms and a rustic "wine cellar" bar are filled with photographs, garlic braids, and hand-painted crockery. Lavishly presented and reasonably priced, the food is outstanding. Don't miss brandy-flamed rosemary chicken or signature Oysters Irene, broiled on the half-shell with a crisp *gratin* of prosciutto and cheese. Share a towering wedge of baked Alaska for your flaming finale.

FOR MORE ROMANCE

Sicilian descendants celebrate their patron's **Feast Day of St. Joseph** on March 19 by building incredible food-laden altars in private homes, restaurants, churches, and businesses all over New Orleans. Later the offerings are donated to the poor, but everyone takes home a "lucky bean" (dried fava) to tuck into his wallet until next year, a protection against going broke. Parades and parties coincide with similar festivities in the Irish community to honor St. Patrick's Day (March 17), so it's a great time to soak in a double shot of local color that most tourists never see, if it suits your schedule. Love and family, hearth and home, the neighboring events celebrate romance that endures for generations.

ITINERARY 13
Two days and two nights

SPLENDOR IN THE GRASS

GARDENS, COURTYARDS, AND PARKS

*T*hough better known for indoor games and unnatural attractions, New Orleans has plenty of pleasant surprises for nature buffs. From the showy landscaping of the Garden District to the secret patios of the French Quarter, from the ancient oaks of City Park to the tropical courtyards of old-line Creole restaurants, you'll find fertile ground with sunny exposure where love is sure to bloom.

Sidewalks and medians are draped with a hot-hued fringe of azaleas, crape myrtles, hibiscus, and bridal veil. Massive magnolia trees shower deep green shade and Old South elegance over the humblest cottages. Even the air is perfumed by sweet olives, gardenias, and night-blooming jasmine. Whether your fantasies are colored by banks of roses in a manicured eden, or jungle fever beneath the banana trees, verdant backdrops await around every corner.

Practical notes: The Park View books up early, especially during special events at nearby Tulane and Loyola universities, so reserve your room two to three months in advance (504–861–7564). Reservations are recommended to dine at Broussard's (504–581–3866), Bayona (504–525–4455), and Feelings Cafe (504–945–2222).

DAY ONE: AFTERNOON

Overlooking the moss-draped oaks and lazy lagoons of the former estate of naturalist John James Audubon, now Audubon Park, you'll enjoy plenty of green space and room to move at **Park View** (7004 St. Charles Avenue at Walnut Street; 504–861–7564; doubles with private bath, $95). Built as a hotel for the 1884 World Cotton Exchange Exhibit and attractively renovated in 1992, this sedate guest house now offers twenty-two rooms graced by antiques, fifteen with private baths, and some with balconies. The rates include morning coffee and croissants in the sunny Audubon Room.

Right next door, **Audubon Park** (bounded by St. Charles Avenue, the Mississippi River, Walnut Street, and Exposition Boulevard) is a 385-acre beauty laid out in the 1890s by John Olmsted, son of Frederick Law Olmsted who designed New York's Central Park. In addition to **Cascade Riding Stables** (504–891–2246) and **Audubon Zoological Garden** (see "Cheap Thrills"), the uptown gathering spot is home to an impressive collection of tropical plants at **Heymann Memorial Conservatory** (504–891–2419).

Take a walk over to the charming shopping area that lines Maple Street, where shops are brightened by window boxes and cottage gardens. Don't miss the miniature trees, gardening tools, and original handcrafted containers at **The Garden Gallery and Bonsai Center** (729 Burdette Street at Maple Street; 504–865–8593), which also specializes in books and supplies for ikebana (Japanese flower arranging). **The Sun Shop** (7722 Maple Street between Burdette and Adams Streets; 504–861–8338) is filled with outdoor ornaments, wall plaques, and other native artifacts from owner Chester "Chick" Fortner's travels throughout North and South America. Continue all the way

Romance at a Glance

♥ *Open your bedroom windows over mossy oaks and moody lagoons at Park View.*

♥ *Wine and dine in historic courtyards at Broussard's, Bayona, and Feelings Cafe.*

♥ *Explore heirloom gardens at the Old Ursuline Convent and Hermann-Grima House.*

♥ *Bring home the blooms with ikebana, bonsai, and water gardening supplies.*

across Carrollton Avenue to the atelier and shop of nationally recognized jewelry designer **Mignon Faget Ltd.** (710 Dublin Street between Maple and Hampson Streets; 504–865–1107), whose works incorporate banana leaves, garden snails, and other nature-inspired themes.

DAY ONE: EVENING

From Carrollton Avenue, catch the St. Charles Avenue streetcar back to the Park View to dress for dinner. Afterward, continue downtown on the streetcar for a cool rumble under the oaks, past meticulously landscaped mansions and pocket parks. Get off at Canal Street and cross to the French Quarter, where you'll linger over luxuriant cuisine, surrounded by one of the city's most extravagant gardens.

Dinner

The lavish courtyard is famous, but the food is just as impressive as the landscaping at **Broussard's** (819 Conti Street between Dauphine and Bourbon Streets; 504–581–3866; expensive). Veteran chef Gunter Preuss and wife Evelyn brought along a loyal local clientele when they took over operation of the historic French Quarter restaurant in 1995. To the established Creole specialties, they added such updates as Louisiana bouillabaisse stocked with shrimp, crabmeat, and oysters; breaded veal medallions topped with herbed crabmeat; and a wild game grill that changes daily. Best of all, dessert lovers who can't make up their minds are offered a sampling platter with generous tastings of the best sweets in the house. Just say yes.

✤

After dinner, stroll along Royal Street to peek around gates and peer down corridors for a glimpse of the French Quarter's secluded courtyards and patios, being careful not to intrude upon private property. Sneak through hotel lobbies to view the illuminated gardens after dark, especially the **Royal Sonesta** (300 Bourbon Street between Bienville and Conti Streets) and the **St. Louis** (730 Bienville Street between Royal and Bourbon Streets).

DAY TWO: MORNING

After breakfast at the Park View, you'll spend the morning exploring two urban edens. **Longue Vue House and Gardens** (7 Bamboo Road at Metairie Road; 504–488–5488) is a Mid-City showplace that features a Louisiana Native Garden, fountain-splashed Portuguese Canal Garden, and formal Spanish Court patterned after the fourteenth-century Generalife Gardens of Spain's Alhambra. The 1942 mansion is also open for tours that highlight European and American antiques, modern art, and pottery. For more details on the estate, see "Glittering Oaks and Bonfires on the Levee."

Nearby, 1,500-acre **City Park** (bounded by Lake Pontchartrain, City Park Avenue, Bayou St. John, and Orleans Avenue; 504–482–4888) is home to more than eighty plant species and 30,000 trees, including hundreds of ancient oaks, the largest stand in the world. The seven-acre **New Orleans Botanical Garden** (Victory Avenue across from the tennis courts), built in the park during the 1930s by WPA workers, is graced by a tranquil water garden and major collections of bromeliads, begonias, and large tropicals. The romantic Art Deco wading pools, fountains, and statues were created by sculptor Enrique Alferez.

DAY TWO: AFTERNOON

From City Park, follow oak-shaded Esplanade Avenue to the French Quarter. Though not as well maintained as tonier St. Charles Avenue, the once-grand drive is lined with historic houses and colorful blooms.

Say It with Flowers

Everyone knows you send red roses to express passion and an olive branch for peace, but what other hidden messages can be conveyed by an innocent-looking bouquet? Some examples from the traditional language of flowers:

Asphodel: *My regret follows you to the grave.*

Bay leaf: *I change but in death.*

Bluebell: *constancy*

Foxglove: *insincerity*

Honeysuckle: *generous and devoted affection*

Jasmine: *amiability*

Nasturtium: *patriotism*

Orange blossom: *virginity*

Oak leaves: *bravery*

Peony: *shame or bashfulness*

Quince: *temptation*

Rosemary: *remembrance*

Snowdrop: *hope*

Veronica: *fidelity*

And roses, it seems, speak a language all their own. Among the thorny remarks:

White rosebud: *too young to love*

White rose full of buds: *secrecy*

Burgundy rose: *simplicity and beauty*

Yellow rose: *jealousy*

Faded rose: *Beauty is fleeting.*

Lunch

One of the city's most respected chefs, Susan Spicer presents her self-styled "New World cuisine" in a nineteenth-century cottage filled with photographs of historic Italian gardens at **Bayona** (430 Dauphine Street between Conti and St. Louis Streets; 504–525–4455; expensive). Tables are also scattered about a *bellisima* courtyard cooled by banana trees, flowering shrubs, fish pond, and fountain. The menu changes with the seasons, offering such Mediterranean-inspired fare as cream of garlic soup, stuffed quail with foie gras and rose geranium sauce, grilled rabbit with lemon and thyme, and double chocolate espresso cake. Among many other honors, Spicer was named best chef in the Southeast by the James Beard Foundation in 1993.

∽⊚⊚∾

Ramble through the French Quarter at your leisure, peeking into secret gardens you missed last night. Visit the **New Orleans Pharmacy Museum** (514 Chartres Street between St. Louis and Toulouse Streets; 504–565–8027) to see the walled courtyard planted with medicinal herbs; the **Coghlan Gallery** (710 Toulouse between Royal and Bourbon Streets; 504–525–8550) to shop for treasures in a courtyard filled with garden ornaments, fountains, and stone angels created by local crafters; and the formal gardens at the **Hermann-Grima Historic House** (820 St. Louis Street between Bourbon and Dauphine Streets; 504–525–5661) and **Old Ursuline Convent** (1100 Chartres Street between Ursulines and Governor Nicholls Streets; 504–529–3040).

Hail a cab for a quick ride to **American Aquatic Gardens** (621 Elysian Fields Avenue between Royal and Chartres Streets; 504–944–0410), a fascinating store devoted to water gardening. Throughout the large indoor/outdoor complex, you'll find pond kits, stone ornaments, handmade fountains, and exotic plants. Almost anything in stock can be shipped, but it's a fun romantic fantasy even if you're "just looking."

DAY TWO: Evening

While you're in the neighborhood, a verdant hideaway is nestled just a few blocks away (but take a cab, especially after dark). **Feelings Cafe** (2600 Chartres Street at Franklin Avenue; 504–945–2222; expensive) is an ultra-romantic local favorite with an unfortunate name but sophisticated food and service. Set in the carriage house of the former D'Aunoy

Plantation, the dining room and piano bar adjoin a lovely courtyard that's surfaced with brick from the old plantation fireplace and shaded by banana trees. House specialties include barbecue shrimp, soft shell crabs, veal d'Aunoy (sauteed in lemon herb butter and garnished with sliced mushrooms and hollandaise), and the infamous peanut butter pie.

FOR MORE ROMANCE

Private entrances to quaint cottage suites and guest rooms open onto a courtyard with a butterfly garden at **The Chimes Bed and Breakfast** (1146 Constantinople at Coliseum Street; 800–729–4640 or 504–488–4640; doubles, $71 to $127). Milkweed, passion flower, and dill serve as host plants for the caterpillar stage; while pentas and blue haze provide nectar for adult monarch and swallowtail butterflies. Spring and fall are best for viewing.

For details on walking tours of the Garden District, see "Rich in Love." For more on City Park and Longue Vue Gardens at Christmas, see "Glittering Oaks and Bonfires on the Levee." To tour grounds of nearby country plantations, see "Sugar Palaces and Sweet Dreams." Two of the state's most famous public gardens are featured in "Cajun Rendezvous."

Other restaurants where you may dine in—or overlooking—some of the city's most beautiful patios and courtyards include **Begue's** (page 205), **Brennan's French Restaurant** (pages 6–7), **Commander's Palace** (page 20), **The Court of Two Sisters** (page 35), and **G&E Courtyard Grill** (page 120). Garden-themed paintings crowd the walls and fresh flowers adorn every table, adding splashes of sunny style to the **Upperline** (page 71).

HOMEGROWN AND HANDCRAFTED

*Y*ou enter through an ancient carriageway edged with tropical blooms, a pocket jungle in the City That Care Forgot. Inside the shop, shuttered French doors open wide to let in tranquil impressions of a slower age, the clop-clop of horse-drawn carriages, a chattering courtyard foundatin, soft glow from gaslights along the street.

Those graceful French Quarter spaces that now rent by the square foot were once filled with working crafters who produced handmade goods by necessity, to supply local colonists and an expanding frontier. Today, many of their traditional skills survive, but the emphasis is on originality and polish to attract craft lovers in search of one-of-a-kind creations. In the same spirit, simple organic ingredients are being fashioned into exciting new dishes, at once cosmopolitan and rustic, by some of the city's best chefs. Humble beer has attracted the attention of connoisseurs via local microbreweries. And you'll enjoy the fruits of all their labors on this tour of the earthy side of New Orleans.

Practical notes: Most of the merchants in this itinerary will ship, a convenience that may also save on sales taxes. Reservations are recommended for G&E Courtyard Grill (504–528–9376).

DAY ONE: AFTERNOON

Surround yourselves with original art and exotic handmade items at **Jana's B&B** (628 Baronne Street between Girod and Lafayette Streets; 504–524–6473). Located in an 1840s townhouse above three working studios, artist Jana Napoli's loft space is divided into two offbeat guest apartments filled with artifacts from her world travels and furnishings from her **628 Gallery** on the ground floor. (For details on her work with **YA/YA** artisans, see "From Gumbo to Gospel." The adjoining **Estudio Gallery** is featured in "Artful Seduction.") A landscaped rooftop deck between the apartments has great views of the Gothic Revival spire of nearby St. Patrick's Church, Mississippi River bridges, and downtown skyscrapers. The two-bedroom, two-bath apartment with a private kitchen and Jacuzzi rents for $200. A smaller, split-level unit (one bedroom, no kitchen) is $125.

Chic vertical mall **Canal Place** (Canal Street at the river; 504–522–9200) may look like an unlikely spot for a nonprofit cooperative, but high-quality merchandise suits the toney surroundings at **RHINO** (504–523–7945). The gallery of fine crafts provides a retail outlet for about eighty Louisiana artisans who market their works "Right Here In New Orleans." In addition to the latest news on the local arts scene (exhibitors take turns minding the store) you'll find sculpture, pottery, textiles, glass, jewelry, furniture, and much more.

Romance at a Glance

♥ *Sin, then repent, in a bed made from an old convent altar at Jana's B&B.*

♥ *Put your lips together and blow at New Orleans School of Glass Works.*

♥ *Bring home a touch of the French Quarter with gaslights or ornamental iron.*

♥ *Feast on regional produce at G&E Courtyard Grill and Chicory Farm Cafe.*

♥ *Sample your way across Louisiana at the Crescent City Farmer's Market.*

Lunch

Crescent City Brewhouse (527 Decatur Street between Toulouse and St. Louis Streets; 504–522–0571; inexpensive) serves a stellar variety of house-brewed drafts, along with beer-friendly appetizers and entrées that showcase seasonal Louisiana products. Raise your glasses next to the towering copper vats (and wonder how they keep them so shiny) or go out on the balcony to catch the breeze off the river and watch the busy street scene below.

⁂

The soft glow of gaslight has always shown this aged city to its best advantage, and the clock winds back more than fifty years when you walk into **Bevelo Gas and Electric Lights** (521 Conti Street between Decatur and Chartres Streets; 504–522–9485). This holdout against the march of industry still handcrafts copper fixtures in the well-worn second- and third-floor ateliers, high above the cobwebs of the dusty old showroom. In fact, the only newfangled addition allowed on the premises is an up-to-date computer that can scan in a photo of your house to help you choose fixtures that are appropriate in scale. Ask for a peek at the ancient machinery that workers will use to fill your order.

If sewing is one of your crafts, look for antique and French enameled buttons in another tiny slice of the past. **Zula Frick's Button Shop** (328 Chartres between Conti and Bienville Streets; 504–523–6557) also sells rare dolls and unique jewelry decorated with unusual old buttons.

Handmade items from Oaxaca and other Mexican towns make for a colorful display at **Trade Folk Art** (828 Chartres between Dumaine and Madison Streets; 504–596–6827). The gallery specializes in antique silver, *santos,* ceremonial masks, and whimsical doodads that celebrate Mexico's Day of the Dead.

Nothing defines French Quarter romance like lacy ironwork balconies (especially those with suitor-proof spikes designed to thwart gentlemen callers who couldn't make it past Papa at the front door). If you'd like to bring home a piece of history, you'll find the right stuff at **Sigle's Antiques and Metalcraft** (935 Royal Street between St. Philip and Dumaine Streets; 504–522–7647). You can order enough for a balcony of your own, or small bits of detailing that have been converted into plant holders and decorations for patio walls.

Hand-carved ducks, giant reproductions of antique fishing lures, and other sports art is featured at the **Crabnet Wildlife Art and Gifts** (925 Decatur Street Between St. Philip and Dumaine Streets; 800–424–3478 or 504–522–3478). Most of the represented artists are Louisiana born.

DAY ONE: EVENING
Dinner

Continue two blocks to cool your heels over a homegrown feast. Chef/proprietor Michael Uddo has attracted national attention at **G&E Courtyard Grill** (1113 Decatur Street between Governor Nicholls and Ursulines Streets; 504–528–9376; expensive) with his innovative cuisine that makes delicious use of organically grown produce. Uddo combines Louisiana ingredients with international techniques to create such dazzlers as Japanese softshell crab rolls with caviar, wasabi, and asparagus. Relax in the formal dining room or go around to the large courtyard, where a wall of twinkling votive candles adds a grace note to lusty aromas from the open-air rotisserie.

⌀⌀⌀

You'll be walking in the footsteps of Native Americans and eighteenth-century colonists when you take an after-dinner stroll through the historic **French Market** (on the river from Jackson Square to Barracks Street). Louisiana's earliest settlers traded goods here long before the lovely colonnaded buildings were added in the nineteenth century. The open-air stands, now the oldest farmers' market in the U.S., sell fresh produce twenty-four hours a day. Remember to pick out some fruit to take back to your apartment for breakfast. (For more on the market's fascinating history, see "Magnificent Obsession.")

DAY TWO: MORNING

Make breakfast (and whoopee) in your own kitchen, then start the day close to home with a ramble through the galleries along Julia Street. Of particular note for crafters are the fine ceramics at **Ariodante Contemporary Craft Gallery** (535 Julia Street between Magazine and Camp Streets; 504–524–3233); pottery, jewelry, and other contemporary crafts at **LeMieux Galleries** (332 Julia Street between Commerce and Tchoupitoulas Streets; 504–522–5988); and stunning handmade furnishings and accessories at **Christopher Maier Furniture Design** (329 Julia Street at Commerce Street; 504–586–9079).

If you have time, sign up for one of the workshops at **New Orleans School of GlassWorks & Printmaking Studio** (727 Magazine Street between Julia and Girod Streets; 504–529–7277). The South's largest contemporary glassworking and printmaking studio also offers exquisite hand-blown glass pieces, along with handmade paper, prints, and books. For details on custom designs, including an opportunity for your own hands to be transformed into a unique sculpture, see "Narcissus Does New Orleans."

DAY TWO: AFTERNOON/EVENING

You may not be able to buy a New Orleans house, but you can certainly take a piece of one back home. Cypress doors, gingerbread trim, heavy worn planks, and other salvage from razed properties become quality furniture at **Charbonnet & Charbonnet, Inc.** (2929 Magazine Street at Seventh Street; 504–891–9948). Choose from beds, entertainment armoires, tables, kitchen cabinets, and other showpieces. Pick your own stain for custom work, or go natural with a polished beeswax finish. Displays are enlivened by a variety of accessories, including some made from rescued architectural details. (If you don't have a car, hop the Magazine Street bus and get off at Seventh Street.)

Lunch

Authentic Southern-style cooking is hard to find in Creole-dominated New Orleans, but locals love the first-rate chicken and dumplings, catfish and hushpuppies, liver and onions, chicken-fried steak with cream gravy, fried green tomatoes, and long lists of daily vegetables at Iler Pope's **Cafe Atchafalaya** (901 Louisiana Avenue at Laurel Street; 504–891–5271; inexpensive). The bright and cozy cottage is also a fine destination for country-style desserts and house-made ice creams.

☙👁👁❧

Reboard the Magazine Street bus to **Shadyside Pottery** (3823 Magazine Street between Peniston and General Taylor Streets; 504–897–1710) to watch a master craftsman at work in his studio/gallery. Charles Bohn studied in Japan, but his work also reflects classical Chinese, Egyptian, Greek, and Roman themes.

Just a block up the street at **Casey Willems Pottery** (3919 Magazine between General Taylor and Austerlitz Streets; 504–899–1174) the house specialty is European-style berry bowls that work like small ceramic colanders. The shop's self-taught namesake loves his craft and loves to talk about it with interested customers. His son, a New York-based animator, adds his own humorous touch to decorative plates when he is in town, and also draws the shop's annual Christmas cards that convey greetings and gift ideas. If you like what you see (and you should), add your names to the mailing list.

You'll need to transfer to the Broadway bus to reach the numerous crafters who offer their goods in the nineteenth-century cottages along Maple Street. For details, see "Splendor in the Grass."

Dinner

The farm came first and the name is real at **Chicory Farm Cafe** (723 Hillary Street between Hampson and Maple Streets; 504–866–2325; moderate). Organic produce and wild mushrooms, grown at their 100-acre operation on the North Shore of Lake Pontchartrain, end up on your plate in this charming old Victorian house turned restaurant. A carefully selected wine list offers the perfect accompaniment to sixteen varieties of aged, handmade

European-style cheeses—also direct from the farm. Meat lovers won't believe what their tastebuds tell them when they discover just how richly flavored vegetarian dishes can be. Try an herbal sorbet for dessert.

⊲◦⊕◦⊳

After dinner, **Coffee and Company** (7708 Maple Street between Adams and Burdette Streets; 504–861–8843; inexpensive) offers an excellent selection of both in a freewheeling atmosphere of hand-painted furnishings, folk art, newspapers, and table games. Meet new friends or monopolize one another, then board the St. Charles Avenue streetcar for a beautiful and breezy rumble back to your room.

FOR MORE ROMANCE

If you are here on a Saturday, don't miss the **Crescent City Farmer's Market** (Magazine Street at Girod Street; 504–861–5898), a weekly gathering in the Warehouse/Arts District from 8:00 A.M. to noon. The beloved community event features the freshest produce from independent regional growers: Chicory Farm cheeses, fresh sorbets, homemade baked goods, preserves, and wines. Most vendors offer samples. The city's best chefs conduct cooking demonstrations, with more tastings, at 10:00 A.M. ("Our motto is it's never too early to start off the morning with garlic," says director Richard McCarthy.)

Another fashionable restaurant that makes excellent use of Louisiana products is **Mr. B's Bistro** (201 Royal Street at Iberville; 504–523–2078; expensive). Local vegetarians adore stylish and cheery **Old Dog, New Trick** (307 Exchange Alley between Bienville and Conti Streets; 504–522–4569; inexpensive).

FOLIES À DEUX

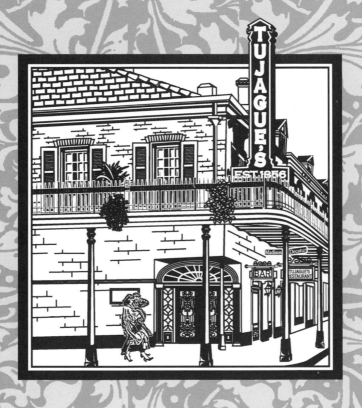

ITINERARY 15
Two nights and two days

RICH IN LOVE

A WEEKEND OF GENTEEL POVERTY

*I*t's no disgrace to be poor and in love, especially in New Orleans, where you'll be in excellent company. Artists and writers thrive in local cafe society, where a few dollars buys a great meal and hours of unhurried table talk. Talented musicians perform on street corners, polishing their craft while collecting donations from grass-roots philanthropists. Even aristocrats take a dim view of conspicuous consumption, a good thing since some of the best families have been penniless for generations.

You don't need money to ramble hand-in-hand through the French Quarter, cruise across the river on the Canal Street ferry, take in dozens of art galleries, or listen to the free concerts presented by the French Market and majestic old churches. And you might as well join the crowd and dress down, because expensive clothes wilt just as quickly on a hot summer day. Meanwhile, if the object of your affection inquires about the state of your finances, just pass along the stock answer our mothers and grandmothers always had for their children, "Darling, we're rich in love."

Practical notes: For inexpensive accommodations in private homes, contact Bed & Breakfast Inc. Reservation Service (800–729–4640 or 504–488–4640) or New Orleans Bed and Breakfast and Accommodations (504–838–0071). The free walking tours offered by the National Park Service are conducted daily except Christmas and Mardi Gras. Reservations are required for the Garden District walk. The French Quarter walk is limited to thirty participants—first come, first served—and each pass must be picked up in person on the day of the tour. The office opens at 9:00 A.M. Neither route enters any buildings and shelter is usually unavailable, especially in the Garden District, so take your umbrellas.

Romance at a Glance

♥ *Indulge in hot French doughnuts and people-watching at sidewalk Cafe du Monde.*

♥ *Add yourselves to the art on display in downtown plazas and sculpture gardens.*

♥ *Gather a feast of Creole delicacies for an impromptu urban picnic.*

♥ *Clang past mansions, parks, and universities on the St. Charles Avenue streetcar.*

♥ *Amble under the oaks to view the magnificent architecture of the Garden District.*

FRIDAY EVENING

A great French Quarter location and informal ambience attract a regular clientele, including many cost-conscious Europeans, to **Olivier House** (828 Toulouse Street between Bourbon and Dauphine Streets; 504–525–8456; doubles, $110 to $155; suites, $165 to $350; cottage, $210). The 1836 mansion was built for Marianne Bienvenue Olivier, widow of a wealthy planter, and her family of fifty grandchildren. It was converted to a guest house by Jim and Kathryn Danner in 1970. Today their courtyard is rather wild and crumbly, an oasis of Southern decadence in a neighborhood of overly manicured commercial properties.

As for the accommodations, decor and rates vary widely, so be sure to specify exactly what you would like. Some of the forty rooms are furnished with antique beds and armoires; others are modern lofts. Suite 216 is well worn, but it has 12-

foot ceilings and romantic old furnishings; French doors open from the bathroom to a corner balcony overlooking Toulouse and Dauphine Streets. Room 306 is haunted by a Civil War soldier. Pricier, but still a bargain for the French Quarter, the eighteenth-century honeymoon cottage is graced by antiques, a deluxe modern bath, working fireplace, and its own private patio. All accommodations have private baths; many are equipped with kitchenettes. Ask about balconies, split-level suites, and noise. (Beware first-floor units with windows facing the street.) Amenities include a swimming pool and complimentary morning coffee. For the price, expect a few rough edges, but plenty of atmosphere.

Dinner

Tonight you'll dine at one of the city's oldest and most celebrated restaurants, thanks to an insider trick. A little-known secret, even among natives, is a great sandwich that is served on request in the bar at historic **Tujague's Restaurant** (823 Decatur Street at Madison Street; 504–525–8676; moderate). A few slices of the famous brisket of beef with Creole sauce has been the traditional first course in the adjoining dining room since 1856. But just say the word and the bartender will arrange for a hefty portion to be sent over, cradled in a loaf of crusty French bread. It's not on the menu, but one sandwich should be enough for both of you, around $10 with two glasses of the house red wine. Meanwhile, you'll be treated to the same Old New Orleans atmosphere and dignified service as diners paying five times the price, and your seats at the bar will be much cozier.

Afterward, stroll around **Jackson Square** (bounded by Decatur, St. Peter, St. Ann, and Chartres Streets). Look for the guy who sets up his huge telescope in good weather, charging a nominal fee for a view of the night sky. Climb the levee to watch the Mississippi from the **Moonwalk** (on the river at Jackson Square), where you'll probably be serenaded by one or more freelance musicians.

SATURDAY MORNING

First stop at 9:00 A.M. is the visitor center for the **French Quarter Unit of Jean Lafitte National Historical Park and Preserve** (916 North Peters Street between St. Philip and Dumaine Streets; 504–589–2636) to pick up passes for a free walking tour of the French Quarter at 10:30 A.M. While you're there, make reservations to join the Garden District walking tour on Sunday.

Breakfast

That done, proceed one block to claim a sidewalk table at **Cafe du Monde** (800 Decatur Street at Jackson Square; 504–525–4544; inexpensive) for steaming café au lait with an order of hot and yeasty beignets dusted in powdered sugar. The elegant old coffeehouse has been open around the clock since the 1860s, "except for Christmas and some hurricanes," at one of the greatest people-watching corners on earth.

⌒⌒⌒

Fortified by breakfast and inspired to join the fascinating parade of humanity, head back to the historical park for your tour. The ninety-minute walk begins with a brief orientation at the visitor center, followed by a journey of approximately 1 mile that takes in Jackson Square, along with other significant architectural and historic sites near the riverfront. Led by a national park ranger, it's a fun introduction to the quirks of geography, politics, and ethnicity that have created the wild local culture.

SATURDAY AFTERNOON

Lunch

By now, the sights and smells of the French Quarter have probably made you hungry again, but don't settle for anything less than the best. The world is your picnic ground in this food-loving town, where romancing in public is an inalienable right and the way to

A Loaf of Bread, a Sack of Crawfish, and Thou . . .

No need to squander your time and money on restaurants, or resort to junk food, when you can gather a moveable feast and head for a bench with a view.

Imported cheeses, sausages, olives, biscotti, and fresh-baked Italian breads are great at side-by-side Sicilian delis, **Central Grocery Company** *(923 Decatur Street between Dumaine and St. Philip Streets; 504–523–1620) and* **Progress Grocery** *(915 Decatur Street between Dumaine and St. Philip Streets; 504–525–6627). Cross the street to the* **French Market** *(on the river between Jackson Square and Barracks Street) for fruits, vegetables, pecans, pralines, and tiny sweet potato pies.*

The French Quarter **A&P** *(701 Royal Street at St. Peter Street; 504–523–1353) is set in a picturesque old corner grocery, probably the only branch where you can squeeze the tomatoes alongside off-duty strippers, mimes, drag queens, and little old ladies who've seen it all. While you're there, pick out edible souvenirs (gumbo and etouffée mixes, chicory coffee, regional beers) for a fraction of the price you'd pay in tourist shops.*

Most casual restaurants will wrap up a couple of "po-boys," French bread stacked with deli meats, fried shellfish, or hot roast beef drenched in gravy. Oyster bars can package spicy boiled shrimp or crawfish to go—but be sure to throw in plenty of napkins and choose a secluded spot for this sloppy splurge.

everyone's heart is through the stomach. Half the fun is shopping at quirky markets, which are also a good source for tasty and inexpensive souvenirs. Pack yourselves a picnic at one of the vendors described in the sidebar.

Once you've decided on the menu, you'll still need to choose your spot. For riverfront drama, spread out on the steps of Moonwalk. For a free floor show, outdoor jazz concerts are scheduled most Saturdays and Sundays from 1:00 to 3:00 P.M. in the French Market, where you should be able to manage a simple meal on a sidewalk bench or fountain ledge.

To feed body and soul surrounded by monumental works of art (or for a spectacular after-lunch hike) make a circuit of downtown plazas and outdoor sculptures. Begin by walking upriver along the levee to view the fanciful masterpieces in **Woldenberg Riverfront Park** (between Toulouse and Canal Streets). Ida Kohlmeyer's *Aquatic Colonnade* is a row of twenty multicolored columns, each 25 feet tall and topped by a fantastic underwater beastie. Nearby, towering stainless steel pylons support huge rings hung with moving paddles for John Scott's *Ocean Song.*

Cross Canal Street to **Spanish Plaza** (on the river between Canal and Poydras) and catch the cool spray from a 50-foot fountain as you stroll around the base to see the Iberian coats of arms. The mosaic-tiled square was a 1976 bicentennial gift from Spain.

In 1979 superstar architect Charles Moore concocted a whimsical "Roman ruin" for his postmodern **Piazza d'Italia** (Poydras Street between South Peters and Tchoupitoulas). The crumbling pastel extravaganza is a playground for adults, a pocket classic graced by archway, campanile, pavilion, and Italy-shaped fountain.

While you're in the neighborhood, it doesn't cost anything to view the exciting works exhibited along **Gallery Row** (Julia Street, between Church and Commerce). The crisply renovated collection of historic townhouses and industrial lofts is the heart of the local contemporary arts scene.

More masterpieces are on view in the **outdoor sculpture garden at K&B Plaza** (1055 St. Charles Avenue at Lee Circle). The stellar display of works by important twentieth-century artists includes Frank McGuire's welded steel *Streetcar Stop,* bronze hand and foot benches by Mexican artist Pedro Friedeberg, British sculptor Michael Sandle's *The Drummer,* and George Rickey's *Four Open Rectangles Excentric, Square Sections.* Towering above all, Isamu Noguchi's *The Mississippi* is a carved granite monolith polished by a sheet of water. A free indoor gallery is open weekdays from 8:30 A.M. to 4:30 P.M. Hop the St. Charles Avenue Streetcar at Lee Circle for a ride back to Canal Street.

SATURDAY EVENING
Dinner

Wood-fired ovens turn out roasted chickens, quiches, crackly baguettes, and savory peasant breads at **La Madeleine French Bakery & Café** (547 St. Ann Street on Jackson Square; 504–568–9950; inexpensive). Start with herb-scented soup and linger over coffee and pastries here in old New Orleans style, framed by high ceilings, tile floors, and dark wood furnishings. Choose a table near the French doors that open wide for fine views of St. Louis Cathedral (oldest in the U.S.) and the bustle around Jackson Square.

⌘

Take your after-dinner stroll along Chartres Street to window-shop the offbeat antique stores and eccentric retailers that still exist in this (relatively) unspoiled region of the French Quarter.

SUNDAY MORNING
Breakfast

Before you view some of the most splendid sights this old city has to offer, tiny **La Marquise Pâtisserie de Roi** (625 Chartres Street between Toulouse and St. Peter; 504–524-0420; inexpensive) is a charming eye opener. European-style pastries, quiches, croissants, cappuccino, and hot mocha are served in a quaintly scruffy dining area with marble-topped tables. Better yet, carry your prizes out to the little rear courtyard.

⌘

The 10:00 A.M. Sunday Mass at **St. Louis Cathedral** (Jackson Square between Père Antoine's Alley and Pirate's Alley; 504–525–9585) is a magnificent show, complete with full choir and pipe organ. If you're not too flashy with the collection basket, you'll have some change left for the street performers outside in front of Jackson Square.

Walk down Pirate's Alley, which runs along one side of the Cathedral, and proceed up

Royal Street to window-shop some of the city's greatest antique stores and galleries. Cross Canal Street to board the **St. Charles Avenue streetcar** (St. Charles Avenue between Canal and Common Streets) for a round-trip through the oaks, past mansions, parks, and universities. Disembark at South Carrollton Avenue.

Lunch

You'll find several inexpensive cafes—and some very expensive shops—here at the point where the Mississippi curves into the picturesque neighborhood known as **Riverbend** (St. Charles Avenue at South Carrollton Avenue). A sentimental favorite with Uptown Brahmins, stately **Camellia Grill** (626 South Carrollton Avenue between St. Charles Avenue and Hampson Street; 504–866–9573; inexpensive) has been a fixture under the oaks since 1946. Waiters in starched white linen deliver first-class burgers, sandwiches, salads, and house-made pies. Breakfasts are simply perfect, especially the omelets, buttery grits, and pecan waffles.

⌘

Afterward, climb the levee to see the impressive bend in the Mississippi and get a feel for the natural shoreline in its wild and grassy state, beyond all the urban development. Catch the streetcar back downtown; then disembark at Washington Avenue and walk one block to the corner of Prytania Street to meet your group for the free Garden District tour at 2:30 P.M. The 1-mile guided walk, past grand mansions and historic churches, takes about ninety minutes.

If you prefer to go it alone, pick up a free map at any tourist information office for a self-guided tour of Garden District architecture. If you've got the time, plan your circuit to end at lovely **Trinity Episcopal Church** (1329 Jackson Avenue at Coliseum; 504–522–0276) for the **Trinity Artist Series,** free performances by local and nationally known musicians every Sunday at 5:00 P.M.

FOR MORE ROMANCE

Admission to the galleries at the **Contemporary Arts Center** (900 Camp Street between Howard Avenue and St. Joseph Street; 504–523–1216) is always free on Thursdays. Otherwise, the price changes according to exhibition, but tops out at $5 per person. Free musical concerts and reasonably priced theater productions are scheduled throughout the season.

Though it's fun to steal a picnic in some unlikely urban spot, more traditional retreats await all over town, and many of those are nearly deserted on weekdays. **City Park** (City Park Avenue at Esplanade Avenue) is perfect for a *déjeuner sur l'herbe* under the ancient oaks, especially near the botanical garden or antique carousel. **Audubon Park** (St. Charles Avenue at Exposition Boulevard) has a few stone gazebos scattered around the lagoons, just right for a semi-private rendezvous. The stepped seawall that lines **Lake Pontchartrain** for 5 miles along Lakeshore Drive has supported lovers for decades, and you're never too old to tailgate the submarine races on "the world's longest grandstand."

You'll find more opportunities to stretch your travel budget gracefully in "Past Imperfect," "Splendor in the Grass," and "Artful Seduction." For rowdier amusements, see "Cheap Thrills in the City that Care Forgot."

ITINERARY 16
Three days and two nights

CHEAP THRILLS IN THE CITY THAT CARE FORGOT

*T*hese days, when two people can drop $45 on dinner at Shoney's and a Terminator movie, it's not hard to see why cocooning qualifies as a movement. But that's why they call New Orleans "The Big Easy;" cheap dates are always just around the corner.

Here are a few romantic quickies to get you going, though you're sure to discover more at every turn. Stop by the tourist information booths for discount coupons and freebies. Read the entertainment listings in the *Times-Picayune* and newsweekly *Gambit*. Check the bulletin boards at coffeehouses and bars. Phone the music, drama, and sports departments at area universities for performance schedules and special events.

Better yet, just ask around. New Orleanians love to share good times, good deals, and their personal opinions. Go native, hang out, watch the parade along the sidewalk. The free shows are the best.

Practical notes: The Mississippi River ferry leaves the Canal Street dock every half hour beginning at 6:00 A.M. The last round trip departs Canal Street at 11:30 P.M. and returns at midnight. The boat ties up for the night at 12:15 A.M. on the opposite bank in Algiers, an isolated riverfront neighborhood and definitely *not* a good place to be stranded.

DAY ONE: LATE AFTERNOON

Don't let that familiar freeway logo scare you away—the downtown **Hampton Inn** (226 Carondelet Street at Gravier Street; 800–HAMPTON or 504–529–9990; $99 to $139) is set in a National Historic Landmark building dating from 1903. High ceilings and huge old windows add a touch of architectural pizzazz to guest quarters decorated in comfortable contemporary style. Centrally located directly on the St. Charles Avenue streetcar line, this is one of the city's better values. (That higher rate of $139 buys a deluxe room with king-sized bed and Jacuzzi, a fraction of the price for comparable accommodations in the French Quarter, just two blocks away.) Be sure to request an upper floor for some view of the city lights and less noise from the streetcar. Complimentary continental breakfast, a generous spread served in the lounge area, adds to the savings.

It may fall short of the Empire State Building, but you can score a romantic high à la *Sleepless in Seattle* on the 31st-floor **observation deck of the World Trade Center** (2 Canal Street at the river; 504–581–4888). Most visitors pay a stiff price to drink in the view from the revolving cocktail lounge on the 33rd floor, but you'll see the same rooftops and river traffic (without handing over $11.50 plus tip for two mint juleps and sitting around for ninety minutes to make a full revolution). Admission to the deck is nominal, and it's open daily until 5:00 P.M. Be sure to notice the art exhibit in the lobby on your way to the elevator.

Back on the ground, stroll a half block to board the **Canal Street ferry** (Canal Street at the river) for a closer look at one of the world's busiest ports, a spectacular experience after dark and always a bargain at $1 per car, free for foot passengers.

Romance at a Glance

♥ *Eavesdrop on world-class jazz musicians without paying a cover charge.*

♥ *Score a package deal for the zoo, aquarium, IMAX, and a riverboat cruise.*

♥ *Taste exotic imports, from Austria to Zimbabwe, at the city's greatest beer joint.*

♥ *Ramble around the shrimp boats and fishing camps of Bucktown Harbor.*

♥ *Dig into fresh seafood on the screened porch at Sid-Mar's.*

DAY ONE: EVEVNING

Catch the bright red **Riverfront Streetcar** (Canal Street at the river) to Esplanade Avenue for a little low-rent nightlife in the bohemian clubs and coffeehouses of Faubourg Marigny. Some of the smaller venues keep irregular hours, but just poke around Frenchmen Street until you hear something you like.

Live music is usually free from 7:00 to 10:00 P.M. nightly at **Café Brasil** (2100 Chartres Street at Frenchmen Street; no phone). Even when the featured bands take the stage around 10:30 P.M., the cover rarely goes above $5. The clientele at this storefront coffeehouse is studiously cool, and the entertainment is hot hot hot, anything from modern jazz to merengue.

Dinner

When you're ready to cross the street for dinner, time your meal to coincide with the 9:00 P.M. show at **Snug Harbor Jazz Bistro** (626 Frenchmen Street between Royal and Chartres Streets; 504–949–0696), where the dining area is well within earshot of the stage, but minus view and cover charge. Bite into fat chargrilled burgers and baked potatoes while you feast your ears on world-class musicians like pianist Ellis Marsalis (father of Wynton and Branford), David Torkanowski, Walter "Wolfman" Washington, Astral Project, and vocalist Charmaine Neville. Tucked inside a lofty space warmed by exposed beams, old brick, and intelligent service, it's a cozy spot to linger over a pitcher of locally brewed Abita beer. By the time you walk back out the door, around 11:00 P.M., the nightly street scene should be in full swing.

For the cheapest thrill of all, stroll back to the hotel along Bourbon Street, where you'll see all you want (and then some) just gawking through the open doors. Whiskey-voiced barkers are a scream, extolling the vices of nude mud wrestling, "French orgies," and other exotica as they flash the passing crowd with quick peeks inside the strip clubs.

DAY TWO: MORNING

Just time for a quick continental breakfast before you embark on a whirlwind adventure. Today you'll spend a little more than $30 each for a ticket that will take you from the Amazon Basin to the mountains of Africa, with a really big show and a boat ride in between to rest your feet. Just pick up an Audubon Adventure Passport when you visit **Aquarium of the Americas** (Canal Street at the river; 504–861–2537). The discount combination ticket also covers admission to the in-house **IMAX Theater** and a riverboat shuttle up the Mississippi to **Audubon Zoo** (6500 Magazine Street at Natatorium Drive; 504–861–2538). Be sure to request the package with a one-way shuttle, as you'll be returning on the streetcar.

Romantic backdrops inside the aquarium are sure to arouse deep emotions. Pursue one another through the tropical blooms and treetops of an Amazon rain forest. Stroll along a Caribbean reef in a clear acrylic tunnel surrounded by 132,000 gallons of seawater. Pet baby sharks in one of the touch pools. Watch the penguins, who mate for life, as they snuggle in their nests or go about their daily business in pairs. Stake out a secluded spot on the bleachers in a darkened room that overlooks the shark exhibit. You can even cuddle on the backseat of a car to view clips from drive-in monster movies, part of the kitschy **Fatal Beauties** exhibit of killer creatures from the deep.

Though you go out of your way to avoid them at the beach, the world's largest collection of jellyfish offers a rare opportunity for a close encounter without getting stung. **Jellies** is set in yet another dark and sensuous retreat, a jewel box of luminous enclosures, water tunnels, and neon waves. A real eye opener for anyone who expects transparent blobs, many specimens are vibrant with other-worldly coloring and some appear to glow in the dark. Hundreds on display range in size from a pencil-tip speck to 8 feet in diameter.

More hand holding awaits in the long shadows of the aquarium's IMAX Theater, where you'll get a larger-than-life look at undersea creatures or other wonders of nature (volcanos, Antarctica, the Rolling Stones) on a silver screen that's more than five stories tall.

DAY TWO: AFTERNOON

After the film, board the **Riverboat John James Audubon** (Canal Street at the river; 504–586–8777) for an eco-cruise up the Mississippi, past tugboats, freighters, barges, and other industrial traffic on one of the world's most important waterways. During the 7-mile journey, you can explore interactive exhibits on regional ecology and natural science, or retreat to a isolated corner of the deck for a little hands-on research of your own.

In about forty-five minutes you'll dock at oak-shaded Audubon Park, home to a beautiful zoological garden graced by tropical vegetation, country estate architecture, classic statuary, and more than 1,800 animals in their native habitats. There's lots to see, so fortify yourselves with a quick lunch in a Cajun cabin surrounded by the world's only urban swamp (no, not New Orleans).

Lunch

Head straight to the **Louisiana Swamp** exhibit for a surprisingly good self-service menu of crawfish pie, red beans and rice, gumbo, jambalaya, and other unlikely zoo fare. The **Cypress Knee Cafe** is surrounded by outdoor decking that overlooks the alligator pond for some fascinating dining companions.

✦

Afterward, make the rounds of this award-winning exhibit, 6½ acres of indigenous varmints and architecture, scattered with antique boats, fishing paraphernalia, duck blinds, and other artifacts from swamp dwellers of the two-legged variety. In this case, maintaining a natural habitat is hardly a stretch.

"We planted the cypress trees and tupelo gums," says curator Rick Atkinson. "Ordinarily our problem is not planting material, but clearing it away. We don't have to look too hard for our livestock either. People call us to remove snakes and alligators from their backyards.

Several of our raccoons were rescued from the eaves of an apartment complex. This is probably the wildest environment they've ever known. We get a lot of our animals from answering the phone, and some just fly in and set up shop. We differ from the rest of the zoo in that most of our stock is common, not endangered or teetering on the edge of extinction. Our emphasis is on what you really would see in a nearby swamp."

One of the most romantic sites in Audubon Zoo is the colonnaded **sea lion pool** that dates back to 1928. Classical music and artworks add to the tranquil beauty of the **Tropical Birdhouse,** where you can stroll through lush foliage ablaze with sixty colorful species. Also fluttering free in the domed pavilion are more than 1,000 specimens from the **Butterflies in Flight** exhibit. Finally, be sure to swing by the **World of Primates** exhibit to catch up on a continuing soap opera. (See page 143.)

DAY TWO: Evening
Dinner

By now you're probably ready for a cold beer, so stroll under the oaks to the front entrance of the park and take the St. Charles Avenue streetcar a few blocks uptown to Carrollton Avenue. You'll see several inexpensive cafes, but **Cooter Brown's Tavern & Oyster Bar** (509 South Carrollton Avenue at the river; 504–866–9104; inexpensive) boasts the city's largest variety of brews, forty on draft and 450 bottled. Start with a couple of local drafts, Turbodog and Purple Haze, as you pore over the incredible list of provocative brands like Alimony Ale, John Courage, Taj Mahal, Old Peculiar, Blue Moon Honey Blond, Evil Eye Honey Brown, Wild Irish Rogue, and La Fin du Monde. While you drink your way around the globe, share a dozen raw oysters, a fried seafood platter, or one of the big sandwiches. Usually mobbed with an easygoing crowd of university students and Uptown residents, this funky old favorite is a great place to misspend your youth. A late-night streetcar ride back to your hotel makes a grand finale.

As the World of Primates Turns

She was hairy, weighed 320 pounds, and had a face that only an environmentalist could love. He was younger, attached, the father of a five-year-old. His mate wisely adopted a wait-and-see attitude.

Longtime companions Bom Bom and Fanya, rare lowland gorillas, had become rather complacent when their keepers imported Binti, a little homewrecker from the Woodland Park Zoo in Seattle. She was introduced to the group with the express purpose of shaking it up a bit, either to mate with Bom Bom or rekindle his lost passion for Fanya.

The *menagerie à trois* was sanctioned by the Species Survival Plan of the American Association of Zoological Parks and Aquariums, which maintains records to ensure that endangered animals are bred for optimum health. In this case, matchmakers culled pertinent data from the SSP's tantalizingly titled "Gorilla Stud Book."

Initial meetings between the rival seventeen-year-old females were less than cordial, as anyone who has witnessed similar confrontations at a sock hop could have predicted.

"We had one keeper on the backstop with a radio and a hose," said Eve Watts, curator of primates, "and another on the rockwork above the exhibit with a hose, radio, and fire extinguisher." Curators and veterinary staff were stationed along the front railing.

Binti's first date with Bom Bom was even more volatile. He bit, she charged. She required stitches and a short period of immobilization.

Since then, the general mood has improved steadily. Binti gave birth to a bouncing baby girl (named Praline) in 1996. Fanya has not been so cooperative, though she could soon produce the zoo's first test tube gorilla. And—this will come as no surprise to males of any species—Binti and Fanya have teamed up on more than one occasion.

"They chase Bom Bom around the exhibit screaming," Watts said. "When the females support each other, it's a very encouraging sign."

DAY THREE: MORNING/AFTERNOON

For generations New Orleanians have headed out to the shore of Lake Pontchartrain for cool breezes and casual good times. (If this inland estuary really were a lake, it would be one of the nation's largest at 640 square miles.) Catch the Canal/Lakefront bus (number 41) at any stop on Canal Street; get off at the intersection of West End and Robert E. Lee Boulevards; walk a half block on West End Boulevard to Lake Marina Drive (you'll be able to see the sailboat masts towering above the marina walls); then continue about six blocks to **West End Park** (West Roadway Drive at Lake Pontchartrain).

Weekends bring the greatest activity to this waterfront square, surrounded by a lively jumble of marinas, boathouses, and casual seafood restaurants balanced over the water on pilings. At one corner is a public boat launch overrun by Jet Ski enthusiasts. At the other is a huge complex of sand volleyball courts where you can join a game or start your own at no charge. (Just trade your driver's license for equipment at the snack bar.) Occasional tournaments are free for spectators.

Lunch

Right behind the volleyball area is a footbridge that crosses to Bucktown Harbor, a picturesque anchorage for independent shrimp boats and other small working vessels. Local favorite **Sid-Mar's** (1824 Orpheum Avenue on Bucktown Harbor; 504–831–9541; inexpensive) is a modest little frame house with a big screened porch. This is the ideal place to launch your final cheap thrill, so order up a feast of boiled lake seafood, spicy new potatoes, French bread, and a pitcher of beer. *Bon voyage!*

FOR MORE ROMANCE

If you're willing to sacrifice a little comfort for a posh address, two can squeeze into an "I.T.," an individual traveler room that is considerably smaller than a standard double at

Omni Royal Orleans Hotel (621 St. Louis Street at Royal Street; 800–THE–OMNI or 504–529–5333; I.T.'s, $109 to $129; doubles, $139 to $364; suites, $239 to $389). In season, the bottom line is about what you'd pay for the deluxe set-up at Hampton Inn, but you'll be in a grand hotel in the heart of the French Quarter with a lavish marble lobby, panoramic rooftop pool, and first-rate service.

Pick up a detailed map at the **Preservation Resource Center** (604 Julia Street; 504–581–7032) for a self-guided tour of the cast-iron facades, Gothic arches, 19th-century townhouses, and other fascinating landmarks in the Warehouse/Arts District—gallery hopping as you go for a full afternoon of free art and architecture. Great places to steal a kiss include the steps of **St. Patrick's Church** (724 Camp Street between Julia and Girod Streets; 504–525–4413) and tree-shaded **Lafayette Square** (St. Charles Avenue between North Maestri Place and South Maestri Place). A good stop for cappuccino or a light meal is the old brick **True Brew Coffee** (200 Julia Street at Fulton Street; 504–524–8441; inexpensive), where you'll also find reasonably priced theater productions at night.

Want to save even more? Check "Rich in Love," "Howling at the Moon," "On the Prowl," and "A Day of Low Culture and High Camp."

ITINERARY 17
Three days and two nights

PAST IMPERFECT
A DALLIANCE IN OLD NEW ORLEANS

*L*et your fingers keep walking if you like slick renovations, history behind glass, or flying Dumbos. You're in the wrong itinerary. Our theme here is New Orleans unplugged, a celebration of the quirky old anachronisms that inspired the developers to move in and molest the French Quarter in the first place. Each year more ground is lost to their manufactured amusements and T-shirt shops. But, like the wispy Spanish moss that clings to the oaks and grows a mere foot per century, some ancient beauties are more tenacious than others.

If you prefer unvarnished nostalgia and simple pleasures, you should be enchanted by these undisturbed corners of the nineteenth century. If you think preservationists fight on the side of the angels, come on in and enjoy the view. Old-fashioned lovers are always welcome.

Practical notes: New Orleans is flat, perfect for cycling, and the 2-mile bike ride to City Park should be within the range of any reasonably fit adult. You'll need a bit need more stamina to continue along Lake Pontchartrain for the late lunch at Bruning's Sea Food Restaurant—plus there's the return trip to consider—so gentler constitutions should return the bike first and take a cab. At any rate, be sure to watch for potholes and maneuver through traffic with care, as New Orleans drivers are notoriously freewheeling. Unfortunately, even the city's best neighborhoods can change dramatically within a few blocks, so stick to the recommended routes.

Romance at a Glance

♥ *Pass through 300 years of scandal and glory at Musée Conti Historical Wax Museum.*

♥ *Pamper your senses in grand style at the three oldest restaurants in New Orleans.*

♥ *Poke around quaint shops for perfumed fans, toy soldiers, pralines, and pipes.*

♥ *Plot against your enemies over Pimm's cups and a muffuletta at Napoleon House.*

♥ *Pedal a bicycle built for two past the mansions of Esplanade Avenue to City Park.*

DAY ONE: AFTERNOON

Check into the **Cornstalk Hotel** (915 Royal Street between Dumaine and St. Philip Streets; 504–523–1516; doubles, $75 to $155, including continental breakfast) for old-fashioned atmosphere and comfortable rooms furnished with canopy beds, marble-topped tables, and assorted Victoriana. Its famous fence, intertwined with cast iron cornstalks and morning glories, was a gift to a homesick Midwestern wife from her husband in 1850.

Though subject to dispute over which came first, the two oldest existing structures in the Lower Mississippi Valley are in your neighborhood. **Madame John's Legacy** (632 Dumaine Street between Chartres and Royal Streets; not open to the public) was originally built in 1724, but may have been reconstructed following a 1788 conflagration that destroyed much of the city. The **Old Ursuline Convent** (1100 Chartres Street between Ursulines and Governor Nicholls Streets; 504–529–3040) was designed in 1742 and completed in 1754, the only undisputed survivor of the eighteenth-century fires and the sole example of pure French Creole architecture in New Orleans. It's open for guided tours, admission $4 per person, Tuesday through Sunday.

As for noteworthy ex-citizens, **Musée Conti Historical Wax Museum** (917 Conti Street between Dauphine and Burgundy Streets; 504–525–2605) is a quaint and cooling retreat graced by exquisitely detailed figures imported from Paris, a charming introduction to Louisiana's heroes and scoundrels. Be sure to notice voodoo priestess Marie Laveau, who created love charms and spells for New Orleanians of all classes; Baroness Pontalba, who nursed an unrequited love for General Andrew Jackson; and the "casket girls," an earlier breed of carpetbaggers who lugged their worldly goods to the colony in search of husbands. Of course there's a Chamber of Horrors, fun for shivery embraces in the shadow of assorted fatal attractions. Among the beauties and beasts on display is the tragic Phantom of the Opera with his lovely Christine.

DAY ONE: EVENING

Before you return to your room to dress for dinner, stop at the **Absinthe House** (240 Bourbon Street between Iberville and Bienville Streets; 504–523–3181) to sample the historic drink that's now made with Herbsaint, a legal version of absinthe minus the narcotic kick of wormwood. Among the countless celebrities who bellied up for the bar's famed absinthe frappé (since rechristened Herbsaint frappé) were Mark Twain, Oscar Wilde, William Thackeray, Walt Whitman, and Grand Duke Alexis. Unfortunately, these days the walls are cluttered by football memorabilia and thousands of stapled business cards, but the famed marble fountains remain.

Dinner

Since the doors first opened in 1840, the city's oldest and most celebrated restaurant has welcomed the world, from Count Albrecht von Bismarck to Mick Jagger. **Antoine's** (713 St. Louis Street between Royal and Bourbon Streets; 504–581–4422; expensive) is a gorgeous time warp of dark woods, gleaming tile floors, potted palms, and antique furnishings. Formally clad waiters weave through a maze of fifteen dining rooms, ranging from public to very private, and the wine cellar stocks more than 25,000 bottles. This is no place for clock (or cholesterol) watchers, so plan to settle in for an authentic Creole binge on a grand scale. Oysters Rockefeller originated here, as did *pompano en papillote,* which was created to honor a visiting French balloonist. (The Gulf fish is covered with lump crabmeat and steamed in an inflated white parchment bag.) Signature baked Alaska serves two with advance notice, so reserve one before the meal begins.

⤿⊙⤾

Be prepared to suffer for someone else's art on the hard benches at **Preservation Hall** (726 St. Peter Street between Bourbon and Royal Streets; 504–523–8939 or 522–2841). Legendary musicians still perform every night in the dank and scruffy space, a living museum of traditional jazz. You'll feel like you've stepped right into a sepia-toned portrait of old Storyville. Sets are scheduled on the hour nightly from 8:00 P.M. to midnight. Admission is $4 per person.

DAY TWO: Morning

If weather permits, enjoy your breakfast on the hotel's graceful front porch. For more antiquated ambience and old curiosities, take a browser's tour of French Quarter shops. You'll have to bypass some garish modernities along the way, so pick up a vetiver-scented fan from **Hové Parfumeur, Ltd.** (824 Royal Street between St. Ann and Dumaine Streets; 504–525–7827) to shield your sensibilities. Better yet, buy a tiny perfume-filled bottle, or *labalier,* to wear on a delicate chain around your neck. (No lady should wander the malodorous city streets without one.)

Next, relive the happy hours of your youth at **Old Children's Books** (734 Royal Street between Père Antoine's Alley and St. Ann Streets; 504–525–3655). A wonderfully creaky

Heartthrob of the Old Town

Look out through the entrance at Old Town Praline Shop and try to picture the scene in 1860–61, when the block was cluttered with lovestruck Creole gentlemen hoping to catch a glimpse of the 17-year-old diva who had taken the city by storm. Adelina Patti made her debut in New York as Lucia di Lammermoor *in 1859, but she traveled to New Orleans to live at 627 Royal Street with her sister, whose husband conducted the orchestra at the French Opera House. Teetering on the brink of financial ruin, the local company was saved by Patti's sold-out performances. Meanwhile, her impromptu recitals, singing from the Royal Street balcony for her ardent young admirers, broke dozens of hearts.*

She went on to become one of the greatest coloraturas—and richest women—of the nineteenth century, commanding $5,000 per performance, a fortune in those days. In 1868 she married Henri, marquis de Caux, divorcing in 1885. Her second husband, tenor Ernesto Nicolini, died in 1898. By 1899 she had taken a third, Swedish baron Rolf Cederström.

"The older she got, the younger the men she married," says Old Town Praline Shop attendant Mary Lou. "She had a heck of a good time, I'm telling you. She traveled in a private railroad car with her own chef; she married royalty; she bought a castle in Wales . . . Our American customers always ask us about the woman in the pictures; but the Europeans, they know who she is."

hideaway straight out of Dickens, it's secluded at the end of a long alleyway, overlooking a patio brightened by antique metal figures from *The Wizard of Oz*. Once inside, old children will discover thousands of familiar and obscure titles dating from the 1800s through the 1970s.

Another playroom for all ages houses the remarkable inventory at **Le Petit Soldier** (528 Royal Street between St. Louis and Toulouse Streets; 504–523–7741). A full-time staff of six artists creates the miniature infantrymen and their leaders, who range from Achilles to Eisenhower. You can also purchase authentic medals, British royal family commemoratives, and other purloined decorations for your family tree.

There's certainly no shortage of praline vendors in the French Quarter, but for vintage atmosphere and a great love story, step into **Old Town Praline Shop** (627 Royal Street between Toulouse and St. Peter; 504-525-1413). The patio out back is filled with wild birds, who await their feeding at the end of the day, when the kitchen door opens and the confectioner scatters leftover samples and pecan dust across the flagstones. Inside, other family members staff the candy counter, surrounded by pictures and programs from the old French Opera House around the corner (destroyed by fire in 1919). This sweet shrine recalls one of the Vieux Carré's most romantic interludes; the story unfolds in the box on page 151.

DAY TWO: AFTERNOON
Lunch

Napoleon House (500 Chartres Street at St. Louis Streets; 504–524–9752; inexpensive) stands firm against the march of progress, an old-world bulwark of crumbling sepia plaster and wobbly chairs, scratchy classical records and irascible waiters. The beloved watering hole was built in 1797 as a residence for then-Mayor Nicholas Girod, who refurbished it to house Napoleon when local supporters plotted his rescue from the island of St. Helena. Unfortunately, the little emperor died in exile before their schemes came true. Today the cognoscenti order Pimm's cups (gin coolers garnished with cucumber) and split a muffuletta, a massive sandwich of Italian cold cuts, cheeses, and olive salad stacked on a seeded bun. Plan to stick around a while and set your inner clocks back about 200 years.

◈

Before heading home to your hotel for a long afternoon nap (another delicious local tradition), spend a few moments exploring a few more antiquities. The Jansen family has custom blended tobaccos for three generations at **Ye Olde Pipe Shoppe** (306 Chartres Street between Bienville and Conti Streets; 504–522–1484), including the house blend, Jansen's New Orleans, a favorite since 1868. In addition to a great name, **Zula Fricks**

Button Shop (328 Chartres Street between Bienville and Conti Streets; 504–523–6557) has rare, antique, and French enameled buttons; plus one-of-a-kind button jewelry and dolls.

DAY TWO: EVENING

Take your time waking up and dressing for dinner. Tonight's entertainments cannot be rushed. The second-oldest restaurant in New Orleans is a no-nonsense beauty graced by dark woods, antique bar, ceiling fans, and traditional service. Established in 1856, **Tujague's** (823 Decatur Street at Madison Street; 504–525–8676; moderate) earned a national reputation with the robust meals Madame Tujague prepared for workers from the nearby French Market. Countless celebrities, including several presidents, have also preceded you. Until recently the nightly menu was set in stone, and every diner was served an identical five-course meal. Today the program is a bit more flexible, though it still begins with shrimp rémoulade, soup du jour, and the signature brisket of beef with Creole sauce. Next comes your choice from three entrées, followed by dessert and dark Creole coffee.

Afterward, walk around **St. Louis Cathedral** (615 Père Antoine's Alley at Jackson Square; 504–525–9585) on two cobblestoned time tunnels known as Pirate's Alley and Père Antoine's Alley. Shadowy and gaslit, filled with echoes, they remain untouched by the twentieth century. Be sure to look through the iron fence behind the cathedral into St. Anthony's Garden, once the favored dueling spot for Creole gentlemen.

DAY THREE: MORNING

Beat the heat with an early start, then slow your pace to jaunting speed. After breakfast at the hotel, rent some two-wheeled transportation just outside the French Quarter at **Bicycle Michael's** (622 Frenchmen Street between Royal and Chartres Streets; 504–945–9505), which even stocks a few bicycles built for two, if you're confident maneuvering through traffic. Head up Esplanade Avenue, where you'll pass some of the city's greatest mansions in various states of repair.

When the French Quarter was New Orleans, Creole gentry built their country homes just 2 miles away on **Bayou St. John.** Today several of these historic houses still stand along Moss Street, which traces both banks of the natural waterway that runs from City Park to Lake Pontchartrain. For an easy side trip, turn left on Moss Street and ride up one side; then cross the small bridge at Orleans Avenue and return along the opposite bank to the park's main entrance at Esplanade Avenue.

Pedal boats and canoes have kept love afloat for more than a century at **City Park** (City Park Avenue at Esplanade Avenue), where you can still drift along miles of oak-draped lagoons and explore tiny islets shrouded by cypress and water lilies. (Don't forget to buy a bag of popcorn to feed the swans.) Afterward take a spin on one of the few remaining carved wooden carousels in the country, a gilt-edged beauty built in 1908, listed on the National Register of Historic Places, and known to generations of New Orleanians as "the flying horses."

Depending upon your inclinations or levels of fitness, you can either continue your ride to the lakefront for a late lunch at West End Park (about 3 miles) or return your wheels to Michael's and arrange for other transportation. To bike, exit City Park at Marconi Drive, heading right to reach Lakeshore Drive. Take a left on Lakeshore Drive, then a right on Lake Marina Drive. Bruning's is about six blocks farther along in West End Park.

Lunch

Though natives could probably guess the first two, most would be surprised to learn that the third-oldest restaurant in New Orleans is a simple fish house set on pilings over Lake Pontchartrain. Established by a German immigrant in 1859, **Bruning's Sea Food**

Restaurant (West End Park; 504–282–9395) has a long and colorful history. In the beginning, a separate entrance for Victorian ladies bypassed the bar. Later, Jazz Age flappers danced on its marble top and guzzled illegal booze. When gambling was outlawed in the 1930s and 1940s, the offshore structure was technically beyond city limits, so slot machines rang wide open. Today it's still a noisy family restaurant with outstanding fried and boiled seafood and easygoing service, the ideal setting for your last hurrah.

FOR MORE ROMANCE

For more antiquated pleasures, check "Rich in Love" and "Haute Creole."

A DAY OF LOW CULTURE AND HIGH CAMP

*O*kay, so maybe we do call it "cultcha," but that don't mean we ain't got any. The architecture, music, food, and *patois* of New Orleans are recognized around the globe. The city definitely has a style of its own.

We gave the world tasseled pasties, truck parades, drive-thru daiquiri stands, alligator sausage, *Crawfish Playing Poker* on black velvet, and *The Drag Queen's Cookbook & Guide to Sensible Living*. Our governors date strippers and gamble in Las Vegas. We brought Jimmy Swaggart to his knees.

In this pragmatic town, where bars outnumber churches, the secular and the spiritual are old drinking buddies and residents are blessed with a wealth of tolerance. Dress codes are practically nonexistent, except on Mardi Gras, when masking is *de rigueur* and the streets are ablaze with square-dancing transvestites, anatomically correct mummies, and soccer moms flashing their breasts in exchange for plastic trinkets. Everyone's welcome at the party. Just bring your own eccentricities and an unhealthy sense of the absurd.

Practical notes: Take a cab to and from Restaurant Mandich and Saturn Bar in the

Ninth Ward. It's a short ride, and the St. Claude Avenue bus is a very unpleasant alternative. A cab is also recommended for Mid-City Lanes, especially for the return trip late at night.

AFTERNOON

The downscale neighborhood known as the Ninth Ward is the cultural low point of New Orleans, bottom of the bowl in a city that's already several feet below C-level. Other than the guy hawking fake Gucci bags from the trunk of his car, there's no shopping to speak of (unless you're in the market for used appliances or a roll of linoleum). Most of the historic architecture is obscured by aluminum awnings and chain-link fences. And you won't be bothered with any galleries or museums, either, so just relax and concentrate on the big issues: Eating and Drinking.

Romance at a Glance

♥ *Trek over to Saturn Bar, where the atmosphere is out of this world.*

♥ *Adorn yourselves like rock stars and royalty at Bongo and Decatur Collectibles.*

♥ *Take a peek at the unmentionables and unfathomables in Second Skin Leather.*

♥ *Chow down at Lucky Chang's, where the service is a drag.*

♥ *Booze it up, dance to live music, and work on your game at Rock 'n' Bowl.*

Lunch

One of the best places to meet the people is **Restaurant Mandich** (3200 St. Claude Avenue at Louisa Street; 504–947–9553; moderate), a bedrock of good old-fashioned, heart-unhealthy cuisine that draws customers citywide. Like fried oysters? You're halfway there. Like fried oysters drizzled with garlicky Bordelaise and a side of tartar sauce for dipping? Then check your cholesterol counts at the door and join the crowd for lunch. Seafood dishes and steaks are good, especially trout Mandich topped with lump crabmeat. A few broiled entrées and salads are on the menu for health Nazis. Geez, live a little.

Crying in the Chapel

Ask anyone who has ever planned or participated in one: A wedding is an invitation to disaster. No event is more carefully orchestrated, nor more likely to spiral into chaos. Even in one of the world's most romantic cities, every stranger you meet can tell a story of love gone horribly wrong.

Friends asked Sam Boyd to record a tape of dance music for their wedding. As a joke, he included a twangy cowboy ballad about a dog named "Old Shep." Unfortunately the bride's father, who had died recently, used to sing the song to her when she was a child. "When it came on, she burst into tears," Boyd said, "and everything stopped cold. I ruined the whole reception."

"The first time I got hitched," said Jerry Bohannan, "was in a little church attached to an elementary school in Oklahoma City. Everyone had snuck in the kitchen and poured whiskey in the punch, which was an old Bohannan family tradition. Well, somehow it got mixed up and the nuns gave it to the second graders for a mid-morning snack. They all got stewed, and the office had to call their mamas to come and get 'em."

"I sang at a big wedding that had candles in glass globes marking every third pew," said Eileen Andrews. "The church was really cold, so during the ceremony all of the globes started exploding. Nobody was hurt, but it was very dramatic."

⌇⌇⌇

Just two blocks away you'll discover one of the city's stellar dives at **Saturn Bar** (3067 St. Claude Avenue at Clouet Street; 504–949–7532). Collecting dust since 1947, this crazy time capsule is a jumble of neon chandeliers, plaster madonnas, vinyl easy chairs, Brazil nut vending machine, stuffed fighting cocks, and other moth-eaten trophies. The ceiling was frescoed with swirling stars and planets nearly forty years ago by native folk artist Mike Frolich. Be sure to view his other works on canvas below, especially *How the West Was Won* and *Benny's Victorious Chicken.*

Take a cab to the French Quarter and stop at **Arnaud's** (813 Bienville Street between Dauphine and Bourbon Streets; 504–523–5433; expensive), celebrated for haute cuisine downstairs and high camp upstairs. You should be hungry again in three or four days, so make a future reservation for the dining room on your way to the second floor. Meanwhile, you're here to view the extraordinary **Germaine Wells Mardi Gras Museum,** which is free and open to the public during restaurant hours.

The daughter of Arnaud Cazenave, who established the famous Creole institution in 1918, Wells was an eccentric socialite who reigned as queen of twenty-two Carnival balls between 1937 and 1968, more than anyone else in New Orleans history. Her elaborate gowns and headdresses make an astonishing display. (She was buried in a replica of the plumed and spangled extravaganza she wore as Queen of Naiades in 1954.) Wells opened her Carnival Memory Room at Arnaud's in 1952, and the spectacular tableaux are maintained—along with a collection of Easter bonnets from her annual buggy parade through the Quarter—by current owner Archie Casbarian. The tangled web of Carnival tradition has always been an enigma for visitors, but after viewing this exhibit, you'll be more mystified than ever.

Thus inspired, it's time to don some regalia of your own. First stop is **Decatur Collectibles** (1224 Decatur Street between Governor Nicholls and Barracks Streets; 504–558–9858) to play queen for a day, digging through a musty treasure trove of rhinestone crowns and scepters, sequined boots, elaborately beaded capes, and other castoffs of Carnival royalty.

Dress for excess, or scoop up outré souvenirs, at **Second Skin Leather** (521 St. Philip Street between Decatur and Chartres Streets; 504–561–8167), "Purveyors of fine leather, latex, sexual hardware, and erotica for men and women." Among countless hard-to-find items, we spotted a chrome bustier with spiked nipples, Roman gladiator skirt, rhinestone-encrusted handcuffs ("Be Mine"), and a bejeweled tiara ("by the same company that makes them for Miss America," the manager boasted). Just picture yourself in one of each.

Top it off with magenta lipstick and spider rings from **Bongo** (415 Decatur Street between Conti and St. Louis Streets; 504–523–ROCK). "Shoplifters Will Be Crucified" at the South's largest outfitter of alternative rockers and ravers.

EVENING
Dinner

By now, you're ready for anything, so here it comes. Dragon "ladies" (accent on drag) who greet customers and wait tables in the studiously murky atmosphere are a scream, but the equally flamboyant Pacific Rim cuisine is no joke at **Lucky Chang's** (720 St. Louis Street between Royal and Bourbon Streets; 504–529–2045; moderate). You'll feel like you've walked into your favorite *film noir* set, surrounded by deep burgundy walls, velvet chairs, gold fringe, embroidered silk pillows, and brittle dialogue.

Hardly a grand finale, but it's not unusual to spot famous faces in the crowd for **Rock 'n' Bowl at Mid–City Lanes** (4133 South Carrollton Avenue between Ulloa Street and Tulane Avenue; 504–482–3133). The vintage 1941 bowling alley is one of the city's wildest music venues, with bands alternating on two facing stages, and walls splashed by 1950s street scenes. Where else can you roll a few strikes while you mambo to Nathan and the Zydeco Cha-Chas and chomp fried alligator from the snack bar?

FOR MORE LOW CULTURE

Bad taste rears its ugly head with pride at **Rivershack Tavern** (3449 River Road at Shrewsbury Street; 504–834–4938), which boasts a famous collection of tacky ashtrays, most traded for free drinks. The choicest specimens (hundreds more are in storage) share the walls with Elvis paraphernalia, biker gear, and roadside flotsam and jetsam. However, co-owner

Jimmy Collings is responsible for the main attraction. His patented "Bar Legs" barstools stand on shrimpers' boots, golf cleats, high heels, and other footwear "from all walks of life." The menu features half-pound burgers, fried green tomatoes, calamari, po-boys, alligator pizza, plus thirty-seven beers on tap. The 100-year-old waterfront building was recently treated to a facelift, when asbestos shingles were removed to reveal vibrant hand-painted advertisements from the 1940s, preserved for a half-century in mint condition. The original Luzianne, Dr Pepper, and Schlitz logos now flank the front entrance.

ITINERARY 19
Two days and one night

BACKFIELD IN MOTION
TOUCH FOOTBALL AT THE SUPERDOME

*J*ust the two of you—and about 70,000 screaming fans—it's the next best thing to being alone. If your team scores, celebrate with kisses. If not, console each other with hugs. And there's no need to feel embarrassed if your guys get stomped in the Louisiana Superdome, which should be rechristened St. Jude Stadium (for the patron of hopeless causes).

You're on home AstroTurf for the New Orleans "Ain'ts," where natives wear bags over their heads and yell "WHO DAT" because they actually believe it makes a mockery of *others*. Here in the City That Care Forgot, life's too short to get your drawers in a twist over football. Win or lose, the game will be followed by a victory celebration.

Meanwhile, why not keep track of your vacation stats for a souvenir? Tally up beers, hurricanes, boiled crawfish, fried shrimp, impromptu dances, team cheers on Bourbon Street, bear hugs, kisses from total strangers . . . Maybe you'll even score a personal best back at the hotel.

Practical notes: Reservations are recommended for Ruth's Chris Steak House (504–486–0810). Guided tours of the Louisiana Superdome are scheduled on the hour from 10:00

A.M. to 4:00 P.M. daily; purchase tickets at the ground level on Poydras Street and enter at Gate A on the mezzanine level.

DAY ONE: AFTERNOON

One of the reasons football fans love New Orleans is that most major hotels are within walking distance of the Dome. However, the downtown stadium is directly connected, via covered walkways, to the second floor of the **Hyatt Regency** (500 Poydras Plaza between Loyola Avenue and LaSalle Street; 504–561–1234 or 800–233–1234; doubles, $109 to $210; suites, $375 to $750). If the tropically landscaped lobby and 27-floor atrium are a little busy for your taste, request the Regency Club, a private floor with its own intimate lounge and other special perks. Big-screen televisions and team paraphernalia pull fans into Hyttops Sports Bar.

Romance at a Glance

♥ *Revel in the homecoming atmosphere and "tailgate party" at the Hyatt Regency.*

♥ *Tackle prime aged beef at Ruth's Chris Steak House, mother of all U.S. branches.*

♥ *Picture yourselves on the cover of Sports Illustrated or Football Digest.*

♥ *Toss back hurricanes and sing along with rah-rah songs at Pat O'Brien's.*

♥ *Dive into the post-game frenzy on Bourbon Street, where anything goes.*

Even though you'll be inside for the game, stroll over and take a guided tour of the **Louisiana Superdome** (1500 Poydras Street at LaSalle Street; 504–587–3810), scheduled on the hour from 10:00 A.M. to 4:00 P.M. The largest indoor arena in the world is twenty-seven stories high and sprawls over fifty-two acres. It seats 70,000 for football games, 87,500 for concerts, and contains 400 miles of electrical wiring, 15,200 lighting fixtures, et cetera, et cetera.

The Hyatt hooks up with the Dome through the **New Orleans Centre** (1400 Poydras Street between Loyola Avenue and LaSalle 504–568–0000). In addition to Lord & Taylor and Macy's, this high-rise luxury mall is home to some sixty shops and eateries. Drop by **Sports World of the South** (504–529–1111) to don matching T-shirts, hats, and jackets emblazoned with the logo of your favorite NFL or top-twenty college team.

Next head to **Riverwalk Marketplace** (on the Mississippi between Canal and Girod Streets; 504–522–1555) for festival shopping on the waterfront. A few minutes in **Amazing Pictures** will frame your mugs on a cover of *Football Digest, Inside Sports,* or *Muscle & Fitness.* And any sissy girl who doesn't want to pose as the first female NFL quarterback can grace the cover of *Modern Bride* (hint hint).

DAY ONE: EVENING
Dinner

Take a cab for romance and red meat at **Ruth's Chris Steak House** (711 North Broad Street at Orleans Street; 504–486–0810; expensive). You'll find clones from coast to coast, but this is the original, where the atmosphere is as thick as the steaks, with soft lighting, deep crimson walls, dark woods, and plush carpeting. Everything is over the top, from prime aged beef served in a sizzling pool of butter to vegetables draped with hollandaise. Health fanatics or vegetarians need not apply.

∽∾⊚∾∾

After dinner, it's a short hop by taxi to the French Quarter to get in on the pre-game action. The spectacle along the pedestrian mall of Bourbon Street, especially when both teams are from out of town, can put any halftime show to shame. Fans congregate in roving groups to cheer and flash their colors. Dense crowds move in slow motion, but the alcohol flows freely, and drunks only attract official notice (from scores of pragmatic cops) if they pass out or start a fight.

The Absinthe House (240 Bourbon Street between Iberville and Bienville Streets; 504–523–3181) is filled to the rafters with vintage football helmets, as well as newer autographed jerseys and other gear, donated to the owner by NFL stars. The walls are plastered with thousands of business cards from other satisfied customers.

Local historians claim the Sazerac as the world's first cocktail, but it's the hurricane that most boozing visitors remember—or wish they could forget. That hot-pink blend of fruit juices does an amazing job of masking 4½ ounces of dark rum until it's too late to turn back. The original source is **Pat O'Brien's** (718 St. Peter Street between Bourbon and Royal Streets; 504–525–4823). A rowdy rallying point for generations, singers at two grand pianos belt out college fight songs and other rousing favorites. It's usually mobbed, but repeat customers would rather wait in line at the piano bar than go on to the larger back patio or the smaller bar to the left of the entrance passageway.

Back out on Bourbon, take a leisurely walk toward Canal Street and head left at Bienville Street. Around the first corner to the right you'll see the grand old Monteleone Hotel, an easy place to find a taxi for the short ride back to your hotel.

GAME DAY: MORNING/AFTERNOON
Brunch

Today is the big day, so fortify yourselves for cheers or tears. The Hyatt lays on a major spread before Saints games, with a brunch buffet in the atrium and a festive "tailgate party" along the second-floor approach to the Dome. Beer stations, disc jockeys, interactive games, and contests are all part of the pre-game lineup. Afterward, it's off to the main event . . .

Just when you thought the scene couldn't get any wilder, some team wins a game in the Dome and victorious fans hit Bourbon Street with an even stronger wave of energy than the night before—time to climb the lampposts, molest strangers, and proceed with other male bonding rituals at an accelerated pitch. Not terribly romantic, but the air is so thick with testosterone it can only lead to a rousing climax back at the hotel. (Please wait.) Meanwhile, go with the flow . . .

You want it in writing, before witnesses? How about a proposal spelled out on an electronic screen—8 feet tall by 88 feet long—in front of about 50,000 of your closest friends?

"At a Saints pre-season game in August 1986," says Bill Curl, director of public relations for the Superdome, "a guy named Chris buys time on the message board. Late in the second quarter, two beating hearts come up with the words: 'Karin, will you marry me?'

"During the third quarter, her response comes up: 'Chris, I love you! The answer is yes!' And the whole place explodes in a cheer.

"Then, at a game in August 1993, we get another sign on the message board: 'Rhonda, you make my life complete. I am the happiest man in the world,'" Curl says. "It's signed 'Chris.' Same guy."

FOR MORE ROMANCE

All those T-shirts that celebrate the winning team the minute you hit the French Quarter —were they printed by psychics? Nope, the back rooms of the shops are stacked with boxes of shirts that proclaim victory for the losers. Ask a clerk to dig one out for you, a unique (if fraudulent) souvenir that is sure to excite comment on the plane home.

The adjoining sports bar is a new addition to **Mulate's** (201 Julia Street at Convention Center Boulevard; 504–522–1492; moderate), local spinoff of the celebrated Breaux Bridge roadhouse. The self-proclaimed "World's Most Famous Cajun Restaurant" has plenty to crow about, with good food, rollicking atmosphere, and foot-stomping live bands nightly.

Local fans hang out at **Parkway Tavern** (5135 Canal Boulevard at City Park Avenue; 504–488–2500). The funky old neighborhood bar, cluttered with sports memorabilia from track shoes to hockey sticks, picks up four or five games at once via cable and satellite hookups.

ITINERARY 20
Five days and four nights

FAREWELL TO THE FLESH
MARDI GRAS MANIA

*D*o you crave unbridled passion, freedom from inhibitions, an invitation to let your love run wild? Once a year in New Orleans, more than a million people hit the streets for a daylong ramble through a dizzy kingdom blessed with an excess of everything but parking spaces and common sense. Most rules are suspended, but overindulgence is *de rigueur.* Everyone from postal workers to burglars takes the day off, as the mayor himself hands the city over to "the lords of misrule."

Here's the deal: Ash Wednesday ushers in forty-five days of atonement and fasting for Lent, so we've all got one last chance to run up the tab on Mardi Gras or "Fat Tuesday." The main event climaxes weeks of parades and balls that celebrate the ancient season known simply as Carnival, from the Latin *carnivale,* or "farewell to flesh."

Along St. Charles Avenue and in the suburbs, families stake a claim on one of the major parade routes for a full day of picnicking and scrambling for "throws," beads and trinkets tossed from the floats. Meanwhile, the French Quarter is another scene altogether, with scantily clad bohemians masquerading as pregnant nuns, topless girl scouts, bottomless cowboys, Elvis zombies—a moveable orgy of bare flesh and blasphemy. Adding to the wild display, fundamentalist preachers (some armed with loudspeakers and neon crosses) hit town by the busload to rage against the wholesale sin. Here is democracy run amok—mass public drunkenness and dancing in the streets—as police maintain a tolerant distance.

By sunrise Wednesday morning repentance is sincere, as groggy work-bound sinners stop into church to get their throbbing foreheads dabbed with ashes, bidding a heartfelt and final farewell to flesh. Until next year.

Practical notes: Make hotel reservations as soon as possible; some are booked up to a year in advance during Carnival. Most require a four-night minimum over Mardi Gras weekend (Saturday through Tuesday), and all charge their highest rates. In general, expect long waits and (friendly) mobs wherever you go. Bring comfortable shoes. If you don't like crowds—or if you're offended by political satire, bare skin, and blasphemy—this is no time to visit New Orleans.

Romance at a Glance

♥ *See Carnival in style overlooking the main parade route at Hotel Inter-Continental.*

♥ *Overdose on glitz at the world's largest masked ball in the Louisiana Superdome.*

♥ *Cruise across the Mississippi for a tour of Blaine Kern's float-building studio.*

♥ *Dance the morning, noon, and night away at Lundi Gras concerts on the riverfront.*

♥ *Don your masks and join the crowd for the greatest free show on earth, Mardi Gras!*

SATURDAY: MORNING/AFTERNOON

Plan to check in around noon at **Hotel Inter-Continental New Orleans** (444 St. Charles Avenue between Commercial and Poydras Streets; 800–332–4246 or 504–525–5566; doubles, $220 to $260; four-night minimum for Mardi Gras weekend). If you arrive later, you'll have to fight your way through parade crowds to reach the front door. Ideally situated on the main parade route, this stylish high rise is flanked by reviewing stands. Ask about "stand tickets" when you call for room reservations; you'll be glad for the seats and extra insulation from the jostling masses. Also, request a room on a lower floor facing St. Charles Avenue for the best Carnival views. The hotel's sleek, rose granite lobby and a fifth-floor sculpture garden are graced by important contemporary artworks. Guest accommodations are turned out in cool and elegant neutrals with sexy marble baths. Amenities include a rooftop pool and health club and twenty-four-hour room service.

Lunch

Daily breakfast, lunch, and dinner buffets at the Inter-Continental are a welcome convenience during Carnival, when even the best French Quarter eateries are jammed and inefficient. In-house restaurants and ballrooms are set up with elaborate spreads of well-prepared seafood, Creole/Cajun dishes, salads, pastries, and more. (Then again, you can always relax with room service between parades—and you'll be relieved to have your own private bathroom when the mobs descend.)

❧

Sponsored by the oldest active women's Carnival organization, the **Krewe of Iris parade** rolls at noon from the intersection of St. Charles Avenue and Napoleon Avenue. It should reach the Inter-Continental sometime between 1:00 and 2:00 P.M. Established in 1917 to present an annual masquerade ball, the group began parading in 1959. Today some 500 members ride in this endearing old lineup of floats, bands, and marching groups—a relatively sedate introduction to local tradition and a good opportunity to develop your skills at catching beads and other "throws" before the crush of bigger parades.

Directly following the socially prominent ladies of Iris, the **Krewe of Tucks parade** is a rowdy local favorite, founded in 1969 by Loyola students who hung out at Friar Tuck's, a popular tavern near the university. Today over 400 members take to the streets for a free-wheeling march colored by scatological, sexual, and political satire.

SATURDAY: EVENING

By the time you head back upstairs to your room to recover from Iris and Tucks, crowds of spectators will already be lining the streets for one of the main events of Carnival. The massive **Krewe of Endymion parade** is an amazing spectacle of extra-large floats, marching bands, pop musicians, and celebrity grand marshals (past honorees have ranged from Laverne and Shirley to Dennis Quaid). Dukes and maids of the krewe are decked out in towering headdresses and elaborate robes overflowing with plumes and spangles.

You have two options here. You could squeeze your way through the multitudes to a seat in the reviewing stands or another vantage point near the hotel, where the parade will pass around 7:00 P.M. Alternatively, you could purchase advance tickets to a one-of-a-kind experience: At the end of the line, the whole shebang pulls into the **Louisiana Superdome** (1500 Poydras Street at LaSalle Street) where thousands of screaming spectators in formal attire watch the parade as it travels through the stadium, followed by a Las Vegas-style revue of epic proportions. The annual **Endymion Extravaganza** (504–736–0160) may be your very own vision of heaven or hell, depending on your idea of a good time, but it's definitely a sight to behold.

Whatever your decision, end the evening with a walk through the French Quarter to lose yourselves in the whirl of mounting excitement. You may have struggled among the begging rabble all afternoon, but tonight you can be benevolent aristocrats—just bring an armload of the beads you caught at today's parades to bestow on deserving exhibitionists. Ah, the rare pleasures of noblesse oblige.

SUNDAY: MORNING
Brunch

Reserve well in advance for jazz brunch at **Arnaud's** (813 Bienville Street between Dauphine and Bourbon Streets; 504–523–5433; expensive). The grand Creole dining palace, established in 1918, is beautifully restored with gleaming woods, potted palms, mosaic tile floors, leaded glass windows, and ceiling fans. Don't miss the restaurant's **Germaine Wells Mardi Gras Museum** (second floor), a fascinating collection of a former owner's opulent ball costumes and Carnival memorabilia. For details, see "A Day of Low Culture and High Camp."

SUNDAY: AFTERNOON

After brunch, glide across the Mississippi on the **Canal Street ferry** (Canal Street at the river) for a close-up look at the busy harbor. Disembark on the West Bank, where a shuttle van meets every landing to convey visitors to **Blaine Kern's Mardi Gras World** (233 Newton Street at the river in Algiers; 504–362–8211). The complex of working studios is home base for Kern, an internationally known designer who creates most of the city's Carnival floats, along with others for the Macy's Thanksgiving Day Parade and the Bastille Day parade in Cannes, France. Within the warehouses and surrounding grounds, you'll see dozens of his rolling behemoths in various stages of completion, along with huge mechanical figures and other props that make fun backdrops for photos. (Don't miss the 20-foot-high Michael Jackson head.) And be sure to walk up on the levee out back for a stirring view of New Orleans across the river. The facility is open daily for public tours, except Mardi Gras. (By the way, if you experience a touch of *déjà vu*, it's probably because someone gets chased through the darkened warehouses full of floats in almost every movie filmed in New Orleans. Now it will make you groan, too.)

SUNDAY: EVENING

By early evening the sidewalks will be lined ten-deep for the ultra-lavish **Krewe of Bacchus parade,** and you'll be glad for easy access to the manic scene just outside your hotel—and for your own four walls of privacy when you're ready to retreat from the mob.

Order sandwiches from room service; then dive into the crowd for this stellar display that has been a highlight of the Carnival season since 1968. Each year a different celebrity wears the Bacchus crown. Past kings have included Bob Hope, Charlton Heston, Danny Kaye, Jackie Gleason, and Kirk Douglas.

MONDAY: MORNING, AFTERNOON, AND EVENING

Nobody ever got much work done the day before Fat Tuesday, so the powers that be finally caved in and declared an unofficial holiday on "Fat Monday." Now Lundi Gras festivities rage all day long on the riverfront at **Spanish Plaza** (Canal to Poydras Streets at the river), featuring a full schedule of free concerts by such stars as Dr. John and the Neville Brothers, climaxing with a big fireworks display shot off from a barge in the middle of the Mississippi. Afterward, most people call it an early night, because Mardi Gras begins bright and early in the morning.

If you didn't bring along costumes for Fat Tuesday, you'll need to put something together, even if it's just wild make-up and crazy hats. Some of the world's greatest maskmakers are located in New Orleans, and their creations can be recycled for dazzling wall art back home. For a guide to the best outfitters in town, see "Haunting Honeymoon." And be sure to complete your shopping today at the latest, because everything shuts down on Mardi Gras.

FAT TUESDAY: MORNING

When the first black organization paraded in 1909, King Zulu (civic leader William Story) mocked the pretensions of white Carnival "royalty" by carrying a banana stalk scepter and wearing a lard-can crown. **The Krewe of Zulu parade** has maintained its satirical bent, still one of the highlights of Mardi Gras. Today multiracial members ride Zulu's towering floats that roll at 8:00 A.M., immediately preceding the main event of the Carnival season, the

A Grand Ducal Dalliance

Though Mardi Gras celebrations came to the New World with European settlers, and have been documented in Louisiana since the 1700s, our reigning King of Carnival was the product of an 1872 romance. Rex and his parade were created to entertain Russia's Grand Duke Alexis, who passed through New Orleans on a cross-country trek in pursuit of actress Lydia Thompson. "If Ever I Cease to Love," a quaint old tune associated with the music hall heartthrob, remains the official anthem of Mardi Gras. And even today, traditional Carnival flags and other regalia are decked in purple (for justice), green (for faith), and gold (for power). The royal tricolor was also the official standard of the Romanoff household.

much-anticipated arrival of Rex.

Most krewes proclaim their own king and queen each year, but Rex and his queen rule over the entire celebration. The annually appointed King of Carnival first appeared in 1872, when a gala procession was organized to honor the touring Grand Duke Alexis of Russia. Since then, other lofty visitors (even the Duke and Duchess of Windsor) have been known to join in the spirit and bow to the reigning "Lord of Misrule." The dazzling **Rex parade** is a classic beauty graced by historic handcrafted floats, masked dukes on horseback, and trinkets tossed by the city's real-life aristocrats. If you only see one parade, this is it.

FAT TUESDAY: AFTERNOON/EVENING

Rex is followed by a couple of wild and crazy truck parades that stretch on for hours, but you've probably seen more than enough floats by now. With more than a million people on the streets, you can pick the kind of crowd you'd like to join.

To be among families and other G-rated festivities, head uptown on St. Charles Avenue.

Enjoy the casual community picnic atmosphere, where large groups dress alike as clowns, Martians, poodles, etcetera.

For racier delights, the French Quarter is where the wild things are. Bourbon Street gets so packed that you'll need fifteen or twenty minutes to travel one block. If it gets too intense, cross over to Royal or Chartres Street, where you'll have enough room to view the bizarre array of passing costumes (or lack thereof) from head to foot. Walk, walk, walk. Circle Jackson Square; go up on the levee. Turn around when the crowd gets too thick; turn around again when it gets too sparse. A block that you just passed will be a totally new scene when you return from the opposite direction.

Save your dining budget for another day. Most fine restaurants are closed, and due to crowds and confusion, quality suffers in places that remain open. Stick to sandwiches, red beans, jambalaya, or gumbo wherever the lines aren't too long.

Throughout the morning and afternoon, be on the lookout for the famous marching clubs, costumed men who promenade with brass bands in rollicking battalions, some dating back to the nineteenth century. The troops become increasingly disheveled and woozy as they wind from bar to bar, dispensing paper carnations to ladies who pay with a kiss, but it's all in good fun and a favorite with spectators.

If by some miracle you're still on your feet, you'll witness an eerie spectacle at midnight, as a double wedge of mounted policemen leads an army of cleaning crews through the French Quarter for the annual rite known as "the reclaiming of Bourbon Street." The message is polite, but unmistakable: Go home!

ASH WEDNESDAY: MORNING

Ask not for whom the bell tolls; it tolls for thee. Join the line at **St. Louis Cathedral** (615 Père Antoine Alley at Jackson Square; 504–525–9585) for face painting of a more somber kind. See you next year.

Savory Kisses

A very proper Uptown lady who has nonetheless collected her share of paper carnations, Priscilla Fleming Vayda is a local writer, artist, and expert on Carnival history. She may not look the part, but once a year her favors are for sale, as detailed in this shameless confession.

"Sweet kisses, paper flowers, strands of shiny pearls, and marching jazz bands," Vayda rhapsodizes, "an unusual combination to some, but in New Orleans as commonplace on a Fat Tuesday morning as flying the flag on the Fourth. Where else would you find jazz clarinetist Pete Fountain dressed one year in a ballerina's tutu, another in ancient Egyptian garb, parading down St. Charles Avenue with his Half-Fast Walking Club, sashaying among the crowd or riding high on a bandwagon? Where else would swaying Half-Fasters pause to hand fake flowers or counterfeit strings of pearls to waiting girls—pretty or ordinary, young or old, stranger or friend—in exchange for a kiss?

"These marching men know that a good supply of flowers and beads will net embraces, quick pecks, and lingering Parisian-style kisses. Flowers and beads, traded one by one, for hugs, squeezes, and kisses.

"The place to watch and grab a share of bounty," she advises, "is along St. Charles Avenue, heading downtown to the French Quarter, just ahead of Rex. Claim a spot on the parade route and look for the Jefferson City Buzzards—marching since 1890—the Lyons Club, Corner Club, and Pete's Half-Fast. And savor the kisses."

FOR MORE ROMANCE

If you prefer to spend your nights in the middle of the French Quarter action, book accommodations at the **Royal Sonesta Hotel** (300 Bourbon Street between Bienville and Conti Streets; 800–SONESTA or 504–586–0300) or **The Inn on Bourbon** (541 Bourbon Street at Toulouse Street; 800–535–7891 or 504–524–7611). Be sure to request a room with a balcony, so you can shower your adoring subjects with beads and trinkets from your own private "float."

For Carnival celebrations in the country, see "Cajun Rendezvous." To join in yet another full-tilt bender during Jazz Fest, see "A Feast for the Ears."

A Feast for the Ears
New Orleans Jazz & Heritage Festival

*E*ver have trouble choosing your aphrodisiacs from a great menu? Just wait 'til you see what the New Orleans Jazz & Heritage Festival serves up: During one hour you may be forced to decide among Dr. John, the Herbie Hancock Quartet, Aaron Neville, Oumou Sangare of Mali, Better Than Ezra, Fats Domino, or the St. John Divine Gospel Drill Team. Next you might have to take your pick from the Allman Brothers, Little Queenie, Santana, Al Jarreau, Rockin' Dopsie Jr. & the Zydeco Twisters, Snooks Eaglin, and the Dixie Cups. Then again, you could always agree to catch the first half of one show and the last of another.

A day at Jazz Fest is the perfect date, a whirl of sexy love songs, adventurous cuisine, dancing in the sunshine, and walking in the rain. The performance schedule is a multicultural orgy that swings from white rockers to gospel choirs, Cajuns to contemporary brass. Meanwhile, food vendors tempt your senses with exotic treats that represent just about every ethnic flavor in Louisiana's melting pot. Sound good? Millions of satisfied music lovers think so, but there's always room for two more.

Practical notes: Try to make room reservations at least six months in advance. Many hotels and guest houses require a four- or five-night minimum during Jazz Fest and rates are always at the upper limit of the range. If you want to book dinner reservations at any famous restaurants, start early and lotsa luck. Festival crowds tend to be smaller during weekdays than on weekends, but the music and food are just as good. Pack extra clothes (after a day of dancing in the sun or rain, you'll probably want to change for the evening). Bring sunblock, a wide-brimmed hat, and sensible shoes that won't be ruined by mud. Nobody dresses up, and some barely dress at all. Food vendors at the fest accept cash only, but several ATMs are located on the grounds.

Romance at a Glance

♥ *Dance the days away at Jazz Fest and hit the city's hottest clubs by night.*

♥ *Wine and dine on the mighty Mississippi aboard the historic Steamboat Natchez.*

♥ *Two-step to Cajun bands and dig into colorful "zydeco salads" at Mulate's.*

♥ *Feast on the famous voice (and red beans) of Irma Thomas at her Lion's Den.*

♥ *Un-jangle your nerves with classical music and Asian cuisine at Genghis Khan.*

DAY ONE: CHECKING IN

You won't be spending many waking hours in your room during Jazz Fest, so a convenient location should be your first consideration. For apres-Fest mobility, **Hotel Le Meridien** (614 Canal Street between Camp Street and St. Charles Avenue; 504–525–6500; doubles, $215 to $280; suites, $600 to $1700) is within walking distance of the French Quarter, Faubourg Marigny, downtown riverfront, Warehouse/Arts District, and St. Charles Avenue streetcar. After slogging through the crowds at the Fair Grounds all day, you'll appreciate the understated elegance of the lobby and guest rooms in this French-owned high rise, plus the sauna and health club should work wonders on those tired muscles. And you can round out the evening with even more live music at **Jazz Meridien** on the first floor, which features first-class performers.

A couple of other downtown hotels present live jazz in their lounges that soars beyond the usual tourist stuff. The **New**

Orleans Hilton Riverside (2 Poydras Street at the river; 800–445–8667 or 504–561–0500) showcases one of the city's most famous sons in its **Pete Fountain Night Club** (504–523–4374 or 504-561-0500). Celebrated pianist Ronnie Kole is a regular on the schedule at the **Mystick Den** in the **Royal Sonesta Hotel** (300 Bourbon Street between Bienville and Conti Streets; 800–SONESTA or 504–586–0300).

If you prefer lodging on a more human scale within walking distance of the Fair Grounds, try **The House on Bayou Road** (2275 Bayou Road at North Miro Street; 504–945–0992 or 504–949–7711). This romantic bed-and-breakfast inn offers four guest rooms in the 200-year-old main house, a three-bedroom cottage, and a tiny private cottage that's perfect for a couple. Set on two landscaped acres, there's also plenty of room for privacy on the tropically landscaped grounds.

Several other properties located near the Fair Grounds are represented by **Bed and Breakfast, Inc. Reservation Service** (1021 Moss Street, P.O. Box 52257, New Orleans, LA 70119; 800–729–4640 or 504–488–4640). This booking agency represents about forty private homes throughout the city for accommodations in a wide range of prices.

DAYS AT THE JAZZ FEST

Like most great affairs, this romantic rendezvous requires both flexibility and advance planning. Here's the scoop: Jazz Fest is always set for three days during the last weekend in April (Friday through Sunday) and four days during the first weekend in May (Thursday through Sunday). The main action takes place at the historic Mid-City racetrack known as the **New Orleans Fair Grounds** (1751 Gentilly Boulevard at Maurepas Street), where continuous musical performances are scheduled from 11:00 A.M. to 7:00 P.M. at several different outdoor stages, tents, parade grounds, and indoor areas. Throughout the week, evening concerts are also sponsored by fest organizers at a wide variety of venues around the city. (Meanwhile, independent music clubs and bars also make the best of the situation by putting on shows of their own, often featuring the same top musicians who are in town to perform at the fest.) Wherever you go, you're likely to spot as many famous faces in the audience as on the stage. For ticket information and complete schedules, contact the office of the **New Orleans Jazz & Heritage Festival** (P.O. Box 53407, New Orleans, LA 70153; 504–522–4786).

There is enormous competition to acquire food booths at the Jazz Fest, plus strict regulations regarding tradition and quality, so you'll eat as well there as in the best restaurants in town. Servings are usually about the size of a generous appetizer, but only cost around $3 to $5. Plan to share and sample twice as many goodies. Dozens of booths offer such temptations as alligator sauce piquante, pheasant and quail gumbo, Jamaican jerked chicken, seafood-stuffed artichokes, slow-roasted pork sandwiches, barbecued ribs, couscous with lamb, tabbouleh, jama-jama, fried green tomatoes, crawfish pie, Caribbean fruit salad, stuffed shrimp, oyster and artichoke soup, blackened chicken pasta, sweet potato pone, fried plantains, bread pudding with praline sauce, Key lime pie . . .

Try to squeeze in some time between sets to treat yourselves to some of the original works for sale in three areas of the infield: Contemporary Crafts, Congo Square Crafts, and Folk Crafts. All of the featured artisans are talented professionals; most take credit cards and will ship your purchases. Official Jazz Fest posters make colorful souvenirs, signed and/or numbered silk screens that are highly collectible. Music and book tents are well stocked with rare regional titles.

NIGHTS ON THE TOWN

After you spend the day gorging on music and food at the Fair Grounds, there's only one choice for the evening. Find more music and more food!

You should have already checked the schedule for the **New Orleans Jazz & Heritage**

Many local fiancees plan their weddings so out-of-town guests can also attend Jazz Fest. Devoted fans who met each other at previous fests return to celebrate their anniversaries every year. Skywriters spell out marriage proposals above thousands of cheering onlookers.

Some couples have even arranged to hook up with friends and family at a designated spot on the Fair Grounds for a quickie ceremony, followed by the world's biggest reception. It sure beats a polka band and tiny meatballs at the VFW Hall.

Festival Evening Concert Series, which often features big-name stars who do not appear at the Fair Grounds. Call **Ticketmaster** (504–522–5555) well in advance to reserve seats at nighttime venues, such as the **University of New Orleans Lakefront Arena** (Lakeshore Drive at Franklin Avenue) and the **Ernest N. Morial Convention Center** (900 Convention Center Boulevard between Girod Street and Pontchartrain Expressway).

For romance on the river, the historic **Steamboat *Natchez*** (Toulouse Street Wharf at Jax Brewery; 504–586–8777; expensive) offers jazz dinner cruises. Sneak out onto one of the decks in the middle of the show, and you won't have any trouble finding a secluded spot to enjoy the passing view in private. The *Natchez* docks right in the middle of the French Quarter, and you'll be back in plenty of time to club hop for the rest of the night.

The New Orleans spinoff of **Mulate's** (201 Julia Street at Convention Center Boulevard; 504–522–1492; moderate) is slicker than the original country roadhouse in Breaux Bridge, but it's still a fun stop for bayou cuisine, dancing to live Cajun music, and casual *bon temps.* Gumbos, etouffées, and fried seafood are true to tradition, and the zydeco salad is an extravagant display of andouille sausage, blackened catfish, shrimp, and quail eggs.

A Booth in the Back in the Corner in the Dark

With around 150 clubs and venues in greater New Orleans, wading through newspaper music listings can be daunting. A famous name could be performing at a rundown joint in a hostile neighborhood to help an old friend. The vague promise of a "gospel show" might mean foot-stomping entertainment and cold beer on tap, or hellfire and hysteria at some fringe church in the suburbs.

For sexy good times in congenial company, the following nightclubs are central, inexpensive, pleasantly funky, and filled with locals. Those with a star also serve food.

IN AND AROUND THE FRENCH QUARTER

Donna's Bar & Grill★
800 North Rampart Street at St. Ann Street; 504–596–6914

Fritzel's European Jazz Pub
733 Bourbon Street between Orleans and St. Ann Streets; 504–561–0432

Funky Butt at Congo Square★
714 North Rampart Street between Orleans and St. Ann Streets; 504–558–0872

House of Blues★
225 Decatur Street between Iberville and Bienville Streets; 504–529–2624

Palm Court Jazz Cafe★
1204 Decatur between Governor Nicholls and Barracks Streets; 504–525–0200

Preservation Hall
726 St. Peter Street between Royal and Bourbon Streets; 504–522–2841 or 504–523–8939

UPTOWN

Carrollton Station
8140 Willow Street at Dublin Street; 504–865–9190

Jimmy's
8200 Willow Street at Dublin Street; 504–861–8200

Maple Leaf Bar
8316 Oak Street Between Dante and Cambronne Streets; 504–866–9359

Tipitina's★
501 Napoleon Avenue at Tchoupitoulas Street; 504–897–3943

FAUBOURG MARIGNY	WAREHOUSE/ARTS DISTRICT AND MID-CITY
Cafe Brasil	**Howlin' Wolf**
2100 Chartres Street at Frenchmen Street; 504–947–9386	828 South Peters Street between Julia and St. Joseph Streets; 504–523–2551
The Dragon's Den at Siam Cafe★	**Mid-City Lanes Rock 'n' Bowl★**
435 Esplanade Avenue between Frenchmen and North Peters Streets; 504–949–1750	4133 South Carrollton Avenue between Tulane and Ulloa Streets; 504–482–3133
Dream Palace	**The Praline Connection Gospel and Blues Hall★**
534 Frenchmen Street between Chartres and Decatur Streets; 504–945–2040	907 South Peters Street between St. Joseph and North Diamond Streets; 504–523–3973
Snug Harbor★	
626 Frenchmen Street between Royal and Chartres Streets; 504–949–0696	

The "Queen of New Orleans," R&B veteran Irma Thomas, usually performs every night during Jazz Fest at her own midtown lounge, **The Lion's Den** (2655 Gravier Street between South Broad and South Dorgenois Streets; 504–822–4693; inexpensive). In fact, she even cooks big pots of red beans and rice as a special treat for patrons who are too weary for restaurants after a day at the Fair Grounds. The atmosphere may be too basic for some, but this neighborhood bar in a working-class area attracts an easygoing mixed crowd that includes plenty of Europeans and other visiting music lovers.

If your ears just can't take any more blues, one of the city's most unlikely venues for classical music is Korean restaurant **Genghis Khan** (4053 Tulane Avenue between South Pierce Street and Carrollton Avenue; 504–482–4044 or 504–484–6552; moderate). Owner Henry Lee was first violinist for the now-defunct New Orleans Symphony Orchestra. He usually performs nightly with a chamber group, pianist, or operatic vocalist in his small and attractive dining room, which offers traditional Korean and Asian dishes that are carefully prepared and beautifully presented. A longtime local favorite, it's a soothing antidote to the excesses of the Fair Grounds.

FOR MORE ROMANCE

Other music-related attractions are detailed in "Howling at the Moon," "From Gumbo to Gospel," "On the Prowl," and "Artful Seduction."

ITINERARY 22
Two nights and two days

HAUNTING HONEYMOON

A HALLOWEEN VISITATION

*N*ew Orleans loves Halloween, the best of 365 annual excuses to dress outrageously, scare the neighbors, take candy from strangers, and have a monstrous good time. We're in our element, virtuosos of the macabre. No need to manufacture cheesy imitations when you're encircled year-round by witches, ghosts, cobwebs, unhealthy snacks, and nameless dread.

Besides, October is the ideal time to hit town. Here in the tropics, where spring is just an ominous prelude to five sweltering months of summer, everyone gets fall fever. Days are clear and brilliant, nights are pleasantly crisp—perfect for outdoor *l'amour* and dancing in the streets. Join us . . . if you dare.

Practical notes: Most downtown cemeteries are dangerous for lone travelers, so visit only with a guided group. Call ahead to join one of the All Saints Day tours sponsored by Save Our Cemeteries (504–525–3377). The Beauregard-Keyes House and Hermann-Grima Historic House are both open for guided tours Monday through Saturday from 10:00 A.M. to 3:00 P.M.

OCTOBER 30: EVENING

For a touch of moonlight madness, check into **Lanaux House** (547 Esplanade Avenue at Chartres Street; 800–729–4640 or 504–488–4640; suites $132 to $252). If you feel a little *frisson* of *déjà vu,* maybe you recognize the 11,000-square-foot mansion from the steamy remake of *Cat People.* (Nastassia Kinski's feline alter ego lived here with an incestuous brother, played by Malcolm McDowell.) Today it's a cordial bed-and-breakfast inn, ideally located on the cusp of the French Quarter and the bohemian neighborhood known as Faubourg Marigny, both prime stomping grounds for urban sorcerers and assorted creatures of the night.

Romance at a Glance

♥ *Doze like* Cat People *in mysterious and moody Lanaux House.*

♥ *Dream of the phantom ball at romance novelist Frances Parkinson Keyes' old home.*

♥ *Follow the leader (in top hat and cloak) on a gaslit hunt for ghosts and vampires.*

♥ *Attack a Mile-High Ice Cream Pie at an historic cafe featured in* The Witching Hour.

♥ *Celebrate the Feast of All Saints among the tombs in the famed cities of the dead.*

The premier Lanaux Suite, originally the library, is a 17-by-28-foot extravaganza with florid Victorian furnishings and fittings, lofty arched windows overlooking the French Quarter, and 14-foot ceilings enriched by the original cornices and gold-leaf molding. More charming and secluded, the Enchanted Cottage is a sunny retreat with wicker bed, polished wood floors, painted brick, and its own little patio splashed by tropical blooms and the soft chatter of a wall fountain. Two other rooms share the communal courtyard, a pocket jungle of shadows and light, cool brick walkways and Deep South greenery. Each of the four accommodations has its own kitchen facilities, stocked with all the makings for a leisurely private breakfast.

Dinner

October is prime time to dine at **Santa Fe** (801 Frenchmen Street at Dauphine Street; 504–944–6854; moderate). That's when chef/owner Mark Hollger whips up Oktoberfest

specials from his native Germany, in addition to his outstanding New Mexican fare. Multiculturalism is always on the menu at the popular Faubourg Marigny restaurant, where many of the traditional Southwestern dishes are stocked with fresh Louisiana seafood. Rellenos are stuffed with crawfish; creamy corn soup is spiked with hot chiles and lump crabmeat. Ambience is casual and breezy, lightened by tall windows and rattan armchairs, and Hollger's margaritas are famous.

❧

Richard Rochester's eerie gaslit rambles have attracted national attention, including featured spots in a couple of network documentaries. He leads **The French Quarter Haunted House, Vampire and Ghost Hunt** year-round, leaving at 8:00 P.M. nightly from the historic bar known as **Lafitte's Blacksmith Shop** (941 Bourbon Street at St. Philip

Street; 504–523–0066). The two-hour tour promises a "nighttime creep around the dark edges in search of the living dead . . . garlic and wooden stakes provided."

"A lot of people don't believe this stuff exists, because it doesn't exist for them," Rochester says. "Others are like lightning rods; for them it's completely natural. I've seen inanimate objects move. And I've heard countless stories from people on my tours." A true original, Rochester openly admits to throwing in a couple of tall tales and more than a little showbiz to entertain his followers, insisting, "If you think men really do turn into bats, maybe you need a psychiatrist instead of a tour guide."

OCTOBER 31: MORNING

Romance author Frances Parkinson Keyes' former home may still be occupied by an especially colorful cast of restless spirits. The **Beauregard-Keyes House** (1113 Chartres Street between Ursulines and Governor Nicholls; 504–523–7257) was also the residence of heroic Civil War General P. G. T. Beauregard, as well as the scene of a bloody shootout in 1908, when three Mafia thugs were gunned down by members of the infamous Corrado Giacona family. (The Giaconas ran a wholesale liquor business on the premises, target of repeated extortion attempts by the Sicilian "Black Hand.") Guided tours of the house are offered daily on the hour from 10:00 A.M. to 4:00 P.M., admission $4.

Keyes, who lived there during the 1940s, once wrote that a houseguest claimed Beauregard's ghost "pokes around nights, looking for his boots. It seems they buried the poor man in his stocking feet and, being a meticulous dresser, especially in uniform, he cannot rest until he finds them."

If it's diehard authenticity you're after, stop in to pay your respects at the 1831 **Hermann-Grima Historic House** (820 St. Louis Street, between Bourbon and Dauphine Streets; 504–525–5661). The National Historic Landmark is always dressed in basic black this time of year for "Sacred to the Memory," a unique exhibit that resurrects the funereal and All Saints

The Phantom Honeymoon Ball

"Sometimes I have to close up alone when it's all shadowy and spooky after dark," says Marion Chambon, director of Beauregard-Keyes House, "but I don't feel afraid. Occasionally you do feel like somebody's near you, but nothing else, other than creaks and groans and the usual goings-on of an old house. If they are here, we leave them alone and they leave us alone."

However, in the spirit of the season, Chambon does allow that there are some persistent ghost stories associated with the property.

"According to legend," she emphasizes, "Beauregard and his second wife Caroline Deslonde were planning their honeymoon ball when he got called away to Fort Sumter. She died during the four years he was gone. They say that in April the mist comes up and the house fills with fog. You can smell magnolias, hear all the preparations going on . . . I wouldn't mind seeing that.

"The other is the Battle of Shiloh," she continues. "They say you see soldiers and blood, dead bodies, arms lying around, Beauregard galloping down the hall on his horse . . . I think if I ever see that, I'm going to leave."

Chambon does admit to one eerie incident, however. "There are two apartments in the complex," she says, "and once, about fifteen years ago, a young girl who lived downstairs in the basement asked, 'Did you have a party last night? I heard music and furniture being moved around.'"

Day customs of the nineteenth century. Guided tours of the property are offered year-round, Monday through Saturday from 10:00 A.M. to 3:30 P.M. on the half-hour. Admission is $5.

"The Creoles were great people for mourning," says director Harriet Bos. "A local saying was, 'If a cat should die in the family, everyone would be in mourning.' In fact, Alfred Grima (1838–1891) wrote a poem on the death of a dog."

Modern-day mourners of the Widow Grima, who died at the house in October 1850, enter a front door that's hung with black crepe. They make the rounds of her parlor, which has been rearranged to accommodate a coffin stand, and her dining table set with lavender dishes. Black crepe also drapes mirrors and portraits, even toys in the nursery. A "retiring room" is equipped with a black-bordered palmetto fan and orange flower water to revive ladies who feel faint. Docents tell of the elaborate rules of etiquette governing Creole grief and the festive Toussaint (All Saints Day) atmosphere in the local cemeteries.

OCTOBER 31: AFTERNOON

Now it's time to outfit yourselves for the wild night to come. The **Vieux Carré Hair Store** (805 Royal Street, between St. Ann and Dumaine Streets; 504–522–3258) was established in 1877 to create wigs for the New Orleans Opera. Today the cluttered and quirky emporium continues under the direction of the founder's great-great-grandson, who also stocks a bedazzling array of masks and makeup.

You can procure even more new identities (or offbeat wall decorations) from some of the greatest maskmakers and costume designers in this Carnival-driven town at **Masquerade Fantasy** (1233 Decatur Street between Governor Nicholls and Barracks Streets; 504–593–9269) and the two neighboring branches of **Rumors** (319 Royal Street, between Bienville and Conti Streets; 504–523–0011 and 513 Royal Street, between St. Louis and Toulouse Streets; 504–525–0292).

Lunch

Catch the **St. Charles Avenue streetcar** (St. Charles Avenue between Canal and Common Streets) to the Garden District and disembark for lunch at **Cafe Pontchartrain** in the venerable **Pontchartrain Hotel** (2031 St. Charles Avenue at Josephine Street; 504–524–0581). The coffee shop was the setting for several scenes in *The Witching Hour* by Anne Rice (who lives just a few blocks away in a pale purple mansion at the corner of First and Chestnut Streets). A good selection of sandwiches and light entrées includes crabmeat-stuffed avocado Bienville, shrimp cakes, fried green tomatoes, crawfish quesadillas, and several pasta dishes.

The main purpose of a meal here, however, is to share a piece of the legendary Mile-High Ice Cream Pie. It's really only 10½ inches high, but you'll forgive the false advertising when you attack a monster slice that weighs in at one pound, two ounces. Each pie is layered with more than two gallons of house-churned strawberry, chocolate, vanilla, and peppermint ice creams, then crowned with lofty white meringue and hot chocolate sauce. The hotel's bakery turns out twenty-five to thirty of these behemoths each week, which adds up to more than 3,000 gallons of ice cream per year. Why should kids be the only ones to succumb to a sugar buzz on Halloween?

⚬⚭⚬

If you still haven't found the right look, try **MGM Costume Rentals** (1617 St. Charles Avenue at Euterpe Street; 504–581–3999). You'll pass the city's largest outfitter on the streetcar trip back downtown.

OCTOBER 31: EVENING

Afterward, return to Canal Street on the streetcar and walk back to your hotel on Bourbon Street to observe the mounting excitement. As soon as you're properly costumed, hit the streets and add yourselves to the free show. Spend the evening wandering throughout the French Quarter and Faubourg Marigny. Other than Mardi Gras, people-watching just doesn't get any better than this.

Dinner

If it's not too chilly, ask for a table on the flagstone carriageway of **The Old Coffee Pot** (714 St. Peter Street between Royal and Bourbon Street; 504–524–3500; inexpensive). The casual and cozy cafe serves up authentic Creole food for a fraction of the cost at tonier French Quarter restaurants. Choose one of the piquant shrimp or crawfish dishes, red beans and rice, or an oysters Rockefeller omelet. And be sure to ask your server about the resident ghost. (See "Victim of Love," page 197.)

NOVEMBER 1: MORNING

You might want to pack a simple picnic lunch as you prepare breakfast in your kitchen, because today you'll visit some of the world's most romantic old cemeteries. When you see the fascinating architecture and catch the festive mood, you could decide to stick around awhile. What better place to pledge eternal love?

The prime opportunity to view New Orleans' famous "cities of the dead" falls on November 1, when the faithful gather in the cemeteries to clean or whitewash their family tombs and deliver fresh flowers for All Saints Day, a.k.a. the Feast of All Saints. **Save Our Cemeteries** (504–525–3377) is a nonprofit preservation group that sponsors walking tours year-round. The tours are always well attended, so you should definitely call ahead to reserve a spot on this busy occasion.

Lake Lawn Metairie Cemetery (5100 Pontchartrain Boulevard at Metairie Road; 504–486–6331) is on the way to the airport if you're headed out of town, and worth a special trip if you're not. An incredible collection of miniature temples, pagodas, cathedrals, and mosques—even a pyramid guarded by a granite sphinx—it's one of the only in-town cemeteries that is safe for individual travelers to visit. Hand over your driver's license to borrow a tape player and recorded tour at the flower shop near the entrance. You'll hear some good tales of doomed romance and undying devotion.

Victim of Love

After more than thirty years as cook at The Old Coffee Pot Restaurant, Louise Johnson has heard her name called countless times, though not always by impatient waiters.

"The first time was in 1975," she recalls, "and when I saw that nobody was there, I was running all over the place, throwing things . . . but now it's happened so often I don't pay it no mind anymore."

Other employees have reported being touched or pushed. One former waitress was startled by the apparition of a woman "in a long evening dress or nightgown" coming down the stairs. Objects sometimes disappear, only to reappear later in the most unlikely spots.

"She likes to play games," says Johnson, who speculates that the spirit is a former resident of the 1829 townhouse, a sad girl who was "married to a mean doctor" and committed suicide.

According to local legend, evil dentist Xavier Deschamps practiced on the premises in the 1850s. Among other vile deeds, he repeatedly hypnotized an enamored young woman in hopes of using her as a medium to locate buried treasure. When his scheme failed, he abused her terribly until she died, officially from an overdose of chloroform.

FOR MORE ROMANCE

Public parties, concerts, haunted houses, and other colorful events are always scheduled all over town for Halloween. Be sure to read entertainment listings in the *Times-Picayune* and in the newsweekly *Gambit*. Also check restaurant and club ads for special menus and promotions.

An international mob of freaks, fetishists, and radical bookworms hits town for **The Gathering of the Coven,** a necromantic ball for **Anne Rice's Vampire Lestat Fan Club** that's usually attended by the Queen of the Damned herself. It's open to members only (annual dues $15), so phone 504–897–3983 for details on joining and party updates.

Walking tours for the annual **Ghostly Gallivant with the Friends of the Cabildo**

(701 Chartres Street at Jackson Square; 504–568–6968) provide a rare entrée to several private French Quarter courtyards, where you'll get an earful from the costumed "ghosts" of ex-citizens like pirate Jean Lafitte, voodoo priestess Marie Laveau, and infamous sadist Madame Delphine LaLaurie. The self-guided afternoon program is usually presented either the weekend before or on Halloween. Again, check newspaper listings or phone the Cabildo at the number above for details.

You'll find other good sources for costumes and masks in "Farewell to the Flesh" and "A Day of Low Culture and High Camp." For more on local cemeteries, see "Saints and Sinners."

GLITTERING OAKS AND BONFIRES ON THE LEVEE
A CREOLE CHRISTMAS

At 7:00 P.M. on Christmas Eve, the fire chiefs will give the signal to torch more than 100 bonfires that line the east and west banks of the Mississippi just above New Orleans. Some claim the towering flames help Papa Noel to find his way through the dense river fog. Others say the annual tradition began during the nineteenth century as a treat for students at the old Jefferson College, or as a way for country churches to light the paths to midnight mass. But in recent years, the festive blazes have served as the flaming dessert for a feast of holiday events set in and around the city.

Treat each other to a Creole Christmas during this month-long celebration that dishes out a full schedule of specials ranging from ice carving contests to teddy bear teas. You'll even be able to afford extra baubles, since hotel rates are slashed and some of the French Quarter's finest restaurants offer table d'hôte Reveillon meals. Join in the joyful noise of the Cathedral concerts, caroling on the river, gospel choirs, and jazz parades. Add your love light to the sum of more than a million twinkling bulbs strung through the branches of City Park's oaks and fireworks exploding over the skyline. Rest assured, Papa Noel will be able to see it for miles.

Practical notes: For the single best source on a wide-ranging lineup of December celebrations and specials, contact the office of **New Orleans at Christmastime** (100 Conti Street, New Orleans LA 70130; 800–673–5725 or 504–522–5730) to receive a full schedule and listings of bargain "Papa Noel rates" at area hotels. Reserve well in advance for holiday meals listed in this itinerary, especially for Christmas, when the few restaurants that remain open book up quickly. However, if you have waited until the last minute, check the entertainment listings in the *Times-Picayune* for news of dinner seatings and events that are still available.

Romance at a Glance

♥ *Nestle all snug in your bed at the Fairmont, high above the famous Angel Hair Lobby.*

♥ *Dash away to the Christmas Eve bonfires that light up the Mississippi River levee.*

♥ *Revive the Reveillon tradition with good deals on great meals at local restaurants.*

♥ *View majestic St. Louis Cathedral by candlelight during midnight mass.*

♥ *Take your pick of lavish Christmas feasts in some of the city's best dining rooms.*

CHRISTMAS EVE: Afternoon

For atmosphere and tradition check into the **Fairmont Hotel** (123 Baronne Street between Canal and Common streets; 800–527–4727 or 504–529–7111; doubles from $229 and suites from $350, with special rates and packages offered for holidays, weekends, honeymoons, anniversaries, and other special occasions). For generations, local families have made the annual pilgrimage to view the block-long lobby decked with a glistening canopy of angel hair, flocked trees, lifesized gingerbread house, and more than 30,000 lights. As always, overnight guests are coddled by down pillows and comforters, big marble baths with oversized towels, twenty-four-hour room service, rooftop swimming pool, two lighted tennis courts, health club, and beauty salon. Ask about December packages that include formal dining in the swank **Sazerac** or Sunday champagne

brunch and dancing to Leon Kelner's big band orchestra in the gilt-edged **Blue Room**. (The majestic old supper club is also one of the hottest tickets on New Year's Eve. See "Fireworks Over the French Quarter.")

One of the grandest places to get into the spirit gracefully is **Longue Vue House and Gardens** (7 Bamboo Road in Old Metairie; 504–488–5488). Interior rooms are trimmed for the holidays in Georgian tradition, befitting the English manor style of the lavish 1942 estate. Now open to the public, the Greek Revival house and formal gardens were created for Sears heiress Edith Rosenwald Stern and Edgar Bloom Stern, a wealthy cotton broker. Twilight tours at 4:00 and 5:00 P.M. are especially lovely. If you don't have a car, the **Holiday Trolley** (800–535–7786 or 504–587–0861) is a narrated loop shuttle that makes the rounds of this and other local attractions. For more on Longue Vue, see "Splendor in the Grass."

If you need to do a little last-minute shopping, the best collections of department stores and clothing boutiques are at **Canal Place Shopping Centre** (333 Canal Street at Tchoupitoulas Street; 504–522–9200) and **New Orleans Centre** (1400 Poydras Street between Loyola Avenue and LaSalle Streets; 504–568–0000).

CHRISTMAS EVE: EVENING

Like all of our other holidays, Christmas Eve in New Orleans has a style of its own. Here's a roundup of perennial favorites that offers a little bit of everything, except snow.

It's a long and rather noisy voyage that takes off from a dock in suburban Kenner at 3:00 P.M. and returns around 10:00 P.M., but the annual **Christmas Eve Bonfire Riverboat Race** (504–524–0814) definitely qualifies as a one-of-a-kind experience. The paddle wheeler *Creole Queen* and newer riverboat *Cajun Queen* chug up the Mississippi to view the famous bonfires along the levee, complete with Christmas buffet, open bar, and a special appearance by Papa Noel. Transportation to the Kenner dock is available from downtown hotels and tickets cost around $90 per person.

If you'd prefer to drive up, refer to the directions outlined in "Sugar Palaces and Sweet Dreams." Bonfires are built by small communities all along the riverfront, with the biggest concentrations around Lutcher and Gramercy. Traffic can be unpleasantly dense, but the mood is merry and you'll have more time to admire the passing scene. Guided bus tours that include dinner are offered by **Gray Line Tours** (800–535–7786 or 504–587–0861) and **New Orleans Tours** (504–592–0560).

You can avoid the crowds by staying in town and still enjoy a **Christmas Eve Cruise Celebration aboard the *John James Audubon*** (Toulouse Street Wharf behind Jax Brewery; 800–233–BOAT or 504–569–1480; expensive). The romantic riverboat ride includes a dinner buffet, open bar, and dancing to the Big Easy Jazz band from 8:00 to 10:00 P.M., with boarding at 7:00 P.M. Tickets cost around $55 per person. The company also offers **Caroling**

Over the River and Through the Woods . . .

Plantation houses in festive trim, bonfires under construction on the levees, and crisp winter days make this the best time of year for a romantic drive through the Louisiana countryside. All of the properties featured in "Sugar Palaces and Sweet Dreams" are aglow with extra baubles and greenery, but you'll be treated to an especially warm welcome at three historic manors where special fetes are on the calendar every December. Ah, the rare pleasure of retreating to some other family's home for the holidays . . .

*The **Christmas Heritage Celebration at Madewood Plantation House** (4250 LA Highway 308 near Napoleonville; 504–369–7151) is usually held on the second Saturday in December. Guests gather by the fireside in the cavernous old kitchen for hot wassail. Seasonal music is performed by madrigal singers during dinner, concluding with the procession of the yule log and candlelight caroling on the winding staircase. Tickets cost about $55. A limited number of overnight rooms books up early. (Meanwhile, regular overnight visitors can enjoy the magnificent Christmas trees and other decorations throughout the month.)*

*The annual **Bonfire Party at Oak Alley Plantation** (3645 LA Highway 18 near Vacherie; 800–44–ALLEY or 504–265–2151) is a big night of dining and dancing that climaxes with a caroling promenade down the avenue of trees to a bonfire on the levee. One of the region's most popular events, it has been expanded to two nights in early December that still sell out by mid-November. Tickets cost about $60. A few overnight cottages are available.*

*The **Bonfire Christmas Celebration at Tezcuco** (3138 LA Highway 44 in Darrow; 504–562–3929) each December features candlelight tours of the gardens, a bonfire, and fireworks display. The Louisiana cottage is done up in Victorian style with poinsettias, nosegays, even a life-sized dollhouse. Tickets cost about $15, or $32.50 with optional buffet dinner. Overnight cottages are available.*

If you prefer to make the rounds on your own, remember that many of the plantation houses are closed to public tours on Christmas Eve and Christmas. However, the magnificent architecture is still a grand sight from the roadside.

and Jazz on the River from mid-December through Christmas Eve. The two-hour cruises aboard the *John James Audubon* depart the Toulouse Street Wharf at 11:30 A.M. daily. Tickets cost around $15 per person.

After attending midnight mass at the cathedral, nineteenth-century Creole families would return home for the **Reveillon,** a traditional feast of "fish, fowl, and flesh" described by one gentleman as "fit to take on a trip to heaven." The meal usually included such local delicacies as *daube glace* (slow-cooked beef brisket), elaborate egg dishes, pastries, meringues, and crystallized fruits—often ending with a jelly-filled cake dripping with wine or rum and whipped cream. Today's Reveillon, served December 1 through 24 during regular dinner hours at participating French Quarter and Central Business District restaurants, preserves the spirit of the original with contemporary style. The four- or five-course meals are usually priced from $20 to $40 per person, and many include holiday *lagniappe* (a little something extra) of *cafe brulot,* eggnog, or wine. It's a (relatively) inexpensive opportunity to sample the wares of some of the city's most celebrated chefs, sponsored by New Orleans at Christmastime (see page 200), which will provide a complete list of menus and prices on request. The long roster of top restaurants usually includes Brennan's, Broussard's, Galatoire's, Louis XVI, Mr. B's Bistro, Palace Cafe, and Tujague's. All are detailed elsewhere in this guide.

For centuries New Orleanians have attended the traditional vigil mass at midnight on Christmas Eve in stately **St. Louis Cathedral** (615 Père Antoine Alley at Jackson Square; 504–525–9585). Doors open at 11:30 P.M., and the pews fill up fast with people of all faiths who come to view the pomp and pageantry. For more on this historic beauty, see "Saints and Sinners" and "Rich in Love."

CHRISTMAS: MORNING/AFTERNOON

If you didn't make midnight mass at St. Louis Cathedral last night, now's the time to see the city's most famous landmark in all of its splendor. However, right across the street from the Fairmont stands another celebrated beauty. Known to most residents as "the Jesuit church," the **Church of the Immaculate Conception** (132 Baronne Street between Common and Canal Streets; 504–529–1477) is graced by a bronze gilt altar, designed by local architect James Freret, which won first prize at the Paris Exposition of 1867–68. Another treasure is a statue of the Virgin Mary that was created for the royal gallery in the Tuileries Palace at an unfortunate moment in time (just before the 1848 French Revolution). Instead, it went on the block and ended up in the Paris of the Americas. *C'est la guerre.*

Brunch

New Orleans has a greater variety of choices than many cities, but it's still best to reserve far in advance to dine on the one day in the year that most local restaurants are closed. Hotels are usually your best bet.

For instance, right under your noses, the Fairmont pulls out all the stops with formal dining in the Sazerac or a festive jazz brunch in the Imperial Ballroom. The **Grill Room at Windsor Court Hotel** (300 Gravier Street between South Peters and Tchoupitoulas Streets; 800–262–2662 or 504–523–6000; expensive) usually offers an elegant sit-down brunch or dinner. Sunny **Begue's at the Royal Sonesta Hotel** (300 Bourbon Street between Bienville and Conti Streets; 800–SONESTA or 504–586–0300; expensive) serves fresh interpretations of classic Creole cuisine in a flower-filled dining room that overlooks the French Quarter courtyard. An extravagant buffet and spectacular river view draws plenty of local business to the high-rise **Riverbend Grill at the Westin Canal Place Hotel** (100 Iberville Street at Wells Street; 506–566–7006; expensive). Right at dock level, **Kabby's at the New Orleans Hilton Riverside** (2 Poydras Street at the river; 504–584–3880; expensive) has great seafood and a 200-foot glass wall for a panoramic view of traffic on the Mississippi.

After any of the above feasts, you'll probably be ready for a long winter's nap. Just remember to be naughty and nice.

For More Romance

If you arrive a day or two early, be sure to take in some of the following attractions that are traditionally closed on Christmas Eve and Christmas. (Traditions change, though, so check with the office of New Orleans at Christmastime, listed above, for the latest updates when you're ready to travel).

Celebration in the Oaks (504–483–9419) creates a festival of light in the ancient trees of **City Park** (City Park Avenue at Esplanade Avenue). Climb aboard the miniature train or a horse-drawn carriage to view the 2-mile spectacle ablaze with over a million twinkling bulbs; then stroll through the illuminated Botanical Garden, Storyland, and Carousel Garden for puppet shows, gospel choirs, and other entertainments. Walking tours cost around $3.

Once a year, during Christmas week, the snow-deprived children of New Orleans are treated to more than forty tons of the white stuff, brought in by a sympathetic local company for **Snowland in City Park** (504–483–9413). Everyone has a grand time from 9:00 A.M. until around noon, when the last few ounces finally melt away.

Historic houses and other landmark buildings of the French Quarter are decked with period trimmings to welcome regular day visitors, plus occasional evening candlelight tours are offered during the season. For details on the individual properties, see "Haute Creole" and "Haunting Honeymoon."

ITINERARY 24
One afternoon and evening

FIREWORKS OVER THE FRENCH QUARTER
A HOT DATE FOR NEW YEAR'S EVE

*T*here's something about ringing in the New Year on the old streets of the French Quarter that adds an extra resonance of tradition to the cheers and noisemakers. And in this nag-free zone, where less momentous occasions have been marked with boozing and braying for the preceding 364 midnights, the party structure is solidly in place. The neighbors won't call the cops, the threshold of shame is astronomical, and nobody's going to run out of champagne.

If Times Square in slow motion is not your style, there are plenty of other annual fetes on the schedule. You can cruise the river beneath the fireworks, mambo to big bands in a majestic old supper club, shout hallelujah at a gospel and blues hall, or just curl up on a cushy sofa for a spot of bubbly and fish eggs *à deux*. Read on and take your pick of invitations.

Practical notes: You should reserve well in advance for most of the New Year's Eve events listed in this itinerary. However, if you have waited until the last minute, check the entertainment listings in the *Times-Picayune* for news of hot tickets that are still available.

DAY ONE: AFTERNOON

If you need to polish up your ensemble, the best collections of department stores and clothing boutiques are at **Canal Place Shopping Centre** (333 Canal Street at Tchoupitoulas Street; 504–522–9200) and **New Orleans Centre** (1400 Poydras Street between Loyola Avenue and LaSalle Streets; 504–568–0000). Menswear is top drawer at **Rubenstein Bros.** (102 St. Charles Avenue at Canal Street; 504–581–6666) and women will find lavishly feminine dresses and accessories at **Fleur de Paris** (712 Royal Street at Pirate's Alley; 504–525–1899). For a huge selection of handcrafted costume jewelry, including more than 10,000 pairs of earrings and glittery masks, go to the two neighboring branches of **Rumors** (319 Royal Street between Bienville and Conti Streets; 504–523–0011 or 513 Royal Street between St. Louis and Toulouse Streets; 504–525–0292).

Even if you've made other plans for tonight, check out the impressive stock at **Vieux Carré Wine and Spirits** (422 Chartres Street between Conti and St. Louis Streets; 504–568–9463) for souvenirs or shipping. The inventory includes some thirty-five French champagnes, forty more from California, and several Italian sparklers, along with 800 wines and 300 beers. Chilled champagnes are always available, and the shop is open until 1:00 A.M. on New Year's Eve.

Romance at a Glance

♥ *Select your bubbly from seventy-five different champagnes at Vieux Carré Wine and Spirits.*

♥ *Sample assorted caviars with all the accoutrements at Le Salon in Windsor Court.*

♥ *Choose your spot, or party hop, from strictly ballroom to full-tilt blues bash.*

♥ *Get up on the right side of the bed with an offbeat brunch on New Year's Day.*

DAY ONE: EVENING

For a New Year's Eve with all the trimmings, get on the phone just after Thanksgiving to secure your hats and noisemakers at one of the better celebrations. Here's a short list

So Many Beaux, So Little Time

"In the nineteenth century, New Year's Day was a time set aside by Creole gentlemen for their annual formal visits to friends and relatives," says Jan Bradford, chief curator at Hermann-Grima/ Gallier Historic Houses. "As a rule, ladies stayed home to receive the calls, which began as early as 11:00 A.M. Prominently displayed in the parlor was a highly decorated cake and a large bowl of eggnog. After older callers had "made their manners," they could go into the dining room to the sideboard, where brandy and whiskey were available.

"Young gentlemen callers often brought cornets (small paper cornucopias filled with candies, bonbons, and sugared almonds) for the young ladies of the household," Bradford says, "and these symbols of popularity were scattered about the reception rooms. If young men failed to produce a sufficient quantity of cornets to suit a young lady, she could either make her own or purchase more in the street."

of perennial favorites to accommodate a wide range of tastes and budgets. Unless otherwise noted, prices range from $60 to $125 per person, cocktail attire is required, and the bands strike up around 9:00 P.M.

If you like to be at the center of the storm, reserve a place at the "Times Square of the South." **The Riverview Room** atop Jackson Brewery (620 Decatur Street at Jackson Square; 504–525–3000; expensive) has the best indoor and outdoor views of the mob that congregates for the ball-drop countdown and fireworks display. The tab covers a buffet dinner, premium open bar throughout the evening, dancing to live music, champagne at midnight, and favors.

For about $95, you can board the historic **Steamboat *Natchez*** (Toulouse Street Wharf at Jax Brewery; 800–233–BOAT or 504–569–1480) for a river cruise that returns just in time to ring in the New Year directly beneath the fireworks. It's a spectacular ride that includes live music, open bar, a holiday buffet, party favors, and more. Similar cruises are also offered aboard the **Paddlewheeler *Creole Queen*** and the newer **Riverboat *Cajun Queen*** (Canal Street Dock at Spanish Plaza; 504–524–0814).

Another prime riverfront destination is **Kabby's at the New Orleans Hilton Riverside** (2 Poydras Street at the river; 504–584–3880; expensive), where a 200-foot glass wall at dock level gives you a ringside seat overlooking traffic along the Mississippi and the midnight fireworks. Reservations are limited for the five-course dinner with live music and a complimentary glass of champagne.

A sentimental favorite for locals is the gorgeous old Blue Room at the **Fairmont Hotel** (123 Baronne Street between Canal and Common Streets; 800–527–4727 or 504–529–7111; expensive) for a nostalgic whirl of dancing to a big band orchestra, sit-down dinner, midnight balloon drop, and other classic festivities. The 1893 landmark also hosts a wilder party with big-name entertainment (e.g. Neville Brothers, Kool and the Gang) in its Imperial Ballroom, plus an elegant five-course dinner dance in the Sazerac Restaurant.

One of the cushiest places to seek shelter from the mob is **Windsor Court Hotel** (300 Gravier Street between South Peters and Tchoupitoulas Streets; 800–262–2662 or 504–523–6000; expensive). Black tie is the preferred attire for an eight-course dinner and dancing in the posh Grill Room, where the price per person will probably top $150. For a more casual evening, you can settle into an overstuffed chair at Le Salon in the hotel's lobby for a variety of champagnes, caviars, and hors d'oeuvres. Also a chic first stop before moving on to a party elsewhere, the special menu is usually offered from 7:00 P.M. to midnight.

If you prefer to welcome the New Year to a funkier beat, head over to the **Praline Connection's Gospel and Blues Hall** (907 South Peters Street between St. Joseph and North Diamond Streets; 504–523–3973; moderate) for a good time that's easy on the wallet (around $40 per person) and music to your ears. Top local artists belt out a full program of gospel, blues, and jazz. Meanwhile, you won't go hungry with a festive buffet of down-home eats that's sure to include the traditional black-eyed peas (for luck), greens (for money), and a wide variety of Creole/Cajun dishes, fried seafood, and desserts.

If all else fails, the French Quarter will be one big street party, with the main action concentrated around Jackson Brewery and—where else—Bourbon Street. For the best view of the fireworks and plenty of elbow room, you can join a few sneaky locals on the upper floors at the Canal Place parking garage (200 Canal Street at the river), but keep it under your party hat. Maybe we'll see you there. BYO champagne.

FOR MORE ROMANCE

There's nothing like a buffet to cure the morning-after blahs. Most local hotels (and many restaurants) lay out massive spreads, but a couple rate special mention. The New Year's Day gospel brunch at the Praline Connection's Gospel and Blues Hall offers a rousing opportunity to repent your sins of the night before—and put off that diet for a few more hours. The Windsor Court's annual pajama brunch is an invitation to come down to breakfast in your robe and jammies; it's served in Le Salon from 9:00 A.M. to 1:00 P.M. on January 1.

Tickets to the annual Sugar Bowl game on New Year's Day in the Superdome are scarce in town. Your best bet is to contact the college athletic offices of the participating teams.

ROAD TRIPS

SUGAR PALACES AND SWEET DREAMS
IN PLANTATION COUNTRY

*T*he Great River Road traces both sides of the Mississippi from New Orleans to Baton Rouge, an old trade route graced by plantation palaces, Creole cottages, country churches, and crumbly, whitewashed tombs. (Love is blind, so you should be able to overlook the occasional petrochemical plant.) It's a grand architectural journey, a quick getaway to a slower world still populated by ghosts and pirates, Creole aristocracy and damn Yankees.

Even day-trippers can get a taste of the sweet life by following this historic loop drive. Start early and enjoy the views from the roadside, bypassing the interior house tours, then return to New Orleans in time for dinner in the French Quarter.

However, if you can spare the time, spending the night in an authentic plantation manor is a rare thrill. Just don't expect it to be Disneyland slick. Consider this gentle reminder from the master of one historic landmark: "If I could afford everything this house needs to be perfectly restored, I wouldn't be renting out rooms."

Practical notes: Though hours vary slightly, all of the houses in this itinerary are open for guided tours between 10:00 A.M. and 4:00 P.M. daily (except major holidays) and admission fees are under $10.

DAY ONE: MORNING

Your first stop is about forty minutes away, so relax and watch for pelicans, egrets, and other waterfowl as you breeze along Interstate 10 West out of New Orleans, high and dry above the cypress-studded wetlands of the Bonnet Carré Spillway. (When conditions call for the massive gates to be opened, this flood plain diverts over 2 million gallons of water *per second* from the Mississippi River into Lake Pontchartrain, preventing crests from swamping the city.) Get off I–10 at Gramercy (Exit 194) and take Highway 641 South across the Mississippi River bridge to Vacherie; then turn right onto the River Road (a.k.a. LA Highway 18).

In about 2 miles, you'll spot the bright tropical pastels of the 1805 main house at **Laura Plantation** (2247 LA Highway 18 in Vacherie; 504–265–7690; one-hour guided tour). Restoration is still underway on the complex of twelve historic buildings—two manors, slave quarters, and Creole cottages—but the project has gained statewide attention for its rare focus on plantation life from the slaves' perspective. It was on these grounds in the 1870s that the West African folktales of Compair Lapin, better known as Br'er Rabbit, were first recorded in America. This fertile soil has also produced some real-life love stories, including the saga of its namesake. (See "If These Walls Could Talk," page 217.)

Romance at a Glance

♥ *Sleep like rich planters in the master bedrooms at Madewood and Nottoway.*

♥ *Play belle and beau in the verdant natural corridor of Oak Alley.*

♥ *Lunch on spicy Creole cuisine at Lafitte's Landing, a former pirate's den.*

♥ *Steal a kiss in the formal garden at Houmas House.*

♥ *Picnic on the river levee or under the trees at San Francisco Plantation.*

If These Walls Could Talk

Laura Locoul longed to be liberated like the socialites she encountered every summer at the Greenbrier resort in West Virginia, where she met her future husband, Charles Gore. But her hopes were shattered at age nineteen, when she promised her father on his deathbed that she would take charge of the family plantation. Laura was twenty-nine before she finally married Gore, sold off her Louisiana properties, and moved to his home in St. Louis. She didn't see her birthplace again until 1931, when she was seventy. She told her husband and children that it had always haunted her dreams.

Laura's cousin, Fannie DeLobel, suffered longings of her own. Unfortunately, her father observed the thirteen-year-old girl mooning over the carpenter's son, Alcée LeBourgeois, a scandal in the class-conscious 1870's. Alcée was promptly ordered off the property by her outraged Papa, provoking the boy's father to challenge him to a duel. After much lobbying amongst the wives, both men were convinced to sign letters of apology and Fannie was packed off to France. She eventually married the French Consul in New Orleans, and that was the end of the story—until more than 100 years later.

"When we got the house, we stripped off the twentieth-century wallpaper in Fannie's room," says Norman Marmillion, president of Laura Plantation. *"And underneath, scribbled on all the walls, was the name of Alcée LeBourgeois."*

DAY ONE: AFTERNOON

Laura is a noteworthy work in progress, but 4 miles up the River Road you'll be dazzled by the polished jewel known as **Oak Alley Plantation** (3645 LA Highway 18 near Vacherie; 504–265–2151 or 800–44–ALLEY; thirty-five-minute guided tour).

Long before it was occupied by Hollywood bloodsuckers for the film version of *Interview with the Vampire*, and more than a century before the house was completed circa 1839, Oak Alley's namesake was planted by an unknown French settler. Today it is one of the South's most famous images: a magnificent stand of twenty-eight live oaks in two rows of fourteen each, 80 feet apart. The ancient branches arch high above a soft carpet of grass to create a deep green corridor, a quarter-mile avenue leading all the way from the river to the Greek Revival manor.

Lunch

Before or after your guided tour, relax over lunch at the oak-shaded Creole cafe set in one of the old plantation outbuildings (breakfast and lunch only; inexpensive). Touristy, yes, but the smoky and complex gumbos are authentic, service is cozy, and calico-curtained windows frame splendid views of the big house.

⁂

All guests are free to roam the grounds, but you don't have to walk far to escape the typical day tourist. Climb the levee to view Oak Alley as it was meant to be seen—from the river—then find a spot under one of those famous trees to make like Rhett and Scarlett.

DAY ONE: EVENING

After that bit of politically incorrect foreplay, maybe you'd like to prolong the fantasy in a massive canopy bed draped in peach silk, then step out onto your veranda to watch nightfall over Bayou Lafourche. Just backtrack a couple of miles to Vacherie; take a right onto LA Highway 20; then turn on LA Highway 308 north to reach the splendid Greek Revival landmark known as **Madewood** (4250 LA Highway 308 near Napoleonville; 504–369–7151; thirty-minute guided tour; all doubles $185, including dinner and full breakfast). Here guests are quartered in the original bedrooms of the main house, second largest in the state, where they sleep like rich planters on soft linens and feather pillows.

Begun by Colonel Thomas Pugh in 1838 and completed over the next eight years, the twenty-four-room mansion sat vacant for a decade (with a $70,000 price tag) before it was acquired in 1964 by New Orleans art dealer Naomi Marshall. Restoration is an ongoing project, but today sun pours through the vast center hall, brightening crystal chandeliers, oriental rugs, and a majestic curved staircase. Grand in scale, but not in attitude, antique-filled parlors are warmed by family mementos and quirky artifacts. You'll meet the other guests over wine and cheese in the library before moving into the formal dining room for a surprisingly down-home meal (shrimp or chicken pie, crawfish etouffée, gumbo, or fried catfish). Afterward you can rock on the screened back porch for awhile; then head for that magnificent bed.

DAY TWO: MORNING
Breakfast

Linger over an old-fashioned Southern breakfast, complete with hot biscuits and buttery grits, before checking out of Madewood. Then continue north on LA Highway 308; take a right onto LA Highway 70 and cross the river on the Sunshine Bridge. One mile north on River Road (known here as LA Highway 44), you'll see the gracious raised cottage called **Tezcuco** (3138 Highway 44 in Darrow; 504–562–3929; thirty-minute guided tour). Aptly named for the Aztec word meaning "place of quiet rest," this impressive 1855 manor is encircled by cool porches and sheltered by a deep-green canopy of oaks. Included in the admission are a tiny Civil War museum, chapel, children's playhouse, blacksmith shop, antique store, and artifact-stocked commissary. Of particular note is the **River Road African-American Museum and Gallery**, a vibrantly mounted collection that traces the history of slavery and celebrates regional culture and heroes.

Continue 2 miles north of Tezcuco to be wowed by magnificent **Houmas House** (40136 Highway 942 in Burnside; 504–473–7841; thirty-minute guided tour), which once commanded the country's largest cane plantation, some 20,000 acres producing up to 20 million pounds of sugar per year. Two octagonal *garçonièrres* originally housed the young men of the household, who undoubtedly broke a few hearts in the formal garden that is still lovingly maintained.

The Greek Revival mansion was built in 1840 by John Preston Smith. It was John Burnside, however, who bought the house and 12,000 acres in 1858 for $1 million, and saved the great estate during the Civil War. To avoid occupation by Union troops, the Irish native simply declared immunity as a British subject.

DAY TWO: AFTERNOON/EVENING
Lunch

Backtrack just across the Sunshine Bridge where you'll spot riverfront **Lafitte's Landing** (Frontage Street at Sunshine Bridge; 504–473–1232; moderate to expensive). Pirate Jean Lafitte's son was married in the historic building, which was moved to its present site from the Old Viala Plantation nearby. Today it is home base for nationally known chef John Folse, whose seasonal menu ranges from homey apple-smoked duckling to cosmopolitan beef tournedos (crusted with blue cheese and topped with jumbo shrimp bordelaise).

⋘⋙

Fat and happy, follow LA Highway 1 through the town of White Castle, named for gargantuan **Nottoway** (LA Highway 1 between White Castle and Placquemine; 504–545–2730; doubles, $125 to $250, including full breakfast and house tour). The largest surviving plantation manor in the South (53,000 square feet) was spared during the Civil War by a gunboat commander who had once stayed there as a guest. The Greek Revival/Italianate colossus was built in 1859 by sugar planter John Hampden Randolph, who introduced such wonders as indoor plumbing and gas lighting. His spectacular 65-foot Grand White Ballroom remains a favorite setting for weddings.

As at Madewood, visitors are offered the rare opportunity to stay overnight in the

Wedding of the Century

Tongues are still wagging about the double wedding that Charles Durand threw for his daughters in 1860 at Pine Alley Plantation near St. Martinville—especially the strange cargo he imported all the way from China. The crates contained thousands of spiders, which were turned loose in the long avenue of trees leading up to the main house to spin a gossamer canopy amongst the branches. On the big day, slaves showered the webs with real gold and silver dust, then laid oriental carpets end to end along the ground. The bridal procession paraded through this bizarre tunnel to an altar that had been erected on the front lawn. More than 2,000 guests attended and the celebration lasted for two days.

Like other antebellum sugar barons, Durand and his family were accustomed to such excess. Even without the added attraction of a wedding, entire families would visit one another for weeks or months at a time. Formal dinner parties often seated fifty guests and concluded with a dozen different desserts. Rooms were sprayed daily with French perfumes. Carriages were trimmed in precious metals. Lavish gardens were populated by swans and peacocks, even white gazelles and kangaroos.

The insular world of the great plantations crumbled after the Civil War. Durand's estate had been raided and plundered. Without the enforced labor of hundreds of slaves, his fields lay fallow, the sugar mill fell into ruins, and the manor was eventually demolished. Like those gilded cobwebs, it was all gone with the you-know-what.

original rooms, including the stately Master Suite and Randolph Suite, as well as Cornelia's Bedroom, a pink charmer with enormous windows overlooking the Mississippi. Comfortable contemporary lodging is also available on the ground floor, where the bridal suite's patio includes a private wading pool. Just outside are the Mississippi River levee, acres of landscaped grounds, a brick-walled swimming pool (formerly the rose garden) and a sun-splashed restaurant that serves lunch, afternoon tea, and dinner.

DAY THREE: MORNING

Mornings at Nottoway are softened by sweet potato biscuits and hot coffee in your room, a gentle wake-up call to fortify you as you dress for a full breakfast in the dining room downstairs. After checking out, backtrack once again to cross the Sunshine Bridge; then head right on the River Road (here called LA Highway 44) towards New Orleans.

Lunch

It's probably too soon, but stop 3½ miles beyond the bridge to pick up sandwiches or boiled seafood to go from **Hymel's Restaurant** (8740 LA Highway 44 in Convent; 504–562–7031; inexpensive). Stick around for a great country meal if you like the picturesque roadhouse atmosphere. Otherwise, pack your goodies for an alfresco feast on the levee or on the grounds of your next plantation, about 25 miles down the road.

Picnicking is allowed under the oaks at **San Francisco Plantation House** (LA Highway 44 between Lutcher and Reserve; 504–535–2341; thirty-minute guided tour). A lively specimen of Steamboat Gothic style, the brightly painted exterior is frilled with ornate grillwork and gingerbread trim, while interior rooms are lavished with ceiling murals and faux marbling. Built in 1856 by Edmond Bozonier Marmillion at great expense, its name is derived from *sans fruscins,* French slang for "without a penny in my pocket."

⚜

Last in our itinerary, but the oldest documented plantation house left in the Mississippi Valley, classic Louisiana Colonial architecture is on beautiful view at **Destrehan Plantation** (13034 River Road in Destrehan; 504–524–5522; thirty-minute tour). Built in 1787, the hand-hewn cypress timbers, pegged attic and West Indies–style roof are unique features of this beauty that stands just 8 miles west of New Orleans International Airport.

Gothic Romance

Destrehan Plantation was the backdrop for a kinky consummation between the Vampire Lestat (Tom Cruise) and his reluctant protege (Brad Pitt) when the "Seduction and Death Under the Oaks" scene was shot on location for Interview with the Vampire. *However, it was not the first time a supernatural flirtation was caught on film.*

"We do not deny or admit that there are ghosts," Destrehan administrator Irene Tastet emphasizes, "but everyone has a lot of fun with the possibility, especially as we do have some pictures taken by visitors that appear to have ghosts in them." The most famous, on display in the gift shop, is pretty convincing. "In 1984 a tourist took a picture of her friend in the downstairs foyer near the staircase," Tastet says. "Lo and behold, behind her on the stairs is the image of a little girl with a sort of orangey glow, who looks like she's sitting down with her arms folded, really bored.

"Another image showed up from a mirror in a photograph that was taken by a wedding guest in the mid-70s," she continues, "but this one looks like a young lady, not a little girl."

As for tales that a certain ex-pirate still stalks the grounds, "Jean Lafitte was a friend of the Destrehans," Tastet says, "but we're more inclined to believe it's their son, Nicholas Noel Destrehan. It's said that after Lafitte disappeared, Nicholas had his boat and kept it maintained and wouldn't let anyone touch it—but that's just hearsay. There are also rumors that a body was picked up in one of the fireplaces, but only rumors.

"If we do have ghosts or spirits," Tastet concludes, "they're pretty well behaved. They don't move things around, but every once in a while you will feel a cold shiver."

CAJUN RENDEZVOUS

*Y*ou could join the international crowd that lines up early outside the restored Liberty Theater in Eunice for *Rendez Vous des Cajuns,* a Grand Old Opry *en Français* broadcast live on Saturday nights. Or you might head over to Breaux Bridge, "Crawfish Capital of the World," to catch the Mamou Playboys at Mulate's, where the cypress floorboards have survived six generations of *bon temps.* Maybe you'll splurge on the Acadiana Symphony Orchestra in Lafayette, or track down an authentic zydeco roadhouse.

Cajun country cranks up about three hours west of New Orleans, sprawling across several South Louisiana parishes from cypress swamps to prairie. Your love is sure to bloom in this crazy landscape of oil fields and formal gardens, lawn madonnas and country churchyards. Meanwhile, your souls will be nourished by one of the state's best plantation inns and a rollicking assortment of cafes and dance halls. Bring along a good road map, loose attitude, and looser clothing. One thing's for certain, you won't go home hungry.

Practical notes: The drive on Interstate 10 West from New Orleans to Lafayette takes about three hours. Once there, be prepared for more car time to travel among small towns and country attractions. Reservations are essential for an overnight stay at **Chretien Point**

Plantation (800–880–7050 or 318–662–5876); be sure to ask for directions when you book the room.

DAY ONE: MORNING/AFTERNOON
Lunch

Romance at a Glance

♥ *Drift through the night in French colonial luxury at Chretien Point Plantation.*

♥ *Eat your hearts out at Enola Prudhomme's Cajun Cafe and Prejean's Restaurant.*

♥ *Play Evangeline and Gabriel in paradise at Avery Island and Rip Van Winkle Gardens.*

♥ *Whoosh through the wetlands at sunset aboard a fast and breezy airboat tour.*

♥ *Two-step to Cajun bands at Mulate's, where good times were born on the bayou.*

If you leave New Orleans around 8:30 A.M., you'll hit the Lafayette area in time for an early lunch near celebrity chef Paul Prudhomme's old stomping grounds. His older sister owns and operates a country charmer known as **Enola Prudhomme's Cajun Cafe** (4676 NE Evangeline Thruway in Carencro; 318–896–3646; moderate), where the day's offerings could include shrimp and crab gumbo, crawfish pasta, crisp boneless duck over rice with sweet potato gravy, or a fried eggplant "pirogue" (sort of a Cajun canoe) stuffed with fresh shellfish. Sound good? At Lafayette, exit I–10 onto Interstate 49 North (a.k.a. Evangeline Thruway) and continue about five miles to Carencro.

Afterward, walk off some of those calories and immerse yourselves in local color at **Vermilionville** (1600 Surrey Street at Evangeline Thruway in Lafayette; 800–992–2968 or 318–233–4077), a living museum that recreates everyday life in an eighteenth-century Cajun village à la colonial Williamsburg. Artisans demonstrate traditional crafts and cooks teach basics of Cajun cuisine, as strolling fiddlers and storytellers lighten the educational load. If you're lucky, you could even see a real wedding at picturesque **La Chapelle.** To get there from Enola

A Study in Scarlett: Two Material Girls

In a successful bid to outshine her other suitors, Hypolite Chretien built the graceful French manor that won his bride's heart. The former Felicité Neda was a dashing and sought-after gentlewoman who wore trousers, rode astride, gambled, and smoked cigars. Today her portrait still graces Chretien Point Plantation, where she is introduced to guests as "Louisiana's Scarlett, our first liberated lady." As it turns out, the antebellum belles had even more in common. Like Ms. O'Hara, Felicité shot a Yankee intruder on Chretien Point's staircase, and the bloodstain remains to this day, a platter-sized blot on the 11th step. A photographer who visited in the 1930s sent both interior and exterior shots of the house to Hollywood, so the ramp knee staircase and a window design could be reproduced for Tara in Gone with the Wind. *Now an old publicity still from the film is framed in a place of honor at the foot of the stairs: Scarlett with the smoking gun.*

Chretien Point was also a favorite way station for pirate Jean Lafitte and his brother, who drafted Hypolite into a vast smuggling network that ranged throughout St. Landry Parish. The buccaneers crossed the prairie with loot from their Galveston outpost, brazenly holding outdoor markets on the plantation grounds and splitting the profits with the Chretiens. Pragmatic to the end, Felicité continued the lucrative association even after her husband died from yellow fever.

"Can you imagine that scene," marvels current owner Louis J. Cornay, "crowds of people coming down from Opelousas for a day of buying and selling with the Lafittes? In those days this was the edge of civilization. There was nothing between here and California but the Alamo and some New Mexico missions."

Prudhomme's, just double back on the Evangeline Thruway into Lafayette and follow the signs.

You'll be treated to authentic mint juleps and hors d'oeuvres when you check into **Chretien Point** (Chretien Point Road in Sunset; 800–880–7050 or 318–662–5876; doubles,

$110 to $200, including full breakfast). At its zenith, the 1831 manor commanded a 10,000-acre plantation, but by the time Louis and Jeanne Cornay took possession in 1975, the house had fallen on hard times. Inside the family found cotton bales, cows, pigs, and chickens. The basic indoor repairs required two tons of concrete just to fill in the biggest holes, plus 400 gallons of patching plaster for hairline cracks, topped off by 275 gallons of paint. Today the faithfully restored manor is one of a handful of Louisiana plantation inns to lodge guests in the main house. All five bedrooms are generously draped in period fabrics with private baths (though only one *en suite*) and magnificent antique furnishings.

Of particular note is the Prime Minister's Room, named for Canada's Jean Chretien, by a double coincidence related to both Hypolite Chretien, builder of the house, and Jeanne Cornay. The massive queen-sized canopy bed is draped in ivory silk and an adjoining red-carpeted bath is fitted with an oversized whirlpool tub and crystal chandelier. French doors open onto the gallery for a sweeping southern view. The downstairs wine room is a brick-floored charmer with garden views and an intricately carved double bed. Dominating one wall, the Chretiens' old 460-bottle wine rack has been converted into bookshelves. Overnight visitors are free to rock the night away on the front gallery or roam the public rooms. Outdoors a swimming pool, tennis court, and fishing pond are set within twenty landscaped acres shaded by moss-draped live oaks, along with pecan, cherry, mimosa, and tallow trees.

Dinner

Mint juleps and old bedrooms were created for comfort, not speed, so savor your surroundings lanquidly, because dinner is just a short drive away and the dress code is casual. A few miles down the road, glass cases are jammed with culinary gold medals at **Prejean's Restaurant** (3480 Highway 167 North in Lafayette; 318–896–3247; moderate). The stellar bayou cuisine has earned a statewide reputation, especially the steamy rich gumbos. The best introductions for newcomers are sampler platters that feature generous tasting portions of shrimp or crawfish pies, gumbos, salads, etouffées, and other regional specialties. Hunting trophies line the walls and a roll of paper towels is upended in a giant yam can on each table, but don't be fooled by the backwoods atmosphere—the chow is sophisticated, and service is professional. Cajun bands take the stage every night at 7:00 P.M., so wear your dancing shoes.

DAY TWO: MORNING
Breakfast

Your feet may be weary if you've danced the night away, but don't sleep *too* late. At 8:30 A.M., guests at Chretien Point are served a full Southern breakfast, complete with hot homemade biscuits, in the sunny breakfast room or formal dining room.

⌒⊙⌒

Afterward, ask for directions to exotic Avery Island, actually the tip of a subterranean salt mountain that's thousands of feet deep. The surrounding marshland is home to more than 20,000 water birds that nest in the 200-acre **Jungle Gardens** (Avery Island; 318–369–6243), which is open daily. The bird sanctuary was established by nineteenth-century naturalist E. L. McIlhenny, who helped rescue the snowy egret from extinction. His father established the adjoining **McIlhenny Company Tabasco Factory** (Avery Island; 318–365–8173), which began manufacturing the ubiquitous red pepper sauce just after the Civil War. Today the quaint facility, open Monday through Friday and Saturday morning for tours, still cultivates, brews, and bottles the tiny capsicum chiles with labels in Chinese, Dutch, French, Italian, Japanese, Spanish, and Swedish for devotees in more than 100 countries.

A short drive leads to the neighboring salt dome of Jefferson Island and lavish **Rip Van Winkle Gardens** (5505 Rip Van Winkle Road; 800–375–3332 or 318–365–3332). On the shore of Lake Peigneur, twenty-five manicured acres draped with ancient oaks are graced by an aviary, lily pool, Japanese tea house, rose garden, and other earthly delights. Tulips, hyacinths, and daffodils join the brilliant display of Oriental azaleas each spring, when more than 50,000 bulbs are imported from Holland. Actor Joseph Jefferson, best known for his role as Rip Van Winkle, built the estate in 1865 as a winter home. His Georgian mansion, also open daily for tours, houses changing exhibits of traditional arts and crafts.

Lunch

The lovely **Cafe Jefferson** (800–375–3332 or 318–365–3332; moderate) in Rip Van Winkle Gardens offers salads, sandwiches, and other light lunches. Ask to be seated on a glassed-in porch overlooking Lake Peigneur.

∽◌∾

Next, make a romantic pilgrimage to nearby **St. Martinville**, one of the state's prettiest small towns and the setting for an epic love story. The real-life model for Henry Wadsworth Longfellow's *Evangeline,* Emmeline Labiche is buried in the graveyard behind **St. Martin de Tours Church** (Church Square at Main Street in St. Martinville; 318–394–6021). The commemorative statue, a gift from the cast of the Hollywood film version shot on site in 1927, is actually a likeness of its star, Dolores Del Rio. Never mind, you can still steal a kiss beneath the celebrated **Evangeline Oak** (on Bayou Teche at Evangeline Boulevard in St. Martinville), where the tragic heroine awaited her lover Gabriel's return.

DAY TWO: EVENING

You'll need to phone ahead to arrange a special sunset tour of the wetlands. **Airboat Tours Inc.** (318–229–4457) takes off from Marshfield Boat Landing near Loreauville for a one-hour glide across Lake Fausse Point, over cypress swamps and floating fields of purple blooming lotus. Expect close encounters with pelicans and herons, maybe even an alligator, on this memorable romantic adventure. Be sure to ask for directions to the dock when you phone. Regular group tours cost $10 per person, or you can pay $50 for a private cruise for two.

This is the forest primeval . . .

Sentimental, yes, but Henry Wadsworth Longfellow's Evangeline *was inspired by the very real plight of French Acadian refugees who made the arduous trek south after being expelled from Nova Scotia by the English. It's also one of the most famous love stories in American literature. Published in 1847, the narrative poem recounts the heartbreaking legend of Evangeline, who was separated from her lover Gabriel, and waited faithfully for years until they were reunited in Louisiana just before his death. After she died, too, they were finally buried side by side. Dig out your old high school English book and give it another go:*

> Ye who believe in affection that hopes, and endures, and is patient,
> Ye who believe in the beauty and strength of woman's devotion,
> List to the mournful tradition still sung by the pines of the forest;
> List to a Tale of Love in Acadie, home of the happy . . .

There's no better place to call it a night than **Mulate's** (325 Mills Avenue at Highway 94 in Breaux Bridge; 800–42–CAJUN or 318–332–4648; moderate) for foot-stomping *bon temps* on the bayou. Old cypress walls at the legendary Cajun country roadhouse are lined with alligator hides, bronzed dancing shoes, rave reviews from newspapers worldwide, and autographed mug shots of the rich and famous. Feast on heaps of boiled mudbugs here in the "Crawfish Capital of the World," where you can two-step to live bands every night and noon.

FOR MORE ROMANCE

If you're in the area on a Saturday night, don't miss the weekly *Rendez Vous des Cajuns,* sort of a Grand Old Opry in French broadcast live throughout the region from the historic **Liberty Theater** in Eunice (300 South Second Street at Park Avenue; 318–457–6577 or phone the Eunice Chamber of Commerce at 318–457–2565). Tickets are first come, first served, so plan to join the line at the 1918 Vaudeville hall well before the show begins at 6:00 P.M.

The Carnival tradition of masked men (and now women) galloping cross-country on horseback to collect chickens and other ingredients for a community gumbo has survived more than 100 years in southwestern Louisiana, a holdover from similar European rituals that date back to medieval times. Known as *courir du Mardi Gras* (the running of Mardi Gras), various celebrations are set in country towns and rural areas throughout the week leading up to Mardi Gras (always the Tuesday before Ash Wednesday). As in New Orleans, everyday business is suspended and power is turned over to the lords of misrule—within reason. Lafayette puts on a five-day weekend of midway rides, fireworks, parades, and other entertainments, including a public pageant and ball with Queen Evangeline and King Gabriel presiding. Vermilionville presents its own mini-*courir* (minus horses), as well as demonstrations on maskmaking and other Carnival crafts. For details and schedules, contact the Lafayette tourist commission at (800) 346–1958. For more on Mardi Gras in New Orleans, see "Farewell to the Flesh."

Two-hour and half-day sightseeing flights from New Orleans to Cajun country are offered by Southern Seaplane, Inc. For details, see "Grand Illusions."

If you can't spare the time for travel, get a taste of Cajun country in New Orleans at **K-Paul's Louisiana Kitchen** (416 Chartres between Conti and St. Louis Streets; 504–524–7394; expensive), home base for chef Paul Prudhomme. Several of his protegés have gone on to open first-class restaurants of their own, including **Brigtsen's** (723 Dante Street between Maple and Hampson Streets; 504–861–7610; expensive), **Gabrielle** (3201 Esplanade Avenue at Mystery Street; 504–948–6233; expensive), and **Kelsey's** (3923 Magazine Street at Austerlitz Street; 504–897–6722; expensive). The city also has its own branch of **Mulate's** (201 Julia Street at Convention Center Boulevard; 504–522–1492; moderate).

SWAMP FLING

LOUISIANA WILDLIFE ON BAYOU BARATARIA

*H*ere's a weekend getaway that doesn't have everything: It's a trek into the wilderness without the menace, dining and dancing without the cover charge, a visit to the country without the relatives. Imagine camping with soft beds, Neverland with real pirates, nature with bathrooms. It's close to town and easy on the nerves.

French maps from the 1700s first identified the area as *Barataria,* a warning of "fraudulence" or "dishonesty at sea," and the name stuck. In 1808 brothers Jean and Pierre Lafitte organized the smugglers and privateers into an armada of 100 ships and 1,000 men. They set up storehouses in the Indian shell middens along the bayou and held open markets for area merchants and plantation owners. Even so, after they helped defend the city in the Battle of New Orleans, General Andrew Jackson pardoned the infamous Baratarians, whose families still live in the maze of swamps and marshland.

Today it remains a secluded and fiercely independent community of fishermen and farmers, some descendants of Lafitte's band, plus generations of Canary Islanders, Filipinos, and Chinese. Just thirty minutes from the French Quarter, you'll have plenty of elbow room and few manmade distractions—a couple of crumbly old graveyards and some plantation ruins. Other than trawling, nightlife is pretty slim, but modern romantics will find adventure *beaucoup* exploring these mysterious backwaters for Louisiana's natural treasures.

Practical notes: The visitor center at the Barataria Unit of Jean Lafitte National Park is open daily from 9:00 A.M. to 5:00 P.M. Trails are open daily from 7:00 A.M. to 7:00 P.M. Admission to the park, guided walks, and canoe treks are all free. Reservations are essential for the canoe treks (504–589–2330). Canoes are available for rent just outside the park entrance at Earl's Bar (504–689–3271) or Bayou Barn (504–689–2663). Both will deliver the boats into the park. Rangers advise all visitors to wear closed-toed walking shoes and carry plenty of water and insect repellent.

Romance at a Glance

♥ *Cruise from Bayou Barataria to the Gulf of Mexico on a six-passenger nature tour.*

♥ *Wander the gardens and woodland of lakeside Victoria Inn.*

♥ *Paddle among the alligators on a canoe trek through the swamp.*

♥ *Hike through ancient Native American mounds and hardwood forest to open marsh.*

♥ *Two-step to Cajun bands at Bayou Barn's Sunday afternoon* fais-do-do.

SATURDAY MORNING

As soon as you touch down in New Orleans, you'll be bombarded with flyers for swamp excursions. However, if you don't want to be herded onto a rattletrap boat jammed with tourists, contact the family-owned **Turgeon Tours & Charters** (800–73–SWAMP or 504–689–2911). Groups are limited to six or less for these nature-based cruises operated by David and Valerie Turgeon, natives of Lafitte on Bayou Barataria. Their passengers are quietly shuttled through healthy freshwater marshes and swamps, past coastal wetlands restoration projects, old fishing communities, historic cemeteries, shrimp boats,

Lovestyles of the Dank and Slimy

Why is that female turtle smiling? What's more fun than a forked tongue? And why do you think they call it snakin'? You're not going to believe this lowdown and dirty gossip from Rick Atkinson, curator of the Louisiana Swamp Exhibit at Audubon Zoo, but it's the cold-blooded truth.

♥ *Relative to their size, turtles have the largest penises of any animal—and the blue ribbon goes to the alligator snapping turtle.*

♥ *Male pond turtles use their front claws for foreplay, tickling the female's head while they circle one another until she's receptive.*

♥ *Male snakes have Y-shaped penises which allow them to be with two females at the same time, sometimes engaging in frenzied orgies.*

♥ *The orgasm of the male honeybee is so explosive he dies shortly afterward.*

♥ *Armadillos are the only mammals besides humans which copulate face to face. The female always gives birth to four identical babies of the same sex.*

oyster beds, and (in warm months) alligators. (Scheduled daily from 10:00 A.M. to 2:00 P.M.) Designed with bird watchers and wildlife photographers in mind, the four-hour run travels all the way from the bayou to the Gulf of Mexico. Tickets cost $45 per person.

For a romantic quickie, shorter cruises are offered for viewing sunrise (6:00 to 8:00 A.M.) or sunset (6:00 to 8:00 P.M.) in the swamp. This friendly small company will also customize individual charters for fishing or other pursuits aboard the deluxe 23-foot Bayliner. Be sure to ask about their special arrangements with local car rental companies for one- or two-day packages.

SATURDAY AFTERNOON/EVENING

When you make your room reservation, arrange for a hearty afternoon tea to help you recuperate from your swamp tour at **Victoria Inn** (LA Highway 45 in Lafitte; 800–689–4797 or 504–689–4757; doubles, $85 to $125). Newly constructed in traditional style, two West Indies houses are charmingly furnished with antiques and collectibles. The complex is on the site of an old plantation, six acres of garden and woodland fronting a large lake. The Magnolia Suite is fitted with Eastlake antiques, heirloom linens, and oriental rugs. The Gardenia Suite is a tropical retreat with rattan furnishings and a Jacuzzi bath.

Rates include full breakfast. An afternoon tea of sandwiches and pastries, served in the patio or herb garden costs $15 extra.

※

Life is slow on the bayou, especially during the late afternoon. In time-honored Louisiana tradition, you could turn on the ceiling fan and try out that bed.

If weather permits, head down to the inn's private dock for Hobie Cat or sailboard rentals and happy hour specials. Otherwise, visit the barn animals or rendezvous in the woods.

Dinner

Near the inn you can take your pick from a couple of casual family-owned seafood houses overlooking Bayou Barataria. Sit upstairs for sunset views and great fried chicken or Cajun/Creole specialties at **Boutte's** (LA Highway 45 in Lafitte; 504–689–3889; inexpensive). Authentic German food and fresh fish dishes are on the menu at **Voleo's Seafood Restaurant** (LA Highway 45 in Lafitte; 504–689–2482; inexpensive).

※

Before you retire to the comfort of your queen-sized bed and ceiling fan, treat yourselves to a moonlight stroll in the gardens and a little stargazing on the dock.

The Moonlight, the Gators, and You . . .

If paddling through a swamp in the morning is not quite thrilling enough, you could even sign up for a full-moon canoe trek, a romantic adventure offered twice each month at 7:00 P.M. on the night before and night of the full moon.

"Either way," says ranger Laura Turnipseed, "the best thing is seeing the park from water instead of from the little bit of land we have out here. You get a whole different perspective on how the animals live—herons and egrets fishing right beside you, owls or hawks flying overhead while you're so low in the water . . . We usually see lots of squirrels and rabbits and there's always the possibility of raccoons. All of the animals use the water much more than the trails, so you really do experience close encounters. The alligators are especially curious. They'll swim right next to you as you paddle along.

"This is Louisiana's Mississippi delta, forest, and swamp," she says. "You're going through the natural habitat for a chance to really see how the animals interact at home, when they're gathering food, making nests, raising their young."

SUNDAY MORNING

Breakfast

The complimentary full breakfast served from 8:00 to 10:00 A.M. at Victoria Inn is a gracious affair, anything from crabmeat omelet with hollandaise sauce to pecan waffles and sausage. Unfortunately, you may have to settle for the earlier continental spread to make your 8:30 A.M. date with a canoe.

Some of us are more than satisfied to keep our feet on terra firma (or even slightly above) via the park's system of eight trails, five of which are raised, paved, or boardwalked. However, guided canoe treks are scheduled every Sunday morning for three to four hours of unspoiled bayou adventure at the **Barataria Unit of Jean Lafitte National Park and Preserve** (LA Highway 45 in Marrero; 504–589–2330).

SUNDAY AFTERNOON

If you'd like to follow up with a land tour, head for the park's Bayou Coquille trail to join the ranger-guided walk scheduled daily at 1:15 P.M. The half-mile trek begins at the site of a prehistoric Native American village (circa 200 to 600 A.D.) on the banks of Bayou Coquille. From this natural levee, 5 feet above sea level, the trail descends the backslope to progressively lower and wetter areas, passing through several vegetational zones. Beyond the live oaks and other hardwoods, damper soils are thick with dwarf palmettos under a canopy of swamp red maple. Next is the swamp, a flooded forest of bald cypress, water tupelo, and pumpkin ash. Near the end of the line, trees thin out to reveal the open marsh, a floating prairie of freshwater grasses, sedges, and aquatic plants.

Lunch

Just outside the park entrance at the **Bayou Barn** (LA Highway 45 in Marrero; 504–689–2663; inexpensive) the Sunday afternoon *fais-do-do* is a fond farewell of jambalaya, gumbo, and Cajun dancing to live bands in a covered pavilion on Bayou des Familles. See ya later, alligator.

FOR MORE ROMANCE

Fresh and saltwater fishing trips are also offered in Lafitte by Ripp's Inland Charters (504–689–2665). For an exotic moonlit experience, sign on for a nighttime shrimp trawling tour with L'il Cajun Swamp and Shrimping Tours in Lafitte (800–689–3213 or 504–689–3213).

Annual good times in Lafitte include the Oyster Food Fest on the third weekend in January, the Blessing of the Shrimp Fleet on the last Sunday in April, the Jean Lafitte Seafood Festival on the first weekend in August, the World Championship Pirogue Races on various dates in September, and Oktoberfest (including a starlight canoe tour of Jean Lafitte Park) on the third weekend in October.

For a quick in-town adventure, visit the world's only urban swamp at Audubon Zoo, home to the award-winning Louisiana Swamp Exhibit detailed in "Cheap Thrills." If you love to fish, see "Hook, Line, and Sinker." Bird watchers and anyone else who likes a good air show should check out the purple martin observation area in "Over the Lake."

OVER THE LAKE

SUNDAY AFTERNOON ON THE NORTH SHORE

*L*ong before you joined the carefree exodus, generations of New Orleanians flocked "over the lake" for a quick getaway from urban chaos and pollution. During the antebellum years, they ferried across on festive steamers such as the *Susquehanna, Ophelia,* and *Ozone.* Later they boarded the Great Northern Railroad for a 54-mile jaunt from the downtown terminal at Canal and Basin Streets. In 1956 the Lake Pontchartrain Causeway spanned the 24 miles from the South Shore in suburban Metairie to the North Shore in Mandeville, shortening the two-hour travel time to a breezy thirty-minute commute.

Such instant accessibility put an end to grand resorts like the old Southern Hotel in Covington, with its tropical lobby populated by caged monkeys and live alligators, where guests could "take the waters" from an artesian fountain. The location of St. Tammany Parish in one of the world's three ozone belts (the other two are in Arizona and Germany's Hartz mountains) was a major draw, and the artesian wells of its towns were credited with legendary healing powers. That same water is now the key ingredient in two thriving local products, Abita Springs Water and Abita Beer.

Your love is sure to flourish on the fresh air and natural beauty as you explore the quaint country architecture, shops, and restaurants. And a growing collection of bed-and-breakfast inns might even entice you to relax and stay awhile.

Practical notes: The Lake Pontchartrain Causeway is well patrolled, so don't even think about speeding, especially in rainy weather. Reservations are essential for La Provence (504–626–7662), which is open for lunch on Sunday only, dinner Wednesday through Sunday. Men should wear jackets.

Romance at a Glance

♥ *Breeze across the world's longest over-water bridge on a 24-mile car cruise.*

♥ *Feast in French country style at La Provence, one of Louisiana's premier restaurants.*

♥ *Stroll past nineteenth-century summer homes on the historic Mandeville lakefront.*

♥ *Join the nightly crowd of spectators for an amazing view of birds in flight.*

SUNDAY AFTERNOON

From New Orleans take Interstate 10 West to the Causeway North exit and continue to Mandeville on the Lake Pontchartrain Causeway. A smooth ride over 24 miles of open water, the world's longest span stretches well beyond sight of either shore for the exhilarating experience of being at sea without a boat.

Lunch

After exiting the Causeway in Mandeville, take the first right onto LA Highway 190 East and continue 7 miles to **La Provence** (LA Highway 190 in Lacombe; 504–626–7662; expensive). Chef Chris Keragiorgiou's country French restaurant, named for his birthplace, attracts culinary pilgrims statewide. Warmed by an open fireplace and polished oak paneling, the woodsy retreat has been rated among America's best restaurants by readers of *Condé Nast Traveler,* among dozens

of other honors. Duck, lamb, and quail are specialties. The seasonal menu features such temptations as veal Marsala with wild mushrooms, shrimp sauteed in olive oil with fresh herbs, broiled oysters with garlic and saffron, roast tenderloin of beef with a sauce of green peppercorns and brandy, and warm scallop salad with mixed greens. The chef began his career as a baker, so the pastry cart is exceptional. Just say yes.

⌘

Aprés le déjeuner, take LA Highway 190 back to Mandeville and follow the signs to the historic district along Lakeshore Drive. Unlike the concrete-reinforced seawall on the New Orleans side, here the lake's natural shoreline is a quiet and grassy retreat shaded by ancient oaks. It's also a great place for a romantic afternoon stroll past a significant collection of historic architecture dating from 1830 to 1860. (All are private homes, so maintain a polite distance.)

Many were built as speculative models for summer vacation houses by the town's namesake, Bernard Xavier Philippe de Marigny de Mandeville. (The colorful Creole aristocrat also subdivided his family plantation on the outskirts of the present-day French Quarter to create the first *faubourg,* or suburb, in New Orleans. The old neighborhood is still known as Faubourg Marigny.)

Nestled among the namesake trees, **The Magnolias** (1635 Lakeshore Drive between Foy and Jackson Streets) is a mid-1850s raised cottage, designed to beat the heat with its deep roof, shuttered windows, and ample porch. Though occupied by more than twenty owners since, it was originally built by Marigny for his ex-wife.

Other simple beauties include **High Tide** (1717 Lakeshore Drive between Lamarque and Foy Streets), **Little Flower Villa** (1721 Lakeshore Drive between Lamarque and Foy Streets), **Mandeley** (1813 Lakeshore Drive between Marigny Avenue and Lamarque Street), **Flagstaff** (1815 Lakeshore Drive between Marigny Avenue and Lamarque Street), **Chateau Marigny** (121 Marigny Avenue between Lakeshore Drive and Claiborne Street), **Danielson House** (127 Marigny Avenue between Lakeshore Drive and Claiborne Street), and **A. Denis Bechac Home** (1925 Lakeshore Drive at Marigny Avenue).

After your walking tour, stake out a spot under one of those sheltering oaks for some lazy necking and l–o–n–g views across the water. Just remember to rouse yourselves in time to make the return trip across the Causeway before sundown to catch a spectacular natural attraction on the New Orleans shore.

Bird watchers travel cross country to observe the phenomenon, but everyone enjoys the nightly air show presented throughout spring and summer by hordes of purple martins. At dusk they fly in from all directions, careening overhead for several minutes before swooping under the Causeway en masse in a truly grand finale. The mammoth roost, used by up to 200,000 birds during peak season in July and August, was discovered in 1983 by local bird-watcher Carlyle Rogillio. Since then, the sundown audience has grown so large that the city built a concrete deck at water level, designated as the **Purple Martin Observation Area** (Lake Pontchartrain Causeway at the New Orleans shoreline). To get there, park in the lot beside the toll booths for the northbound lanes and make your way carefully across traffic to the stairs leading underneath the southbound span.

FOR MORE ROMANCE

If you'd like to stay overnight, or longer, one of the most romantic bed-and-breakfast inns on the North Shore is **Magnolia House** (904 Main Street at St. Francis Street in Madisonville; 504–845–4922; doubles, $125). Two guest rooms are furnished in antiques with all-natural linens, goose-down comforters, and private baths (one has a clawfoot tub). Built around 1830, the house is located just one block from the Tchefuncte River. Rates include a large breakfast, usually quiche with fresh fruit and pastries.

The **Tammany Trace** (504–867–9490) is an asphalt trail that follows an old railroad bed through a linear park of woods and countryside for about 17 miles from Abita Springs to Lacombe. Cyclists, equestrians, skaters, runners, and walkers enjoy the trail. You can rent bikes, even a tandem, at the Trace headquarters, housed in an old caboose in Mandeville. (To get there from New Orleans, stay on the Causeway after crossing the lake; then take I–12 East to the Mandeville/Abita Springs exit; turn left onto LA Highway 59 and continue about one-third mile; take a left on Koop Drive to reach the caboose.) Horses are also available for hire at the same site, but only by advance reservation with **Wildlife Trails, Inc.** (504–796–3794). When completed, the Trace will extend for 31 miles.

One end of the Trace is anchored by the woodsy **Abita Brew Pub** (72011 Holly Street at LA Highway 59; 504–892–5837; moderate), a great place to sample beers from the most popular regional brewery, along with a stylish menu of salads, appetizers, pasta, and unique entrées.

Covington is a genteel little town filled with charming architecture, ancient oaks, and sophisticated shops. Antiquing is especially good along Lee Lane, where you'll also find a stellar collection of boutiques and stylish cafes.

For more information on the outstanding restaurants, natural attractions, and country towns of the area, contact the **St. Tammany Tourist Commission** (68099 LA Highway 59, Mandeville, LA 70471; 800–634–9443).

HOOK, LINE, AND SINKER

FISHING FOR LOVE IN THE SPORTSMAN'S PARADISE

*I*f you've promised one another that your love will last to the End of the World, here's some alarming news: It only takes an hour to drive there from the French Quarter. The boat launch with the apocalyptic name is located on an isolated tip of land in lower St. Bernard Parish, a favorite joke among residents. As the two-lane blacktop narrows, the shoulder gradually drops off into water on the passenger's side, then the driver's, and finally in front of the car. Once you spot the sign, there's nothing to do but fish, cut bait, or turn around and head back the way you came.

When you get right down to it, the entire city of New Orleans is surrounded by water, but don't picture beaches. This is delta country, and, like the region's other hidden charms, great fishing spots are hard to find without an experienced guide. Still, you don't have to sign on with one of those big operations that crowd twenty or thirty people into the same boat, when the two of you can reserve a guided trip of your very own. Just pack your overnight bags and lucky hats and head toward the End of the World.

Practical notes: Advance reservations are essential for Fishing Guide Services (504–243–

2100; fax 504–241–4311; beeper 504–595–0727). Under a special provision for charter captains, you can obtain one-day, out-of-state licenses directly through the service at a bargain rate. Also be sure to request gear and tackle if you aren't bringing your own. Though the company offers pickup from any downtown hotel, you should rent a car to explore the offbeat charms of St. Bernard Parish at your leisure.

Romance at a Glance

♥ *Spend the night in an isolated fishing camp at the edge of the coastal marshland.*

♥ *Boost your love with a potent aphrodisiac, Louisiana oysters fresh off the boat.*

♥ *Shove off at dawn to wind through remote waterways in search of the big one.*

♥ *Pledge your troth before the net-draped altar of St. Peter the Fisherman Church.*

♥ *Dream of pirates and redcoats at the historic site of the Battle of New Orleans.*

DAY ONE: AFTERNOON

If four or five fish are a good day's catch back home, it may be hard to imagine topping that in less than thirty minutes, but it often happens in the "Sportsman's Paradise" of Louisiana. Captain Dee Geoghegan (say *go haygan*) won't promise such spectacular results every time, but he does offer a ten-fish-minimum guarantee for his **Fishing Guide Services** (504–243–2100; fax 504–241–4311; beeper 504–595–0727). A conservationist who joins in efforts with Louisiana State University, Geoghegan also writes the fish forecast for *Louisiana Outdoor* magazine and does guest shots for local and national television. Retired from a successful family business, he charters trips to support his favorite pastime in grand style—from the new leather-interior Suburban that picks up clients at their hotels to a deluxe 25-foot boat that only draws 11 inches of water, perfect for shallow marsh areas.

To drive out on your own, follow St. Claude Avenue to suburban Arabi, where the name changes to St. Bernard Highway (a.k.a. LA Highway 46), and continue through Chalmette, Mereux, Violet, and Poydras to Ycloskey. Just stay on Highway

46 (now called Ycloskey Highway) until you see the sign on a metal boathouse that reads FISHING GUIDE SERVICES at 1625 Ycloskey Highway.

Guests gather in the main cabin for sit-down dining in a big kitchen. The 15-foot climb up the stairs to the porch of your own little cottage may seem a daunting at first, but you'll be rewarded by long views over wild growth of the coastal marshland. After getting settled into your basic but comfortable digs, cross the street and go out on the dock to watch as dozens of shrimp and oyster boats come in, heading for the processing plants you passed about a mile back. Wave some money, and one will stop to sell you a sack of the freshest oysters anywhere, quite a catch if you know how to open them yourselves (and choose to ignore recent health warnings about consumption of raw shellfish).

Dinner

Here near the End of the World, as way down yonder in New Orleans as you can get on dry land, dinner is a homestyle meal in the main cabin from old family recipes. The simple menu always features jambalaya (à la Geoghegan's grandma) and fresh fillets from that morning's trip. Afterward, there's plenty of time for trading fish stories, but you should turn in early since your boat shoves off at the crack of dawn.

DAY TWO: MORNING
Breakfast

With no strict rules about the menu, start the day with anything from rolls and coffee to a hearty spread with all the trimmings. Meanwhile, make your choices for a packed lunch of po-boys (from a nearby deli) that Geoghegan takes along on the boat.

Be sure to bring a camera for this early morning voyage through the Chandeleur Islands, Breton Sound, and a large section of Louisiana marsh. Although fishing is the name of the game, you'll spot thousands of birds—pelicans, egrets, storks, marsh hens, plus a large kingfisher rookery. Depending on the season (and where the fish are biting) the route could also pass otters, nutria, wild hogs, alligators, deer, and raccoons. Watch for the haunted remains of old Fort Proctor and the rowdy community that sprang up next to it, famous for wide-open casinos and bawdy houses.

"Even a church," Geoghegan says, "so a guy could gamble away most of his money, spend the rest on women, then stop in for confession and go home in a state of grace—all in one trip."

DAY TWO: AFTERNOON

By 2:00 P.M. you'll probably be back at the camp, where your catch can be filleted and packed with ice into Styrofoam containers to make a secure carry-on for the flight home.

On the trip back if you're driving your own car, take time to stop at **San Pedro de Pescador Church** (LA Highway 46 near Florissant; 504–676–3719), named for St. Peter the Fisherman. Shaped like the inverted bow of a boat, the picturesque structure is raised high above the ground on stilts, like the houses of its parishioners. Inside, the altar is draped with handmade nets and other nautical offerings created by members of the rural fishing communities that it serves. The door on the left side is left unlocked every day from 8:00 A.M. to 5:00 P.M., if you'd like to view the interior.

The Dish on Fish from the Aquarium of the Americas

Sharks and rays like rough sex. The male grabs his mate by biting and holding on. Special "graspers" also help to anchor his beloved, who will be permanently scarred by the encounter. (Sound familiar?)

Several species of fish, including wrasses and hogfish, are transsexuals. All are female at birth, but one switches to become dominant male of the group. If he dies, the most dominant female changes sex to replace him.

It must be the moon! Every year all coral reproduce at the same time, depending on the lunar cycle, as males and females release their sperm and eggs into the water at once for a massive gang spawn.

Talk about a long way to go for a date! Steelhead salmon travel back to the stream where they were hatched in order to spawn, sometimes up to 3,000 miles.

Sausalito hummers serenade the objects of their affection for a month each year. The male mating call is a low buzz that carries up to a mile. The nickname comes from houseboat residents in the California town, who were unable to sleep because the humming echoed through their hulls all night. In addition to this musical talent, Sausalito hummers make good fathers, guarding the clutch of bright orange eggs until the young hatch.

The male seahorse is even more accommodating. He carries the pregnancy and gives birth to the babies after the female deposits up to 200 eggs in his brood pouch.

About 7 miles farther along, you'll see a cottage museum designated as the **Isleño Center** (1357 LA Highway 46 in Toca; 504–682–0862). This outpost of the Jean Lafitte National Park and Preserve is named for the Canary Islanders who settled lower St. Bernard Parish in 1778. The free exhibit showcases a small collection of fishing and trapping artifacts, ship models, maps, crafts, and household items.

The Battle of New Orleans was fought at **Chalmette Battlefield and National**

Cemetery (8606 West St. Bernard Highway in Chalmette; 504–589–4430), where the Jean Lafitte National Park and Preserve maintains the oak-shaded graveyard, a driving tour of the ramparts, and a restored historic house. Stop by the visitors' center for an introduction to this colorful episode in the War of 1812 that pitted British redcoats against General Andrew Jackson, a ragtag army of Tennessee sharpshooters, and pirate Jean Lafitte's band. Climb the levee for great views of downtown New Orleans.

FOR MORE ROMANCE

If you just want to play a little hooky right in the center of town, **City Park** (City Park Avenue at Esplanade Avenue) is a gorgeous escape. Anglers can pick a quiet spot from more than 7 miles of lagoons surrounded by 22½ miles of shoreline. Hand-dug in 1930 by the Works Progress Administration (WPA), one is a miniature replica of Lake Pontchartrain, another of Lake Maurepas. The lagoons are well stocked with all of the species found in the fresh or brackish waters of South Louisiana. The boat dock, located behind the park's concession stand, sells one-day permits. Phone (504) 483–9371 for seasonal schedules.

City Park hosts the annual Big Bass Fishing Rodeo, the oldest freshwater fishing contest in the U.S., established in 1945. It's usually set for the last Saturday in March or the first Saturday in April, but dates vary. Phone the number listed above for updates.

For other fishing charters available nearby, including an after-dark trawling tour, see "Swamp Fling." Spectacular underwater exhibits at the Aquarium of the Americas are detailed in "Cheap Thrills."

ROMANTIC RESTAURANTS

Restaurant price categories in this index, represented by one to four dollar signs, designate the cost of an appetizer, an entree, dessert, and one cocktail for one person. The approximate price for each category is indicated in the following key:

Inexpensive ($): Less than $15
Moderate ($$): $15 to $30

Expensive ($$$): $30 to $60
Very Expensive ($$$$): More than $60

ROMANTIC PLACES TO STAY

NIGHTLIFE

GENERAL INDEX

Note: For Restaurant, Hotel, and Nightlife listings, see the special indexes, which begin on page 253.

About the Authors

Constance Snow is a food columnist for the *New Orleans Time-Picayune* and the author of four books. Kenneth Snow is a teacher, freelance illustrator, and regular contributor to the newspaper's entertainment section. This is their second guidebook to the city and they frequently collaborate on travel articles for national and regional publications. They spent the day and night of their tenth (aluminum) wedding anniversary at their computers, desperately trying to meet one of the deadlines for *Romantic Days and Nights in New Orleans.*

Romantic Days and Nights in New Orleans

OTHER TITLES IN THE ROMANTIC DAYS & NIGHTS SERIES INCLUDE:

Romantic Days and Nights in Seattle $14.95
Let the subtle and seductive charms of Seattle unfold before you
in these romantic locales.

Romantic Days and Nights in San Francisco $14.95
Selected getaways in and around this most romantic of cities—the "City by the Bay."

Romantic Days and Nights in Boston $14.95
Intimate and sophisticated, these wonderful itineraries show romantic Boston at its best.

Romantic Days and Nights in Montreal $14.95
Intimate escapes in the Paris of North America

Romantic Days and Nights in New York City $14.95
Find the ultimate romantic escape in the city that never sleeps!

Romantic Days and Nights in Chicago $14.95
Enjoy great days and nights in the Windy City with themed getaways for every budget.

Available from your bookstore or directly from the publisher. For a catalog or to
place an order, call toll-free 24 hours a day (1-800-243-0495), or write to
The Globe Pequot Press, P.O. Box 833, Old Saybrook, Connecticut 06475-0833.